AN ILLUSTRATED DIRECTORY OF
AMPHIBIOUS
WARFARE VESSELS

AN ILLUSTRATED DIRECTORY OF
AMPHIBIOUS WARFARE VESSELS

A COUNTRY-BY-COUNTRY GUIDE TO 130 LANDING SHIPS AND LANDING CRAFT, WITH OVER 210 WARTIME AND MODERN PHOTOGRAPHS

BERNARD IRELAND

southwater

This edition is published by Southwater
an imprint of Anness Publishing Ltd
Blaby Road, Wigston
Leicestershire LE18 4SE
info@anness.com

www.southwaterbooks.com
www.annesspublishing.com

Anness Publishing has a new picture agency outlet for images
for publishing, promotions or advertising. Please visit our website
www.practicalpictures.com for more information.

© Anness Publishing Ltd 2013

A CIP catalogue record for this book
is available from the British Library.

Publisher: Joanna Lorenz
Senior Editor: Felicity Forster
Production Manager: Steve Lang

Produced by JSS Publishing Limited, Bournemouth BH1 4RT
Editor: Jasper Spencer-Smith
Designer: Nigel Pell

Previously published as part of a larger volume,
The World Encyclopedia of Amphibious Warfare Vessels

PUBLISHER'S NOTES
Although the information in this book is believed to be accurate and true at the
time of going to press, neither the authors nor the publisher can accept any legal
responsibility or liability for any errors or omissions that may have been made.
    The nationality of each vessel is identified in the relevant specification box
by the national flag that was in use at the time of service.

ACKNOWLEDGEMENTS
Picture research for this book was carried out by Jasper Spencer-Smith, who has
selected images from the following sources: JSS Collection, Cody Images, Getty Images,
Imperial War Museum and US Navy Archive (l=left, r=right, t=top, b=bottom, m=middle).
Cody Images: 6b, 7bl, 7br, 13b, 14t, 15b, 25b, 29b, 30b, 44t, 46t, 56b, 57t, 64t, 65t, 69,
70t, 72t, 73t, 76b, 77tl, 79, 87t, 90, 91t, 92, 94t, 96t, 98tl, 98b, 102t, 108t, 109, 110b,
111, 113, 122t, 123t, 123m, 124–5, 126t, 127b, 130t, 131t, 132, 136b, 137b, 145, 148,
150–1. US Navy (public domain): 10t, 10b,11t, 93, 102b. UK MoD Crown Copyright
2010: 1, 2, 3, 6t, 8–9, 56t, 58b, 59t, 60b, 61, 62t, 127m, 136t, 156b.
    Every effort has been made to acknowledge photographs correctly, however we
apologize for any unintentional omissions, which will be corrected in future editions.

PAGE 1: **HMS Fearless.**
PAGE 2: **HMS Albion and a combat boat from the Royal Norwegian Navy.**
PAGE 3: **Landing Craft, Medium, LCM (9).**

Contents

LEFT: **HMS *Albion* conducting amphibious operations with a Landing Craft, Utility (LCU) during "Exercise Grey Heron" off the coast of Portsmouth in 2007. The Landing Platform, Dock (LPD) ship's primary function is to embark, transport, deploy and recover troops, equipment, vehicles and cargo.**

Introduction

In the 14th century, small expeditions of determined men could achieve great things – Cortés and Pizarro waded ashore with battalion-sized forces and overthrew established civilizations in the name of gold and religion, resulting in the mainly Spanish-speaking subcontinent of South America. Since then, empires have been built and have collapsed, and colonies have been won and lost.

European colonial powers emerged, each with its own "sphere of influence". Each new colony developed fortified and garrisoned settlements and, as the new wealth was extracted, the hidden arm of seapower supplied the forces of administration and protection. Like tectonic plates, the spheres of influence tended to overlap to create great frictional forces along their boundaries. Great Britain, France, Spain and the Netherlands waged new-style wars, not on each other's sovereign territory but in lands far away. These, necessarily, were expeditionary wars and, as fortified settlements became better defended, so grew the requirement for the seaborne movement of military forces.

By more recent standards, however, numbers remained relatively small: Rooke's 2,000 marines sealed the fate of Gibraltar; Clive triumphed at Plassey with under 3,000 troops, while the disastrous capitulation of Cornwallis at Yorktown involved a force of only 7,000.

Ever-ambitious as a colonial power, Britain remained vulnerable to defeat by invasion. Unlike France, a rival and foe, Britain maintained no great standing army and the first, and effectively only, line of defence was the Royal Navy. This service also policed and protected a growing empire and trade routes; each ship on station was an amphibious force in miniature, able to field a self-contained "naval brigade" to calm any colonial uprising.

The South African ("Boer") War at the turn of the 20th century demanded considerable numbers of merchant ships, chartered to transport the horses upon which the mobility of the British Army depended. It really marked the end of the old-style colonial war, heralding a new era of alliances pitted against alliances, mechanization and modern weapons capable of inflicting death on a massive scale. With conflict in a worldwide arena, armies expanded, with constant movement not of thousands, but millions of troops.

A new front involved not only infantry but also transport and equipment. To rely on landing all this through established ports was to compromise the advantage of surprise.

RIGHT: **With no earlier experience upon which to draw, planners of the Dardanelles campaign in 1915 placed too much reliance upon the use of various boats carried by the merchant ships and warships used in the campaign.**

The operations at Gallipoli thus showed the way forward with the landing over the beach of an initial one and a half divisions. The resulting casualties and variable pace of the operation demonstrated the need for, among much else, more specialist craft. Stalemate caused by a resolute defence resulted in valuable shipping being positioned offshore until enemy submarines arrived to make the situation untenable.

Between the wars Gallipoli was studied in detail, the lessons learned being tempered with the widely held opinion that the added dimension of air power might make such future operations impossible.

The 1930s nonetheless saw the development of the great assault fleet. Although operations were still envisaged on a relatively small scale, a clear requirement was apparent for two major categories of vessel, namely "ships" for shore-to-shore movement, possibly over considerable distances, and "craft" for ship-to-shore movement, the critical phase whereby the military component was landed.

The development complete, it needed only the requirements of World War II to initiate a combination of design ingenuity and industry to realize a large fleet, the likes of which the world had truly never seen.

Amphibious warfare is again receiving considerable attention and investment by governments around the globe, and this book is, perhaps, a timely reminder of that fact.

The book is divided into two fully illustrated sections: the first a directory of landing ships that transport personnel, cargo or vehicles; and the second a directory of landing craft, the majority of which are transported aboard specialist ships. Detailed specification panels are included for each vessel, giving information about country of origin, displacement, dimensions, armament, machinery, power and endurance.

RIGHT: **A vital element in amphibious operations in World War II was the pre-landing naval bombardment of enemy postions. Ships such as USS *Tennessee* (BB-43) would provide this massive firepower.**

ABOVE: **Japan successfully overran South-east Asia in 1942 without specialist amphibious equipment, by boldly exploiting the unpreparedness and low morale of the poorly equipped defending forces.**

ABOVE: **The speed of the Landing Craft, Air Cushion (LCAC) permits, for the first time, Over-The-Horizon (OTH) operations, greatly reducing the vulnerability of valuable multi-purpose amphibious warfare ships.**

A Directory of Landing Ships

Where landing craft were, in general, smaller, open-topped vessels, designed to take the ground in the final phase of an amphibious operation, landing ships were essential to the preliminary moves of transporting troops and equipment to the actual location. Landings during World War II were often mounted from considerable distance, for instance from the US West Coast directly to the western Pacific, or the US East Coast to operations in the Mediterranean.

Stripped of pre-war luxury, passenger liners were converted to move previously unimaginable numbers of troops. Other ships, loaded with assault craft, moved troops to the exact point at which they were required. Dock ships were developed to transport sufficient numbers of assault craft.

Most landing ships were not intended to beach, but the LST was an exception. The vessel carried armour, vehicles and troops. Not only were small craft and amphibious vehicles carried but the type was used as a platform for their repair. The LST was converted for many other roles. The LST and the later LPD were to provide the means for a post-war revolution in the transport by sea of heavy military loads. Many of these vessels are detailed in this chapter.

LEFT: **With the end of the Cold War, amphibious warfare has assumed a greater importance with the world's navies. This Royal Navy assault group led by HMS *Ocean* includes a tanker, store ship and anti-air/submarine escort.**

Landing Ship, Tank, Mark 2 (LST [2])

LST production in the USA began with a British requirement for 200 "Atlantic Tank Landing Craft", dated January 1942. Redesignated Landing Ship, Tank, Mark 2 (LST [2]) to differentiate the type from the British Maracaibo type (a converted oil tanker), the basic specification was progressed into a practical design by the renowned marine architect bureau of Gibbs & Cox. President Roosevelt considered specialist landing craft unnecessary but, just one month after the placement of the above order, the retired admiral overseeing the Lend-Lease Program advised the Chief of Naval Operations (CNO), Admiral Ernest J. King, of the crucial requirement for the type in the future. With Japan just completing the conquest of the Far East, the LST order had, by June 1942, been increased to 390 vessels. By August 1945 it would have exceeded 1,150.

The general British requirement had been for a vessel of some 91.5m/300ft in length, able to carry 20 medium tanks and to cross the Atlantic. As designed, all were some 8.54m/28ft longer at 100m/327ft 9in. Box-shaped, with a long, rectangular-sectioned midbody and tightly rounded bilges, all had bluff bows with clamshell doors backed by a hinged ramp, lowered for cargo access. The tank deck was located just above the load waterline and, as it was closed-off at the after end, vehicles were both loaded and unloaded through the bow doors.

The open upper deck was also used to carry wheeled transport. On the first 530 built, upper deck access was by a basic elevator. Later vessels had a rather steep, folding ramp, with the access opening covered by a hatch. Earlier LSTs had a vehicle deck ventilation system which required ten cylindrical trunks, protruding from and obstructing the upper deck. In later vessels these were removed, leaving space sufficient to carry an LCT (5) or (6) on skids or, alternatively, a wooden deck for the

ABOVE: **The prototype of the US Navy's LST. Very high sides to the hull combined with shallow draught, two small-diameter propellers and moderate-sized rudders made the vessel difficult to steer.** RIGHT: **Five of the 15 post-war LST-1156 class on exercise. Four maintain alignment with forward power, the nearest appearing to be reversing off. Controllable-pitch propellers removed the requirement for stern anchors.**

operation of light observation aircraft. Superstructure was minimal, and the diesel engines, housed in machinery spaces below the tank deck did not require a funnel. Twin propellers and rudders were located within the tunnel formed by protective skegs.

Steering, however, was rarely better than unpredictable. In ballast, this was worsened by the vessel's high sides which caught the wind, and the relatively low power of the locomotive-type diesel engines.

To be able to beach in the shallowest possible water, draught was critical. Matching the natural slope of a beach, the draught aft was greater than that forward. For stability, sea-going draught was considerably increased with water ballast, pumped

out prior to beaching. With a considerable beam and (usually) low centre of gravity, the LST had a high degree of stability, but with a rapid, lurching roll, which made securing cargo difficult. To assist in refloating after beaching, a stern anchor and winch were fitted as standard. Along either side, suspended from the underside of the upper deck, were spaces used for troop accommodation. This proved to be a bonus, which allowed the carrying of two LCVPs, under davits, to be increased to four, then to six.

Many LSTs were fitted with heavy, often unauthorized, armament. On the stern was a single 3in gun, elsewhere up to seven 40mm and/or twelve 20mm cannon could be mounted.

ABOVE: **As with so many LSTs, 733 had a useful service life of barely two years, during which time the vessel had no real refit, being kept running by a combination of skill and ingenuity by the crew.**

LSTs were not used in action until early 1943, but quickly proved to be versatile. To enable the vessel to be beached further from the shoreline when required, modular pontoon units could be secured against the hull sides. These, once released, were either self-propelled or linked to form a causeway. In the Pacific campaign the tank deck could be loaded with LVTs, to be floated off over the bow ramp. LSTs carried every type of cargo, some being converted to forward-area hospital ships and others equipped with emergency repair facilities.

ABOVE: **"Drying out" could impose enormous strains on the hull of an LST if the beach was less than flat. While it solved the problem of a short ramp, the beach gradient could still be too steep.**

Landing Ship, Tank (2)

Displacement: 1,625 tons (light); 2,365 tons (beaching); 4,080 tons (loaded)
Length: 96m/316ft (wl); 100m/327ft 9in
Beam: 15.3m/50ft 2in
Draught (beaching): 0.94m/3ft 1in (forward); 2.89m/9ft 6in (aft)
Draught (loaded): 2.4m/8ft (forward); 4.37m/14ft 4in (aft)
Armament: 1 x 3in gun, 7 x 40mm (2x2, 3x1), 12 x 20mm (12x1)
Machinery: 2 diesel engines, 2 shafts
Power: 1,343kW/1,800bhp for 10.8–12 knots
Fuel: 590 tons oil
Endurance: 16,560km/9,000nm at 9 knots
Protection: 13mm/0.5in splinter protection
Complement: 211–229
Capacity: Up to 1,900 tons distributed load on tank deck

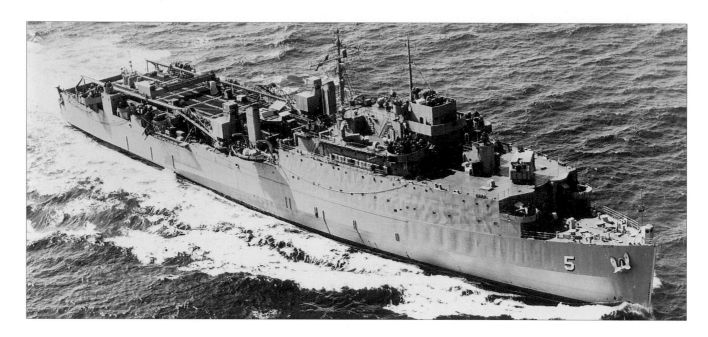

Landing Ship, Dock (LSD), Ashland class

Included in the British list of required ships of January 1942 (known to the US Government as the "1799 Program" from the number of hulls involved) were ten large vessels of an entirely new concept. The British were still thinking in terms of invading occupied Europe but, in order to use heavy armour in such action, the LST or LCT would be required. As the low speed of these types would put any attacking force in jeopardy a larger type of 17-knot vessel was specified, capable of carrying pre-loaded landing craft. The latter would be too large to be launched and recovered by davit or crane, so a "float-on, float-off" approach was proposed. In essence, the resulting ship would be a self-propelled floating dock.

The British draft specification was for a "TLC Carrier", reflecting both use and likely size, but the US Navy Bureau of Ships (BuShips), with a view to US military requirements, redrew the design around a docking well to accommodate 16 of the early type LCMs, then referred to as "tank lighters". With each LCM pre-loaded with a tank or support vehicle, an LSD would be able to lift 25 per cent of a full US Army tank battalion. Gibbs &

Cox again completed the final production design, now able to carry alternative loads of 16 LCMs, three US-pattern LCT (5), or two of the larger British LCT (3). A removable spar deck was added for stowage of "second-wave" vehicles.

In these early LSDs, the docking well extended forward as far as width permitted. All accommodation, including that for crews of military vehicles, was placed above. Bordering the docking well, sided casings extended from

ABOVE: **The relationship between an LSD and a floating dock is clearly shown in this picture of USS *Oak Hill* (LSD-7). The docking well extends to beneath the bridge structure.**

amidships to the square-shaped transom. An almost full transom wide, bottomed-hinged gate closed off the docking well. The gate was operated by two winches. Spanning the docking well was the removable spardeck, referred to as a "superdeck". A 35-ton crane was mounted on each side.

In the sea-going condition, the docking well, (i.e. dock bottom) was the freeboard deck and, thus, situated above the load waterline. To float cargo out, it was necessary to ballast the ship down to put sufficient water over the well deck. With levels equalized, the stern gate was lowered. In calm weather it was permissible to lower the gate while in the unballasted condition, allowing LVTs to drive straight off, using the gate as a ramp.

Although the LSD concept presented naval architects with some challenges, stability at all stages of flooding-down proved to be more than adequate.

Flooding-down took around 1¹/₂ hours and pumping-out around 2¹/₂ hours. To prevent a difficult motion, excess stability was reduced by adding pronounced flare to the lower hull. Ballasted the LSD had a slight stern-down trim, drawing nearly 9.46m/31ft aft, so propellers and rudders were partially recessed into the hull to reduce the danger of damage.

Steam turbine propulsion was originally specified but, because of a shortfall in manufacturing, the first group of eight LSDs were fitted with Skinner-patent "Uniflow" reciprocating steam engines. Other than in machinery, all 27 LSDs were essentially similar. Only four, numbered LSD 9 to 12, were eventually allocated to the British.

The LSD proved the ideal vessel for US military in Pacific operations, which relied on the use of large numbers of LVTs. The Casa Grande

ABOVE: **USS *Oak Hill* (LSD-7). The large gate to the docking well is clearly visible.**

class (LSD-13 to LSD-27) were equipped with double-level superdecks, permitting the carriage of LCMs on the well deck, with over 90 LVTs (or even DUKWs) above. First of class, USS *Ashland* (LSD-1) commissioned in June 1943, and with the USS *Belle Grove* (LSD-2) were fully worked-up for the forthcoming Operation "Galvanic", Gilbert Islands, in November 1943. At Makin, the USS *Belle Grove* (LSD-2) carried LCMs, each pre-loaded with a medium tank and it is recorded that all 26 craft were off-loaded in 12 minutes.

LEFT: **USS *San Marcos* (LSD-25), a Casa Grande-class vessel, carrying two utility LCVPs amidships. Lacking davits, the LCVPs are handled by the massive 35-ton capacity cranes. Note the spardeck ("superdeck") over the docking well.**

Landing Ship, Dock (LSD), Ashland class

Displacement: 5,910 tons (light); 7,930 tons (loaded, seagoing); 15,530 tons (loaded, ballasted)
Length: 138.5m/454ft (wl); 139.6m/457ft 9in (oa)
Beam: 22m/72ft 2in
Draught: 4.8m/15ft 10in (mean, seagoing); 9.2m/30ft 3in (mean, ballasted)
Armament: 1 x 5in gun, 12 x 40mm (2x4, 2x2), 16 x 20mm (16x1)
Machinery: Steam turbines, 2 boilers, 2 shafts
Power: 5,222kW/7,000shp for 16.5 knots
Fuel: 1,500 tons oil
Endurance: 13,800km/7,500nm at 15 knots
Protection: Limited splinter protection
Complement: 326
Capacity: 3 loaded LCT (5) or (6), or 2 loaded LCT (3) or (4), or 14 LCMs, or 41 LVTs, or 47 DUKWs

LEFT: **Introduced in 1944, the LSM (R) was designed to saturate enemy beach defences immediately before craft with troops landed. Over 1,000 rockets could be fired within one minute at a fixed range of 4,572m/5,000yd.**

Landing Ship, Medium (LSM) and Landing Ship, Medium (Rocket) (LSM [R])

With planning for amphibious warfare developing rapidly, requirements arose for more specific types of craft. Building programmes for these and, particularly, the demands for engines, competed with those for other urgently needed types of vessel. Firm production priorities were required.

The Landing Ship, Medium (LSM), of which no less than 350 were ordered between September and November 1943, was one priority. LSTs were proving very successful but, by prioritizing cargo capacity and simplicity, were slow. During a major operation this caused the type to be deployed in separate convoys. The smaller LCT was unsuitable for long sea passages. A speed of 12 knots was

demanded for the new craft, thus necessitating an improved hull shape. It was first designed as an LCT (7) but, in view of its unavoidably larger size, was redesignated as an LSM.

The existing LCT (6) could carry four 32-ton M4A-3 Sherman medium tanks. The dimensions were 36.72 x 9.76m/120ft 4in x 32ft , but range and speed was poor at 1,127km/700 miles and 7 knots.

The new LSM drew considerable uninformed criticism because the slender 62.07 x 10.37m/203ft 6in x 34ft hull, necessary to achieve 12 knots had room to accommodate just one extra Sherman. The vessel thus appeared too large for the task but, in naval ship design, speed is very much a defining

parameter. In addition, the LSM at cruising speed had a respectable range of 5,633km/3,500 miles, invaluable for a Pacific deployment.

Being so much longer, the LSM had to be deeper to keep hull stresses within acceptable limits. One disadvantage was the closed stern, dictating that vehicles loaded and disembarked over the bow ramp. The latter, once stowed, was protected by LST-type bow doors, the stowed height of which required a high

BELOW: **The light construction of the type gave rise to some criticism but, during the final 18 months of World War II, more than 550 were delivered.The LSM was a faster vessel than the standard LST.**

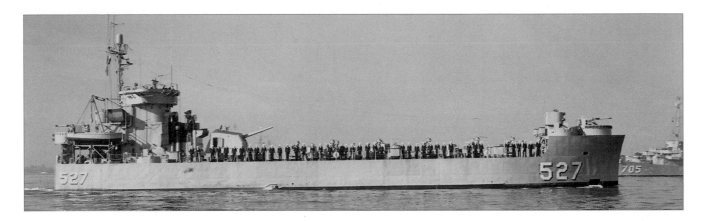

bow profile which was beneficial for seakeeping. The bows were bridged by a short foredeck upon which was a twin 40mm cannon mounting, useful for fire support over the beach. On the starboard side, amidships, the deck supported a narrow but high superstructure. This was two decks deep with an open compass platform at the top, the structure having a distinctive cylindrical shape.

Beneath the tank deck was crew accommodation for over 50 and up to 75 army personnel, mostly vehicle crews. The vessels twin propellers were powered by diesel engines similar to the type used in destroyer escorts and submarines. The LSM was seen as complementary to the rather smaller, troop-carrying LCI (L).

Like other amphibious vessels, the LSM had two significant displacements. One, around 1,100 tons, was a sea-going cargo carrier. To beach, however, the vessel could displace no more than about 740 tons. Thus, considerable water ballast capacity was required to guarantee adequate stability in all conditions. This ballast would be discharged to bring the vessel to beaching trim and displacement.

In September 1944, by which time some 80 LSMs had been delivered, a new role was defined as rocket-firing support craft, LSM (R). Heavy bombardment preceding an assault would be lifted as the first wave approached the beach. The defenders, however, could have survived and been able to rake the beach

with gunfire. By December, the first of over 50 LSM (R) had been built. The vessels were to accompany the first assault wave and to saturate the landing area with a barrage of rocket projectiles to destroy mined areas and obstacles.

LSM (R) were decked over, the vehicle deck being divided into ammunition handling rooms and magazines. Armament varied considerably, with rapid development, culminating in 85 launchers, each mounting 12 projectiles. A 1,000-plus rocket salvo could be discharged in one minute, but a reload took 45 minutes. In addition to automatic weapons, a single 5in naval gun was mounted in the stern.

RIGHT: **On this standard LSM, note the characteristic starboard-side bridge structure and the ramp protruding above the bow doors. The rubbing strake was a necessary later addition.**

Landing Ship, Medium (LSM)

Displacement: 520 tons (light); 1,095 tons (full load); 743 tons (beaching)
Length: 62.07m/203ft 6in
Beam: 10.52m/34ft 6in
Draught (full load): 1.95m/6ft 5in (forward); 2.55mm/8ft 4in (aft)
Draught (beaching): 1.07m/3ft 6in (forward); 2.16m/7ft 1in (aft)
Armament: 2 x 40mm (1x2), 4 x 20mm (4x1)
Machinery: 2 diesel engines, 2 shafts
Power: 2,148kW/2,880bhp for 13 knots
Endurance: 9,016km/4,900nm at 12 knots
Protection: Splinter protection to guns, bridge and pilot house
Complement: 58
Capacity: 5 medium tanks, or 3 heavy tanks, or 6 LVTs, or 9 DUKWs

Landing Ship, Vehicle (LSV)

The US Navy used the designator AP for transports (*cf.* British "troopship"), for the movement of troops. More precisely, the APA was an "attack transport", intended to carry troops directly to a combat zone and to be self-contained when unloading. The common distinguishing feature of an AP was the large number of LCVPs, carried under davits and/or on deck.

Early in 1943 (just six months after Operation "Watchtower", the initial amphibious landing on Guadalcanal) two large minelayers and four very similar netlayers, almost complete, were identified as ideal for conversion to APA.

Displacing up to 8,000 tons fully loaded, these were large ships. The minelayers differed somewhat from the netlayers (not least in having a second funnel) but all featured long gallery decks, extending over half the length of the ship and flanking a narrow centreline casing. To facilitate the movement of vehicles from these spaces, a ramp gate was fitted into the wide flat stern.

ABOVE: **USS *Catskill* (LSV-1), originally classified as AP-106, was launched on May 19, 1942.**
LEFT: **The inclusion of a stern ramp made the class effective carriers of both tracked and wheeled amphibious vehicles.**

Because of the vehicle component, the type designator was changed from APA to LSV, although the ships were not designed to be beached. Vehicle capacity proved to be disappointingly small, the gallery decks being low and badly ventilated. Capacities were as follows:

	LVT	DUKW	Troops
LSV-1 and 2	None	44	800
LSV-3 and 4	19	29	880
LSV-5 and 6	21	31	800

Without vehicles, around a further 1,000 troops could be accommodated. The ships were valuable in being relatively fast but proved to have limited stability when damaged, resulting in planned defensive armament being considerably reduced.

Only the six were built and, having seen little combat use, survived to serve as support ships in the post-war US fleet.

LEFT: **USS *Montauk* (LSV-6) from the LSV-5 to LSV-6 group converted in October 1944. The vessel retains the original squared-off netlayer bow.**

Landing Ship, Vehicle (LSV)

Displacement: 5,615 tons (light); 7,927 tons (full load)
Length: 137.56–138.47m/451–454ft (oa)
Beam: 18.3m/60ft
Draught: 5.19–5.49m/17–18ft
Armament: 3/4 x 5in guns (3/4 x1), 8 x 40mm (4x2), 18/20 x 20mm (18/20 x1)
Machinery: Steam turbines, 4 boilers, 2 shafts
Power: 8,206kW/11,000shp for 19.5 knots
Fuel: 2,020 tons oil
Endurance: Not known
Protection: Not known
Complement: 481

Amphibious Force Flagship (AGC)

Even before US forces undertook the first amphibious operation in August 1942 the need for a headquarters ship, fitted specifically for overall control was appreciated. The US Navy had inspected HMS *Bulolo* upon completion in June 1942, a visit which highlighted the advantages of equipment space and accommodation when using a merchant ship hull as compared to the cramped conditions aboard even a large warship.

In October 1942, following the inspection, the US Navy allocated three standard C2 hulls, already under construction, for conversion to what were first called "Administrative

Flagships", then "Amphibious Force Flagships" (AGC). The "A" in the designator represented auxiliary status. Not being warships, fitted with no more than defensive armament and with relatively low speed, the vessel would not be used in the course of an operation to act as a regular warship.

The C2s were built over half the length with an extra deck to give more space for senior officers and staff of all forces deployed in the assault. Essential was the detailed plot in the command room and a comprehensive suite of communications with adequate backup equipment. All elements supporting the dynamics of the operation were in continuous two-way contact, so that any delay or complication could be quickly addressed by an appropriate decision direct from command staff. All requests for fire support or close air support

ABOVE: **This vessel was a passenger liner until 1942, when it became US Army Transport USS *Ancon* (AP-66). On May 8, 1943, USS *Ancon* entered service, after conversion, as an amphibious command ship (AGC-4).**

were also actioned through the flagship. Only when the battle situation stabilized were the military headquarters staff move ashore.

A total of 15 AGCs were commissioned during the war, with others still completing. Although most were C2 conversions and were generally known as the Appalachian class, they varied considerably. Indeed, a converted passenger liner USS *Ancon* (AGC-4) was the first of the type to be commissioned in August 1942. Some Attack Transports (APA) were fitted with basic command facilities.

Amphibious Force Flagship, USS *Appalachian* (AGC-1)

Displacement: 7,430 tons (light); 12,800 tons (full load)
Length: 140.07m/459ft 3in (oa)
Beam: 19.22m/63ft
Draught: 7.32m/24ft (maximum)
Armament: 2 x 5in guns (2x1), 4/8 x 40mm (2/4x2), 18 x 20mm (18 x1)
Machinery: Steam turbines, 2 boilers, single shaft
Power: 4,476kW/6,000shp for 16.5 knots
Fuel: Oil
Endurance: 9,200km/5,000nm at 14 knots
Protection: Nominal
Complement: 520 (ship) plus 470 (staff)

USS *Henderson* and *Doyen* (AP-1 and AP-2)

The US Marine Corps (USMC) is the primary amphibious attack force in the US military, and AP-1 and 2 are significant because they were the first ships designed around integrated USMC formations. Marines operate in self-sufficient tactical units, which require to be transported to, and landed directly at, the point of attack. By definition, therefore, the ships would be the original attack transports.

Approved in 1912, USS *Henderson* (later AP-1) accommodated a USMC regiment of 75 officers and 1,600 other ranks with space for recreation and exercise. Four of the ship's 5in guns could be dismounted for transport ashore on special lighters. Fewer troops

would be carried in winter but stores and a water-distilling plant occupied a large space in the hull.

Hull design concentrated less on speed than on survivability, manoeuvrability and the moderate draught required to work close inshore. Commissioned shortly after the United States entry into World War I, USS *Henderson* was used during the war as a troop transport, and was not tried in the designed role under wartime conditions.

With further such construction denied by Congress, USS *Henderson* was used on various operations between the wars. Only during 1940, on reports of the successful British conversion of four fast Glen Line cargo liners to LSI (L), were the

first similar ships approved for the US Navy. USS *Doyen* (AP-2) (originally named USS *Heywood*) and USS *Feland* (AP-11) became the first purpose-designed attack transports, but did not enter service until 1943. However, numerous other mercantile hulls had already been converted to the role. The ships were unique in having a slipway incorporated in the stern, large enough to launch and recover a tank-carrying LCM (2). The ships were badly overweight, so the tank and LCM were not carried together as part of weight-saving measures. However, sixteen 30ft "landing boats" were carried for the USMC force of 60 officers and 670 other ranks.

ABOVE: **USS** *Doyen* **(AP-2) was launched in 1918 as SS** *City of Baltimore*, **and was originally named USS** *Heywood* **before adopting the name of a cancelled successor to Henderson. Note the unusual counter stern.**

USS *Doyen* (AP-2)

Displacement: 4,500 tons (standard); 6,350 tons (full load)
Length: 122m/400ft (wl); 124.75m/409ft (oa)
Beam: 17.08m/56ft
Draught: 5.29m/17ft 4in (maximum)
Armament: 1 x 5in gun, 4 x 3in guns (4x1)
Machinery: Steam turbines, 2 boilers, 2 shafts
Power: 5,968kW/8,000shp for 19 knots
Fuel: Oil
Endurance: 18,400km/10,000nm at 16.5 knots
Protection: Nominal
Complement: 234

LEFT: USS *Bower* (APD-40) was originally built as a Buckley-class destroyer escort (DE-637) and launched on October 31, 1943. The vessel was converted in 1945 and redesignated on June 25, 1945.

Destroyer Transports (APD)

By the late 1930s, the US Marine Corps (USMC) was preparing for the role of capturing forward bases in a Pacific campaign. Some operations would be on a small scale, for which a large transport ship would be unsuitable. The requirement was for a small vessel capable of a fast passage carrying a USMC unit, which could be landed and supported by the ship's guns. Many

World War I flush-decked destroyers remained in low-grade reserve and were proposed as suitable for modification.

The prototype conversion was that on USS *Manley* (DD-74), later designated APD-1. The four banks of torpedo tubes were removed and replaced with four sets of davits for "Surf Boats". Also fitted were handling frames for two of the anticipated new

landing craft. As passages of only 12 to 24 hours were envisaged, no special facilities were built in for the some 100 Marines to be conveyed.

Exercises showed that longer passages of several days, with troop contingents of 150, plus stores, were possible. Despite the forward boiler space being converted to troop accommodation, sufficient speed could still be developed. "Surf Boats" were replaced by Landing Craft, Ramped (LCP [R]) and the old 4in guns were replaced by the more versatile 3in weapon.

Twenty-six DD vessels were converted to APD before new destroyer escort (DE) hulls became available. No less than 100 Buckley and Rudderrow-class DEs were allocated but not all conversions were actually completed. These were built with a long amidships accommodation deckhouse for 162 Marines. Heavy double davits could each handle two LCVPs. Around 130 tons of cargo could be carried aft, handled by two derricks ("booms") stepped to a lattice-type mast. Typical armament included a 5in gun, three twin 40mm and six 20mm cannon.

Despite the role remaining viable, surviving APDs were scrapped without replacement during the 1960s.

Destroyer Transport (DE) conversions

Displacement: 1,400 tons (standard); 2,130 tons (full load)
Length: 91.5m/300ft (wl); 93.33m/306ft (oa)
Beam: 11.29m/37ft
Draught: 3.86m/12ft 8in (maximum)
Armament: 1 x 5in gun, 6 x 40mm guns (3x2)
Machinery: Turbo-electric, 2 boilers, 2 shafts
Power: 8,952kW/12,000shp for 23.5 knots
Fuel: 350 tons oil
Endurance: 10,120km/5,500nm at 15 knots
Protection: Nominal
Complement: 214

ABOVE: Early APDs were converted from World War I "flush-decked" destroyers. The forward boiler room has here been removed and funnels reduced from four to two. Note the four LCVPs in davits. USS *Barry* (APD-29) was converted from DD-248 in 1944.

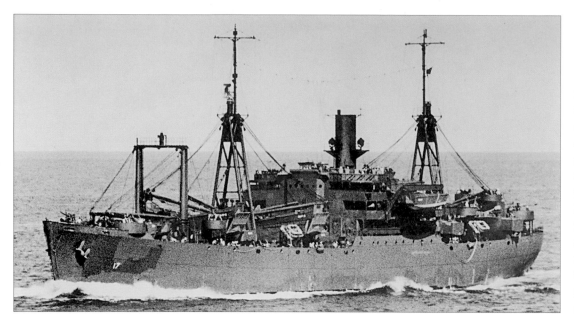

LEFT: **The war-built Andromeda class were completed as either AKA or APA. Both types carried troops, as seen on USS** Centaurus **(AKA-17). Note the heavy cargo mast aft, the LCVPs under davits and one of the two LCMs, just visible forward of the bridge. Also note the paravane cable at the bows.**

Attack Cargo Ships (AKA)

Attack Transports (APA) and Attack Cargo Ships (AKA) were complementary, one type to accommodate combat troops, the other, equipment. In general, personnel require more space, so APAs were converted mainly from standard C3 hulls, and AKAs from the C2. US Maritime Commission (USMaC) codes defined a C2 as a cargo carrier of 122–137.25m/400–450ft waterline length. A C3 was larger, at 137.25–152.5m/450–500ft.

Urgency dictated the use of available shipping, but it was far from ideal. Designed for maximum capacity and ease of access, cargo spaces were large and open. By naval standards, which emphasized survivability through watertight compartments, combat cargo ships were considered vulnerable.

To support the Pacific campaign of 1944, the US military joint staff planners requested a massive total of 133 APAs, 53 AKAs and 13 AGCs. Of these, the AKAs fell into five classes of which four – the Arcturus, Andromeda, Tolland and Charleston – had similar overall dimensions. The smaller S4s of the Artemis class were faster and accommodated over 250 troops.

Hold spaces were divided horizontally by two or three decks. By standardizing headroom, problems were created as military equipment became larger.

Across the hatches were stowed the craft by which the cargo was landed. A typical complement was made up of six LCM (6), two LCM (3), 13 LCVPs and one LCPL. To handle these, two tetrapod-type masts were constructed with at least four derricks ("cargo booms") of 30- to 40-ton safe working load. By the end of the war, 55-ton derricks were being trialed.

Although considerably reduced in post-war reserve, the above classes remained in the US Navy's cargo inventory until the mid-1960s.

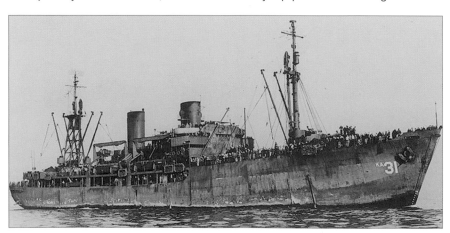

ABOVE: **USS** Medea **(AKA-31), an Artemis-class vessel, with her decks crowded with troops, probably upon arrival in San Francisco Bay, California, circa late 1945 or early 1946.**

Attack Cargo Ship (AKA), Andromeda class

Displacement: 6,990 tons (light); 13,355 tons (full load)
Length: 132.68m/435ft (wl); 140.07m/459ft 3in (oa)
Beam: 19.22m/63ft
Draught: 7.93m/26ft (mean, full load)
Armament: 1 x 5in gun, 8 x 40mm (4x2), 18 x 20mm (18x1)
Machinery: Steam turbines, 2 boilers, single screw
Power: 4.476kW/6,000shp for 16 knots
Fuel: 2,000 tons oil
Endurance: 29,450km/16,000nm at 12 knots
Protection: Nominal
Complement: 368 (war), or 247 (peace)

LEFT: **The Auxillary Motor Minesweeper YMS-373 was redesignated as Motor Minesweeper AMS-21 and named USS *Jackdaw* on February 18, 1947.**

Motor Minesweeper (AMS)

As it was general policy to assume that waters within the 183m/100-fathom line would be mined, it is obvious that clearance was a necessary prelude to any amphibious operation.

The Japanese military had not developed sophisticated magnetic mines – but it could never be assumed that they had not. A potential landing beach was as obvious to the defenders as to the attackers. Extended shallow approaches, unswept, could see the valuable transports in the assault fleet anchored miles offshore, increasing the vulnerability of the assault forces, and slowing the follow-up resupply

Despite the risk of alerting the enemy, therefore, a necessary preliminary was a high-speed sweep of the proposed Transport Area(s) by Destroyer-Minesweepers (DMS). Closer inshore, the very shallow approaches (such as those at Leyte) were swept by Auxiliary Motor Minesweepers (YMS), later called Motor Minesweepers (AMS). These, the Albatross class, were 41.48m/136ft in length. The Pacific Ocean was often found to be of greater hazard than the enemy to the small ships. Sweeping the 18.3m/10-fathom line, a DMS could counter fire from shore batteries with a 5in gun and 40mm cannon. Inshore the AMS mounted a single 3in gun and two Oerlikon 20mm cannon. A destroyer support was always required.

From 1942 the AMSs were built by a wide variety of small shipyards with workers skilled in wooden ship construction. As a result there was a considerable variation in detail. Common to all was the short raised forecastle and heavy, full-length rubbing strake. Some, however, had two tunnels, some one and others none. Mainmasts, sometimes with derricks fitted, were optional. All were equipped to sweep magnetic or contact mines.

Following the Korean War, the improved Bluebird class was built to the same basic design.

ABOVE: **Motor Minesweeper USS *Firecrest* (AMS-5), when in service as YMS-192.**

Motor Minesweeper (AMS), Albatross class

Displacement: 270 tons (standard); 350 tons (full load)
Length: 41.48m/136ft (oa)
Beam: 7.47m/24ft 6in
Draught: 2.44m/8ft (maximum)
Armament: 1 x 3in gun, 2 x 20mm (2x1)
Machinery: 2 diesel engines, 2 shafts
Power: 746kW/1,000bhp for 15 knots
Fuel: 16 tons oil
Endurance: 10,120km/5,500nm at 12 knots
Protection: Nominal
Complement: 50

LEFT: **USS** *Tallahatchie County*, **ex-LST-1154, was, with her only steam-powered sister, USS** *Talbot County* **(LST-1153), converted to an Advanced Aviation Base Ship (AVB) in 1962. Here, the vessel appears to be being used as a landing ship.**

Landing Ship, Tank (LST), LST-1153 type

After World War II, rapid evolution of new weapons systems made the LST look especially vulnerable. Studies to develop a 20-knot version, however, resulted in a vessel that would be expensive, over-large and no longer expendable.

Two prototype steam turbine-powered variants of the LST-1153 (later Talbot County) type were completed in 1947. The modest increase in speed proved expensive. The new ships were not liked. The steam plant was unreliable due to over complexity, and required more skilled personnel. Endurance was inferior to that of the earlier, diesel-powered LST, and the hull still pounded heavily in a head sea.

Gibbs & Cox were charged with refining the LST-1153 design further, producing in 1951 the LST-1156 (Terrebonne Parish) type. Fifteen of these were built between 1952 and 1954. All had four diesel engines, driving two propeller shafts and, for the first time, controllable-pitch propellers for easier reversing off a beach. Displacement and forward beaching draught again inevitably increased, necessitating a longer ramp. This needed to be strong enough to load a 60- to 75-ton tank (the M60A1 Patton main battle tank weighed 52.6 tons). An internal turntable for moving vehicles was also provided. An additional requirement was

accommodation and facilities for 380 troops to support the embarked vehicles. The increase in length, however, made it possible for 14 knots to be achieved on the same 6,000 bhp engine power.

The Korean War raised a demand for a 17-knot LST. The resulting LST-1171 (De Soto County) type was 15 per cent longer and of nearly 40 per cent greater beaching displacement. No longer cheap or expendable, the LST could be refined no further.

ABOVE: **Speed and refinement proved to be expensive. Here, USS** *Washtenaw County* **(LST-1166) is at anchor, loaded and ready to sail from Subic Bay, October 1969. Note also the stacked LCVPs.**

Landing Ship, Tank, LST-1153 type

Displacement: 2,585 tons (light);
   3,330 tons (beaching); 5,780 tons (full load)
Length: 112.24m/368ft (wl);
   117.12m/384ft (oa)
Beam: 16.93m/55ft 6in
Draught (beaching): 1.09m/3ft 7in (forward);
   3.36m/11ft (aft)
Draught (loaded): 2.49m/8ft 2in (forward);
   4.9m/16ft 1in (aft)
Armament: 6 x 3in guns (3x2)
Machinery: 4 diesel engines, 2 shafts
Power: 4.476kW/6,000bhp for 14 knots
Fuel: Oil
Endurance: 18,400km/10,000nm at 10 knots
Protection: Nominal
Complement: 157
Capacity: Maximum 1,395 tons distributed load

LEFT: **USS** *Plymouth Rock* **(LSD-29)**, a Thomaston-class LSD, may easily be identified from earlier classes by the staggered funnel arrangement.

Landing Ship, Dock (LSD), Thomaston class

Vessels deployed for a World War II amphibious operation needed to be organized into fast (15–16 knots) convoys for larger ships and slow (11-knot) convoys for LSTs. Until 1945 this was a necessary inconvenience but the Cold War greatly enhanced threats which resulted in such formations looking highly vulnerable. From 1947, therefore, all new ships had to be designed as an all-20-knot amphibious force.

The design for a replacement LSD was a predictable balance between cost and capability. The vessel was required to transport 21 LCM (6), each of around 17 x 4.3m/56 x 14ft. The welldeck was covered with a light spardeck ("superdeck") and, forward, a temporary mezzanine deck, on which to carry 48 LVTs. This was 13 more than in war-built ships. Alternatively, the spardeck could be used as a helicopter landing deck.

Much sleeker in looks than the utilitarian, war-built predecessor, the eight new ships had three times the engine power, and easily exceeded 23 knots. The engine room was located below the docking well and laid out on the unit principle. The need to exhaust the steam turbines on each side resulted in the characteristic staggered positioning of the funnels.

The area between the funnels was not bridged by the spardeck, allowing the well to be served by the two large cranes. A 7.5-ton capacity gantry crane which spanned the full width also ran the length of the well.

A secondary role for the LSD was in the long-distance transport of smaller warships such as minesweepers or PT boats. The LSD was also used as a temporary dry dock, although facilities for heavy repair were limited.

ABOVE: **USS** *Thomaston* **(LSD-28)**. Most of the 3in gun armament fitted to this class was quickly removed, as it was ineffective against attack by modern aircraft.

Landing Ship, Dock (LSD), Thomaston class

Displacement: 6,880 tons (light);
11,270 tons (full load)

Length: 155.55m/510ft (oa);
waterline length variable

Beam: 25.62m/84ft

Draught: 5.8m/19ft (mean, loaded)

Armament: 16 x 3in guns (8x2),
16 x 20mm (8x2)

Machinery: Steam turbines, 2 boilers, 2 shafts

Power: 17,904kW/24,000shp for 23 knots

Fuel: Oil

Endurance: 23,290km/13,000nm at 10 knots

Protection: Nominal

Complement: 405

Capacity: 21 LCM (6), 48 LVTs, or 2,400 tons
cargo load

LEFT: Simply a modified version of an LSM (R), USS *Carronade* (IFS-1), launched on May 26, 1953, and commissioned into US Navy service on May 25, 1955, remained the only one built. Rapid series production could be started in an emergency.

Inshore Fire Support Ship (IFS)

Although highly valued for close-in fire support, the war-built LSM (R) had limitations, not least in that it took a considerable time to reload between salvoes. Nor was it equipped to pinpoint and neutralize mortar fire, which caused considerable disruption and casualties on the beach.

The US Marine Corps wanted a suitably armed, shallow-draught, manoeuvrable vessel with sufficient protection to attack from a short range. For the designer, this created a clash of priorities in matching shallow draught and limited size with the new overall 20-knot requirement in amphibious warfare vesels. Possible future series production demanded a simple design, while the cost constrictions imposed saw the concept considerably reduced.

The one-off USS *Carronade* (IFS-1) was the post-Korean War compromise to the above specification. Although looking superficially like a landing craft, the new classification emphasised a considerable difference. The laws of hydrodynamics conspire against light displacement hulls being driven at high speed and, by accepting a 15-knot maximum for the vessel USS *Carronade* could be 15 per cent shorter and required only 50 per cent the engine power of a 20-knot equivalent. Hoping for a new, high-velocity, flat-trajectory gun, the US Marine Corps was probably disappointed in the ship mounting a standard, forward-firing 5in Type 38 gun and two mountings of twin 40mm cannon. The long foredeck, however, carried eight of the new Mk 105 twin rocket launchers each capable of launching six rounds per minute. To support such massive firepower, a 6,000-round magazine was provided, although the lack of depth in the hull did not allow this to be located entirely below normal load waterline.

USS *Carronade* was stricken from the US Naval Register on May 1, 1973 and sold for scrap September 1, 1974.

LEFT: USS *Carronade* (IFS-1) was placed on US Navy reserve on May 31, 1960, after just five years in service. The ship was recommisioned as LFR-1 on January 1, 1969, and served during the Vietnam War as the flagship for Inshore Fire Division 93.

Inshore Fire Support Ship, USS *Carronade* (IFS-1)

Displacement: 1,040 tons (light); 1,500 tons (full load)
Length: 72.59m/238ft (wl); 74.73m/245ft (oa)
Beam: 11.9m/39ft
Draught: 3.05m/10ft
Armament: 8 x launchers, 1 x 5in gun, 4 x 40mm guns (2x2)
Machinery: 2 diesel engines, 2 shafts
Power: 2,313kW/3,100bhp for 15 knots
Fuel: Oil
Endurance: Not known
Protection: 19mm/0.75in splinter deck over magazine
Complement: 162

LEFT: **USS** *Vancouver*
(LPD-2) was launched
on September 15, 1962,
and served with the
US 7th Fleet. During
the Vietnam War, the
ship was awarded
11 battle stars.

Landing Ship, Personnel, Dock (LPD), Raleigh class

By the late 1950s, it was apparent that the helicopter would become a potent complement to the landing craft, and studies began for the specification for a ship to accommodate both. Helicopter development was in its infancy, however, and to build such a large and expensive vessel would be a considerable gamble. As an interim measure, therefore, the functions were divided between two new classes of ship, Landing Ship, Personnel, Helicopter (LPH) and Landing Ship, Personnel, Dock (LPD).

It was hoped that the LPD would carry a "balanced load" of assault troops, equipment and transport together with the assault craft and helicopters for a landing. If successful, this might lead to the phasing-out of the APA and AKA ships.

Superficially similar to the Thomaston class, USS *Raleigh* (LPD-1) was recognizable by the permanent helicopter deck in place of the "superdeck". The square transom and stern gate were retained but the docking well was reduced to 51.24 x 15.25m/168 x 50ft, large enough for nine LCM (6). Forward of the well, and linked via ramps, was vehicle garaging and cargo spaces on several levels.

The standard assault helicopter was the Sikorsky CH-46A Sea Knight, the size of which dictated space for only two landing spots and no hangar facilities. A small foldable hanger was added but this could accommodate only one Bell UH-1 "Huey", the ubiquitous combat helicopter. Although capable of carrying over 900 troops, a Raleigh-class LPD was considered suitable to support only a company-level operation. It became necessary to view an LPD and the more expensive LPH as a working combination.

Obviously in need of further refinement, building of the LPD-1 design was limited to just three ships. The last, USS *La Salle* (LPD-3) had better accommodation and was equipped with improved communications for the role of flagship.

ABOVE: **LPDs were built with a permanent helicopter deck in place of the temporary "superdeck" on the LSD. USS *La Salle* (LPD-3) was the third and last of the class to be built.**

Landing Ship, Personnel, Dock, Raleigh class (LPD-1 and 2)

Displacement: 8,040 tons (light); 13,900 tons (full load)
Length: 152.5m/500ft (wl); 159.15m/521ft 10in (oa)
Beam: 25.62m/84ft
Draught: 6.41m/21ft
Armament: 8 x 3in guns (4x2)
Machinery: Steam turbines, 2 boilers, 2 shafts
Power: 17,904kW/24,000shp for 21 knots
Fuel: Oil
Endurance: 17.664km/9,600nm at 16 knots
Protection: Nominal
Complement: 490
Capacity: 9 LCM (6), or 3 LCM (6) plus 1 LCU, or 4 LCM (8), or 20 LVTs

Landing Ship, Personnel, Dock (LPD), Austin class

ABOVE: **The LPD was designed to be a complement to the more expensive LPH. Its layout was based on that of existing LSDs, but with a shorter well deck. This is the USS *Ponce* (LPD-15).**

Continuing the programme initiated with the Raleigh class, the 12 Austin class were very similar, but with an extra 14.64m/48ft in hull length to rectify the shortcomings of the earlier class. Cargo capacity was increased by over 50 per cent and the docking well dimensions to 120 x 15.24m/393ft 6in x 50ft This allowed two LCM (6) and four LCM (8) to be transported. As the LCM (8) had almost twice the displacement of an LCM (6) , it was capable of carrying a M60 Patton main battle tank which weighed 53.6 tons. All landing craft were loaded by gantry cranes running the length of both well and other decks.

Although the helicopter deck was also enlarged, the hangar facilities for a flight of four CH-46A Sea Knight helicopters still proved impracticable on a ship of this size. The lack of full maintenance facilities for helicopters were to limit the ship operating as an independent unit.

During the time in service of the class, the LCAC and the LCU have been introduced. As these were designed to fit the docking well in existing amphibious warfare ships, the Austin class can transport an LCAC, or one LCU plus four LCM (8) or 28 LVT. It is worth noting that, as LVTs have become considerably larger since World War II, fewer can be accommodated.

By design, six of the LPDs were built as flagships for either an amphibious squadron or transport division. These ships can be distinguished by an extra deck on the superstructure. So spacious are these facilities that USS *Coronado* (LPD-11), like the Raleigh-class USS *La Salle* (LPD-3), has seen long service as a fleet flagship.

Phased retirement for the class would probably have commenced in the late 1990s but for repeated delays to the replacement LPD-17 (San Antonio-class) programme. Service Life Extension Programs (SLEP) will probably now see at least five of the Austin class operational until 2014.

Landing Ship, Personnel, Dock (LPD), Austin class

Displacement: 10,000 tons (light); 16,900 (full load)
Length: 173.85m/570ft (oa)
Beam: 25.62m/84ft
Draught: 7m/23ft 3in (mean)
Armament: 8 x 3in guns (4x2)
Machinery: Steam turbines, 2 boilers, 2 shafts
Power: 17,904kW/24,000shp for 23 knots
Fuel: Oil
Endurance: 14,168km/7,700nm at 20 knots
Protection: Nominal
Complement: 490 (plus 90 in flagship)
Capacity: 2 LCM (6) plus 4 LCM (8)

RIGHT: **Twelve Austin-class vessels were built and numbered LPD-4 to LPD-16, with the first being launched on June 27, 1964. Note the carrier-style side galleries at the helicopter deck on the USS *Ponce* (LPD-15).**

LEFT: **The Anchorage class was built after the introduction into service of the high-speed Type 1610 LCU, and designed to carry three of the type. USS *Portland* (LSD-37) was the second to enter service.**

Landing Ship, Dock (LSD), Anchorage class

By the late 1960s the war-built LSDs were becoming obsolete and, to maintain the force, five replacements had to be built. Although the starting point for the design was that of the preceding Thomaston class, the hull was lengthened considerably in order to accommodate three LCU-1610. These craft had become the replacement for earlier LCTs. Each was capable of lifting three 55-ton M103 heavy tanks. The resulting docking well was 131.15m/430ft long which, even in a hull lengthened by some 12.2m/40ft, extended into the bow section.

Externally, the new vessel resembled the earlier class but had a longer superstructure and a braced tripod mast to provide a vibration-free platform for the SPS-40 air-defence radar antenna.

Accommodation was provided for 376 troops. For landing, two LCM (6) were carried topside, together with two LCPLs. All of these were handled by the two 50-ton cranes.

As with the Thomaston class, the helicopter deck did not extend fully to the stern, ending some 15.25m/50ft forward of the stern gate. Again similarly, this deck was removable, with no permanent hangar facilities. However some 90 tons of aviation fuel was carried for the aircraft. Only one Sikorsky CH-53 Sea Stallion aircraft could be handled at a time.

As built, the class had the usual eight 3in DP guns in twin mountings spaced around the superstructure. Later the forward port and aft starboard mountings were removed. US Atlantic Fleet units were then fitted with a single Close-In Weapons System (CIWS) mounting.

None of the class remained in US Navy service beyond 2003.

ABOVE: **The stern of the Anchorage-class vessel has the short helicopter deck and one-piece loading gate. A total of five Anchorage-class vessels were built: USS *Anchorage* (LSD-36), USS *Portland* (LSD-37), USS *Pensacola* (LSD-38), USS *Mount Vernon* (LSD-39), and USS *Fort Fischer* (LSD-40).**

Landing Ship, Dock (LSD), Anchorage class

Displacement: 8,200 tons (light); 13,700 tons (full load)
Length: 162.87m/534ft (wl); 171.41m/562ft (oa)
Beam: 25.62m/84ft
Draught: 6.1m/20ft (mean)
Armament: 8 x 3in guns (4x2)
Machinery: Steam turbines, 2 boilers, 2 shafts
Power: 17,904kW/24,000shp for 22 knots
Fuel: Oil
Endurance: 25,760km/14,000nm at 12 knots
Protection: Nominal
Complement: 322
Capacity: 3 LCUs, or 15 LCM (6), or 8 LCM (8), or 50 LVTs

LEFT: **This excellent overhead of USS *Guadalcanal* (LPH-7) clearly shows the rounded bow and the lack of catapults and arrestor gear that defined the ship as a helicopter carrier.**

Landing Ship, Personnel, Helicopter (LPH), Iwo Jima class

In essence, the Landing Ship, Personnel, Helicopter (LPH) and the Landing Ship, Personnel, Dock (LPD) were complementary. As the designators indicate, both carried personnel (the LPH around twice as many as the LPD) but, for landing operations, one carried helicopters, the other, assault craft. The LPH force would thus establish the beachhead and the LPD force would land with heavy equipment. Together the craft could land a fully equipped US Marine Corps combat formation.

US Marine Corps interest in an initial assault by helicopter ("Vertical Envelopment") dated back to 1947, it having been appreciated that a World War II style of amphibious landing was no longer possible. The vast assemblies of shipping could now be virtually destroyed by a single nuclear strike.

Post-war funding, for what would be an entirely new type of warfare, was limited and initial trials were made with modified war-built escort carriers (CVE). These culminated in the successful conversion of the USS *Thetis Bay* (CVE-90, redesignated CVHA-1 (Carrier, Helicopter, Assault) which, in 1956, could carry some 950 troops and 20 helicopters.

A second escort carrier, USS *Block Island* (CVE-106), was also listed for

ABOVE: **USS *Inchon* (LPH-12) was fitted with the later addition of SPN-35 radar, housed in a conspicuous dome.** RIGHT: **Even with rotors and tail units folded, Sikorsky CH-46 and CH-53 helicopters take up a lot of space on the flightdeck of USS *Tripoli* (LPH-10). The deck-edge elevators are great spacesavers.**

LEFT: **Boeing Vertol CH-46 Sea Knight** helicopters are here visible forward with larger Sikorsky H-53 Sea Stallions aft. Up to 25 helicopters can be carried. This is the converted Essex-class carrier *Boxer*, renumbered (LPH-4).

conversion. This was cancelled, but the ship was significant in being designated the first Landing Personnel Helicopter (LPH-1) ship.

Rendered obsolescent by the new "super carriers", several war-built Essex-class carriers were made available for limited conversion. These large ships could accommodate 2,000 troops and a considerable quantity of cargo. Designed for the steady motion required for flightdeck operations, all were popular with troops unaccustomed to sea travel. Still capable of 27 knots, the ships were usefully fast but, because of heavy usage, all were becoming expensive and difficult to maintain. The type proved the LPH principle, but clearly needed to be superseded by purpose-built ships.

A continued restricted funding resulted in considerable debate over the specification for the new ship. The US Marine Corps' preference was for vessels flexible enough to carry either two-thirds helicopter/one-third assault craft, depending upon circumstances.

The LPH design adopted, therefore, was based on that of a proposed but abandoned 21-knot, single-screw escort carrier. Carrying only the smallest of assault craft under davits, the vessel would be effectively an all-helicopter ship designed to work with LPDs. Without angled deck, catapult or arrestor gear, the LPH could operate only specialized fixed-wing aircraft.

In order to maximize deck space for eight helicopter spots (and, rapid troop loading) both elevators were positioned on the side of the ship. This necessitated large access doors in the hull plating.

A Sikorsky CH-53 Sea Stallion weighs 10,200kg/22,444lb empty and up to 19,090kg/42,000lb on take-off. With larger aircraft in mind, the LPH was fitted with 18,181kg/40,000lb capacity elevators and a flight deck stressed to 27,273kg/60,000lb. The hangar deck headroom of 6.09m/20ft gave the relatively small ship a high profile and generous freeboard. Conversely, it put the hangar deck and, thus the lowered

elevators, close to the waterline, limiting permissible ship movement.

The ship could transport as many troops as a converted Essex class, with around half the crew. An LPH could, however, carry less cargo.

The type was also expected to work as anti-submarine escort carriers (a role which was never seriously practised) or as a base ship for minesweeping variants of the CH-53. In view of the latter, it was ironic that when USS *Tripoli* (LPH-10) hit a mine in the Arabian Sea (Persian Gulf), this resulted in the cancellation of a planned amphibious operation in favour of land attack.

Less than a year after the launch of the last LPH (USS *Inchon* [LPH-12]), the first LHA (USS *Tarawa* [LHA-1]), which combined the roles of LPH and LPD, was launched on December 1, 1973.

ABOVE: **USS *Guadalcanal* (LPH-7) was fitted with a Sea Sparrow Point Defence Missile System (PDMS) forward of the island and on the port quarter. Note the deck-edge elevator.**

Landing Ship, Personnel, Helicopter (LPH), Iwo Jima class

Displacement: 10,990 tons (light); 18,300 tons (full load)
Length: 169.58m/556ft (wl); 180.56m/592ft (oa)
Beam: 25.52m/83ft 8in (wl)
Draught: 8.08m/26ft 6in (maximum)
Armament: 8 x 3in guns (4x2)
Machinery: Steam turbines, 2 boilers, single shaft
Power: 16,785kW/22,500shp for 21 knots
Fuel: Oil
Endurance: 18,400 km/10,000nm at 20 knots
Protection: Nominal
Complement: 594
Capacity: Up to 25 helicopters

Landing Ship, Tank (LST), Newport class

LSTs were valued particularly highly as, due to being the largest vessel routinely capable of beaching, the type could deliver the greatest quantity of cargo ashore during the earliest and most critical phase of a landing. The post-war requirement to produce an LST capable of 20 knots was, however, a long time in planning, as a radical change in hull design was necessary. A fine forward entry would lack buoyancy and would be compensated by deeper draught, causing the vessel to be beached further from the tideline. This was overcome by the provision of a 34m/111ft bow ramp, stowed at sea on the long foredeck and positioned over the bows using a projecting gantry. To facilitate this, the doors in the rounded bow section above the knuckle line opened outward. The ramp could be supplemented by four rectangular pontoon sections which were stowed against the sides of the after hull.

Deploying the main ramp uncovered a second vehicle exit from the covered tank deck. The decks were stressed for 75-ton vehicles, in excess of the current M1A2 Abrams tank at 63 tons. LVTs and other heavier vehicles were loaded and discharged through a gate and ramp set into the stern. Lighter vehicles could be carried on the upper deck, the fore and aft ends linked by a tunnel passing through the amidships structure.

To satisfy the general endurance requirement for 16,093km/10,000 miles at 20 knots, diesel propulsion was specified, the six engines being exhausted through two side funnels, conspicuously unequal in size. Reversing was achieved through the use of controllable-pitch (CP) propellers. Alignment for beaching was assisted by a bow thruster. In the restricted-draught beaching condition, around 400 troops and some 500 tons of cargo could be transported.

ABOVE: **USS Frederick (LST-1184), showing the arrangement of projecting horns to operate a sliding ramp. Note the vehicle access through the superstructure.**

LEFT: **The stern door on USS Cayuga (LST-1186) has been lowered to provide the entry ramp for an LVT. Note the side shelves to carry pontoons, and the frame for the stern anchor.**

Landing Ship, Tank Newport class, LST-1199–1205

Displacement: 4,950 tons (light); 8,525 tons (full load)
Length: 159.26m/522ft 2in (wl); 171.15m/561ft 2in (oa)
Beam: 21.2m/69ft 6in
Draught: 1.8m/5ft 11in (forward); 530m/17ft 4in (aft)
Armament: 4 x 3in guns (2x2)
Machinery: 6 diesel engines, 2 shafts
Power: 12,309kW/16,500bhp for 22 knots
Fuel: 1,750 tons oil
Endurance: 26,220km/14,250nm at 14 knots
Protection: Nominal
Complement: 262

Amphibious Force Flagship (AGC), Mount McKinley class

During World War II, the US Navy commissioned 15 AGCs, and three more shortly afterwards. Numbers were driven by the fact that no single ship was equipped to handle the mass of incoming and outgoing communications and intelligence traffic. Besides the precaution of a back-up vessel, additional AGCs could share the operation rather than simply "double up". As an interim measure, some APAs were fitted to function as basic "relief flagships".

The enemy was quick to appreciate the significance of the AGC, which needed to be anchored inconspicuously in the transport area, worsening the general problem of electronic interference. Electronic Support Measures (ESM) and Electronic Countermeasures (ECM) were fitted to counter the extra complication of enemy jamming

activities. The main function of the AGC still included the joint embarked staffs' maintenance of the master plot of the operation as it developed, and providing a base for the military headquarters staff until developments enabled it to be landed ashore.

By the late 1960s, with the amphibious force much reduced, only five AGCs remained in service and these, headed by USS *Mount McKinley* (AGC-7), were beginning to deteriorate. Badly cramped for the large crew required, the AGC lacked sufficient generating capacity and were unable to accommodate the large automated combat information systems now becoming universal.

The type appeared ever more overloaded. Extra accommodation was added on the superstructure, the after 5in gun being removed

ABOVE: **Equipped with a late-1944 electronics suite, USS *Teton* (AGC-14) is seen here in company, unusually, with an LSV, probably USS *Ozark* (LSV-2). Note how the forward cargo derricks are used to handle small craft.**

and replaced with a helicopter pad. Kingposts, masts and derricks were retained both to handle a wide range of small craft and to support (at the required separation) a carrier-scale electronics outfit, including pencil-beam height finder, air search radar and Tactical Air Navigation (TACAN).

No longer capable of exceeding 15 knots, and beyond effective modernization, the ACGs were replaced in the early 1970s by Blue Ridge-class command ships.

ABOVE: **USS *Mount McKinley* (AGC-7) was originally built in 1943 as a transport ship USS *Cyclone*. The vessel was renamed on December 27, 1943, and commissioned on May 1, 1944.**

Amphibious Force Flagship (AGC), Mount McKinley class, 1960s C2 conversion

Displacement: 7,200 tons (light); 15,300 tons (full load)

Length: 132.68m/435ft (wl); 140m/459ft (oa)

Beam: 19.22m/63ft

Draught: 8.62m/28ft 3in

Armament: 1 x 5in gun, 8 x 40mm (4x2)

Machinery: Steam turbines, 2 boilers, single screw

Power: 4,476kW/6,000shp for 15 knots

Fuel: 3,875 tons oil

Endurance: 61,180km/33,250nm at 12 knots

Protection: Nominal

Complement: 520

Attack Transport/Cargo Ship (APA/AKA), Mariner class

ABOVE: **USS** *Tulare* **(AKA-112) with a full complement of nine LCM (6) carried on the hatch covers. LCVPs are nested in some LCMs, with three more LCVPs on No. 2 hatch. Others are carried under davits.**

The C2 and C3 standard ships that were widely converted to APAs and AKAs during World War II were designed as merchant ships by the US Maritime Commission. With the post-war requirement for an all-20-knot amphibious force, the commission was again tasked with designing a commercial carrier suitable for conversion to military use.

The US Marine Corps wished to lift the same cargo weight (i.e. deadweight, or dwt) as a C3. But, with finer lines, the 20-knot ship would have to be over 30.5m/100ft longer, thus falling into the C4 (Mariner) category. Few commercial operators had trading patterns that suited so large or fast ship, and they could be used only with the assistance of a government subsidy.

The huge hull included seven holds, each with two between deck levels. Commercially, these were served by seven pairs of kingposts but, for the two APAs, USS *Paul Revere* (APA-248) and USS *Francis Marion* (APA-249), and one AKA, USS *Tulare* (AKA-112), (the only three converted from the 35 completed C4-S-1A/B) this standard cargo gear was removed in favour of the already familiar quadripod-type masts, one forward and one aft of the superstructure.

The two completed APAs retained only the earlier Nos. 3 and 6 holds, with Nos. 2, 4, and 5 retained as access trunks. The superstructure was extended aft to provide further accommodation for a 1,650-strong

US Marine Corps battalion and facilities for the ships to operate as flagships. Six LCM (6), 12 LCVPs and two LCPLs were carried. In both types of conversion the area aft, above the No. 7 hold, was built as a helicopter pad, without a hangar.

The AKA retained holds Nos. 2 to 6 inclusive, together with the trunk of the earlier No. 1. The original short superstructure was retained but on the raised forecastle there was a gun platform for a twin 3in mounting with fire director. The AKA carried nine LCM (6) and 14 LVCPs.

Attack Transport/ Cargo Ship (APA/AKA), Mariner class

Displacement: 10,700 tons (light); 16,850 tons (full load)
Length: 161.04m/518ft (wl); 172.02m/564ft (oa)
Beam: 23.18m/76ft
Draught: 8.24m/27ft (maximum)
Armament: 8 x 3in guns (4x2)
Machinery: 2 steam turbines, 2 boilers, single shaft
Power: 16,412kW/22,000shp for 21 knots
Fuel: Oil
Endurance: 18,400km/10,000nm at 20 knots
Protection: Nominal
Complement: 529

ABOVE: **Both USS** *Paul Revere* **(APA-248) and USS** *Francis Marion* **(APA-249) ex-SS** *Prairie Mariner* **were sold to Spain in 1980. The latter, seen here, was later transferred to Spain, undergoing little change.**

Attack Cargo Ship (AKA), Charleston class

The Mariner class conversions proved expensive and, being vessels with commercial features, not ideal. US Navy planning was also moving in the direction of ships with docking wells, not least because handling an LCM (6) by derrick hoist while in an open sea or rolling in an exposed anchorage, could be dangerous. The conversions were limited to just three ships as it appeared that LPDs and LSDs, working jointly, incorporated the functions of both the APA and AKA type. As far as cargo was concerned, however, the assumed demise of the AKA proved premature, with five Charleston-class vessels added to the force in the late 1960s.

The design was purely that of a military cargo carrier, with no concessions to alternative commercial service. The hull form was developed from that of the already-efficient Mariner class and showed a one-knot improvement in speed with the same power plant. The deep-load displacement was increased by nearly 17 per cent. A bulb-type bow assisted efficiency at service speed while more cutaway underwater stern sections reduced radiated propeller noise, and also improved rudder response and manoeuvrability, important for Replenishment At Sea (RAS).

A transom stern increased afterdeck width, enabling the provision of a helicopter pad capable of accepting the largest transport machines. The pad was connected to all four cargo levels by one of seven elevators on the ship. There were just four holds, served by derricks stepped on two heavy goalpost-type and two Stülcken-type masts. The latter, then popular commercially, permitted the 70-ton heavy-lift derricks to serve adjacent hatches. Their precise control allowed the number of landing craft carried and type to be up-rated safely to four LCM (8), five LCM (6), seven LCVPs and two LCPLs.

The last of the classic lift-on/lift-off AKAs, the Charleston class were decommissioned between 1992 and 1994.

Attack Cargo Ship (AKA), Charleston class

Displacement: 13,725 tons (light); 18,650 tons (full load)
Length: 167.75m/550ft (wl); 175.53m/575ft 6in (oa)
Beam: 25.01m/82ft
Draught: 7.76m/25ft 5in (maximum)
Armament: 8 x 3in guns (4x2)
Machinery: 2 steam turbines, 2 boilers, single shaft
Power: 16,421kW/22,000shp for 22 knots
Fuel: Oil
Endurance: 18,400km/10,000nm at 20 knots
Protection: Nominal
Complement: 336

ABOVE: **Decommissioned for over a decade but still a valuable reserve, USS *Mobile* (AKA-115), USS *El Paso* (AKA-117) and USS *Charleston* (AKA-113) are standing idle, stripped of electronics and running rigging.**

LEFT: **USS** *Tarawa* **(LHA-1) was the first of the new class of amphibious assault ships. The vessel was launched on December 1, 1973 and commissioned on May 26, 1976. Decommissioned on March 31, 2009, the vessel was expected to be towed to Hawaii to be used as a target.**

Landing Ship, Helicopter, Assault (LHA), Tarawa class

The US Navy's amphibious force of the mid-1960s comprised a large number of ships, crewed by highly trained personnel. Tight budgets demanded that crew numbers be reduced, and it was this, rather than requests from the US Marine Corps, that encouraged the "all-in-one" approach to the design of the LHA. A Marine battalion would be embarked on the vessel along with armour, transport and general equipment, together with helicopters and landing craft. However arranged, a 20-knot ship combining the functions of existing LPH, LSD and AKA was going to be large and expensive, but a significant overall reduction in crew numbers allowed improved in-service costs. Fewer and larger ships would also reduce building and maintenance costs.

The US Marine Corps was somewhat critical of a ship offering a target as large and as distinctive as a World War II strike carrier (CVA) and capable of being rendered inoperative by a single major mechanical failure.

The new LHA, was subject to lengthy design studies which indicated that a fleet of four, with supporting LSD and LST, could replace a force of over twice the number of existing vessels.

This argument was sufficiently strong for the procurement of further LPH and LPD to be cancelled from mid-1966.

For a battalion-sized lift, a force of six Sikorsky CH-53A Sea Stallion transport helicopters (each lifting around 55 troops), 18 Boeing CH-46A Sea Knight twin-rotor assault helicopters (17 troops each) and two Bell UH-1E Iriquois was required, with tankage for 1,200 tons of aviation fuel. To achieve lift-rate, nine deck landing

spots were necessary. Flight deck and hangar space were maximized by locating one elevator on the centreline at the stern and a second close by on the port deck edge. The latter is folded against the hull when not in use, to keep overall width to within the limitations of the Panama Canal.

Above water, the hull was essentially parallel and rectangular in section. A massive stern gate enclosed an 80 x 23.4m/262 x 77ft docking well,

ABOVE: **USS** *Peleliu* **(LHA-5) listing majestically in a tight turn. The empty pockets at the bow were originally for fire-support 5in guns. Both elevators are located aft, and the hangar area covers only half the length of the ship.**

ABOVE: **USS *Saipan* (LHA-2) flooding down to exercise LCUs, of which she can accommodate four.**

LEFT: **A later image of USS *Saipan* (LHA-2), now fitted with two CIWS. Proven to be difficult to modernize, USS *Saipan* was stricken in 2007.**

large enough to carry four LCU-1610, but also able to carry the LCAC that entered service later. A crane behind the island structure was used to handle two LCM (6) and two LCPL.

As if to emphasize that the ship was not an aircraft carrier, the island was large and located inboard, to allow vehicles to pass outboard. No aircraft catapults or arrestor gear were fitted but vertical/short take-off and land (V/STOL) aircraft worked aboard satisfactorily. Indeed, in "strike" configuration an LHA could carry up to 20 McDonnell Douglas AV-8A Harriers and six helicopters.

Despite the size of the ships, the overall design was very compact, with the 1,900 troops and vehicles being accommodated on several deck levels.

Original armament included three 5in guns, considered necessary for fire support and a Raytheon/ General Dynamics Sea Sparrow Point Defense Missile System (PDMS) launcher. These were located in boxes set into each "corner" of the flight deck. All 5in guns were later removed, the forward mountings being plated-over to improve flight deck layout. The Sea Sparrow was superseded by two 21-round Rolling

Airframe Missile System (RAM) launchers and two 30mm Close-In Weapon System (CIWS).

Although fitted with a comprehensive electronics suite, the LHA were not expected to function as amphibious flagships. Perhaps not surprisingly with so ambitious a concept, the ships, while impressive, had proved to be something of a disappointment in service. Planned Service Life Extension Programs (SLEP) appeared to be too complex to be cost effective. All new ships were, therefore, cancelled and those surviving are due to be withdrawn from service between 2011 and 2015. USS *Belleau Wood* (LHA-3) was in such poor condition that the vessel was used as a target in 2006. During 2007, USS *Saipan* (LHA-2) was decommissioned.

Planned replacements, LHA (R) or LHA-6 class, will begin to be commissioned in 2012. Of nearly 55,000 tons, these vast ships are reportedly mainly for aviation and do not have docking facilities.

LEFT: **The side opening and elevators allow access to the hangar deck. The docking well is now entered through the stern gate. USS *Belleau Wood* (LHA-3) is armed with two CIWS and two RAM launchers. One of each is visible on the after quarters.**

Landing Ship, Helicopter, Assault (LHA), Tarawa class

Displacement: 25,120 tons (light); 39,400 tons (full load)
Length: 237.14m/777ft 6in (bp); 254.2m/833ft 5in (oa)
Beam: 32.31m/105ft 11in (wl); 40.23m/131ft 10in (overall width)
Draught: 7.91m/26ft (mean)
Armament: 3 x 5in guns (3x1), 1 x 8-cell Sea Sparrow BPDMS
Machinery: Steam turbines, 2 boilers, 2 shafts
Power: 57,442kW/77,000shp for 24 knots
Fuel: Oil
Endurance: 18,400km/10,000nm at 20 knots
Protection: Not known
Complement: 940

Landing Ship, Dock (LSD), Whidbey Island/Harpers Ferry class

By the late 1970s, the question of whether to modernize or replace the Thomaston class was raised. Built for a nominal 30-year life, the class might have given further service through a Service Life Extension Program (SLEP), but some showed material deterioration, and none could meet modern accommodation standards without major work. Most importantly, however, the size of the ships was not compatible with the transportation of the new Landing Craft Air Cushion (LCAC), due to enter service in 1984.

Amphibious vessels laying offshore were, by now, vulnerable to attack by shore-based Surface-to-Surface Missiles (SSM). The LCAC was seen as the means by which the LSD could operate from safely Over The Horizon (OTH).

A force of 66 amphibious warfare ships was required to lift US Marine Corps troops in combat ready units. The SLEP would have allowed a delay, but at very considerable cost, while the question of eventual replacement would remain. A new type, designated the LSD-41 (Whidbey Island class) was, therefore, adopted as a ship-for-ship replacement programme for the Thomaston class. Confusingly, many of the new ships had the same names as used on earlier LSDs.

The design parameters for the class were a docking well large enough for four LCACs, together with accommodation for 400 troops and ever-bulkier equipment. A new factor was the high noise levels of the LCAC, which required all berthing to be removed from the wing walls of the well deck and moved forward, another factor which seriously increased vessel size and cost. At 130 x 15.24m/ 440 x 50ft, the docking well could accommodate three LCUs, ten LCM (8), or 64 amphibious assault vehicles (AAV).

Facilities for the LCAC dominated the design, with a requirement for extensive maintenance facilities and accommodation

LEFT: **USS *Tortuga* (LSD-46)**, one of the class built to replace earlier Thomaston-class vessels. BELOW: **USS *Fort McHenry* (LSD-43)** anchored off the coast of North Carolina, with the amphibious assault ship **USS *Bataan* (LHD-5)** in the distance, while embarking personnel and equipment from the 22nd Marine Expeditionary Unit.

for 64 specialist personnel. Free ventilation of the docking well was important as were the guidance systems to allow the LCAC to dock and undock with the ship stationary or moving. A barrier across the docking well closes off forward areas.

As is customary, no hangar facilities are provided for the helicopters, but the elevated flight deck is large enough to provide landing spots for two Sikorsky CH-53Es or similar types. The port and starboard cranes are each rated at 60 tons to enable a main battle tank to be lifted over the side and on to an LCAC.

No medium-calibre guns were specified as the class is designed to operate beyond the range of enemy fire. The defensive armament of two Raytheon Phalanx (CIWS) has, however, been supplemented by two 21-round RIM-116 RAM launchers.

A new innovation was the adoption of medium-speed diesel engines, two driving each shaft. The superior fuel economy allowed fuel storage to be reduced by almost 33 per cent. The planned 12-ship Whidbey Island-class programme saw ships being delivered at around one-year intervals but, within this timeframe, US Marine Corps strategy had evolved to meet changing threats. It became apparent that the increasing amount of equipment could not be accommodated in the class, as completed. A new class was developed in the externally, almost-identical LSD-41 Cargo Variant, or LSD-49 (Harpers Ferry class)

The primary difference between the classes is the docking well of the LSD-49 being large enough for only two LCACs. Simply reprioritizing the various spaces aboard a standard LSD-41 was not possible as the revised weight distribution would reduce the stability range of the ship to below an acceptable minimum. Alternatively the docking well load is

reduced to one LCU or four LCM (8). Two LCPLs and a utility craft are carried on deck, where a 30-ton crane mounted on the starboard side replaces two 60-ton cranes on the LSD-41. For cargo, the LSD-49s can offer over 1,200m²/12,917sq ft of vehicle parking and around 1,330m³/46,996cu ft of cargo stowage.

The importance of the capacity shortfall is underlined by an intention to extend the LSD-49 series to 12 ships. It was, however, terminated at four due to the building programme overlapping that of the latest LPD-17 (San Antonio class).

Landing Ship, Dock, LSD-41 class

Displacement: 11,350 tons (light), 16,220 tons (full load)
Length: 176.8m/579ft 8in (wl); 185.8m/609ft 2in (oa)
Beam: 25.6m/83ft 11in
Draught: 6.25m/20ft 6in (full load)
Armament: 2 x 21-cell RAM PDMS, 2 x CIWS
Machinery: 4 diesel engines, 3 shafts
Power: 31,034kW/41,600bhp for 22 knots
Fuel: Oil
Endurance: 14,720km/8,000nm at 18 knots
Protection: Kevlar patches over limited vital areas
Complement: 315

ABOVE: **A cargo variant of the design, the Harpers Ferry class is indistinguishable externally. Internally, USS *Harpers Ferry* (LSD-49) has a larger cargo space and a shorter docking well.**

Landing Ship, Helicopter, Dock (LHD), Wasp class

ABOVE: **USS *Makin Island* (LHD-8) is powered by two General Electric LM-1500 gas turbine engines.**

The LHD is best considered as an LCAC-capable version of the Tarawa class (LHA), the change of designation being political rather than implying any significant change of function. Hull form and size are similar, the major difference being in the provision of a longer, narrower docking well, 98 x 15.2m/322 x 50ft. This was capable of accommodating three LCACs, compared with only one in an LHA. Alternatively, an LHD can load two LCUs or six LCM (8). The stern gate on an LHA lifted in two sections, horizontally divided, but on the LHD this has reverted to the older LSD type, where the bottom section lowers. This provides a ramp to facilitate launching an LCAC from a dry well.

Larger-area bilge keels have been fitted, presumably to reduce the roll of the ship at lower speeds. A bow-bulb has also been added, probably for greatest efficiency at service speed.

Accommodation for 1,900 troops is on the same scale as in an LHA. The steam power plant is also similar. USS *Makin Island* (LHD-8) is an exception, however, and was commissioned in 2008, some eight years after USS *Bonhomme Richard* (LHD-6). As no further steam-powered ships will be built for the US Navy, LHD-8 is powered by two General Electric LM-1500 gas turbines.

Changing political conditions show in the aviation arrangements. To underline the fact that an LHA was not an aircraft carrier, the efficiency of the flight deck was reduced by mountings for medium-calibre guns (since removed) and a large intrusive island structure. From the outset, armament on the LHD was totally defensive, allowing the flight deck to be squared-off both forward and aft. Flight deck and hangar areas are increased by the adoption of two deck-edge elevators, one aft of amidships, port side, the other on the starboard quarter. The latter replaces the aft centreline elevator on the LHA. Greater usable flight deck width is enabled by the narrower island, reflecting a more flexible attitude to what are essentially specialized aviation requirements.

LEFT: **Despite the width of the superstructure, USS *Wasp* (LHD-1) can easily accommodate the Bell Boeing MV-22 Osprey flown by the USMC.**

LEFT: **A Sikorsky CH-53 Sea Stallion about to land on USS *Kearsarge* (LHD-3). The docking well on the vessel is large enough to accommodate three LCACs. Note the CIWS on either quarter and the centreline Sea Sparrow launcher.**

The LHD can be a multi-purpose vessel, albeit an expensive alternative to a small conventional aircraft carrier. Operations in the "Harrier Carrier" mode have been a little restricted by the requirement to maintain nine landing spots for helicopters.

A new factor is the certification of the long-awaited Bell Boeing V-22A Osprey VTOL aircraft. These are operated from an LHD's flight deck but are very large for existing elevators. In vertical take-off mode, the Osprey weighs up to 23.4 tons as opposed to a Super Stallion at 18.7 tons, but is well within the 34-ton lift capacity of the elevator. The Osprey carries less than half the troops, but at twice the speed, thus doubling flight deck activity for operations at the same range. It does, however, have over twice the range of an SH-53E, and the US sees it as a possible replacement for helicopters in spearhead operations.

LEFT: **Flagship of an Amphibious Ready Group (ARG), the USS *Essex* (LHD-2) is shown leading an Austin-class LPD and a Harpers Ferry-class LSD. The vessel would normally be used in conjunction with a carrier group.**

Landing Ship, Helicopter, Dock, LHD-1 to LHD-7

Displacement: 27,900 tons (light);
 40,750 tons (full load)
Length: 237.14m/777ft 6in (wl);
 257.3m/843ft 8in (oa)
Beam: 32.31m/105ft 11in (wl)
Draught: 8.53m/28ft (full load)
Armament: 2 x 8-cell Sea Sparrow BPDMS,
 2 x 21-cell RAM launchers
Machinery: Steam turbines, 2 boilers, 2 shafts
Power: 57,442kW/77,000shp for 24 knots
Fuel: 6,200 tons oil
Endurance: 18,400km/10,000nm at 20 knots
Protection: Not known
Complement: 1,082

Landing Ship, Personnel, Dock (LPD), San Antonio class

LPD construction appeared to have ended in 1971, with the commissioning of the last of the LPD-4 (Austin class). LPD-16 was never built, and a new type of welldeck ship was being developed. The Austin-class vessels were planned to last 45 years, but the expensive SLEP modernization was cancelled, and the class began to be phased out in 2005. Their characteristics nonetheless having proved useful, they were given replacements in the LPD-17 (San Antonio class) currently being built. As is the way of these things, however, the new ships are also expected to replace the LSD-36 (Anchorage class), and surviving assault cargo ships and LST-1179s (Newport class). Not surprisingly, therefore, they are larger (displacing around 50 per cent more than the average LPD-4) and are very expensive (the first of the class was a reported $1.16 billion, reducing to around a more moderate $700 million by LPD-20).

The LPD-17 programme coincided with post-Cold War western fleets being reorganized with a new emphasis on expeditionary and "littoral" warfare.

Against an unpredictable enemy, rapid intervention appeared the best form of standing response, and amphibious warfare the means of application. The strength of the US Marine Corps was some 180,000

ABOVE AND BELOW: **The total enclosure of all electronic antennas within low radar-signature towers gives USS *San Antonio* (LPD-17) a very angular appearance. The class follows the new trend for diesel propulsion.**

personnel in 2008, who manned 12 Amphibious Ready Groups (ARG), each supporting a Marine Expeditionary Unit (MEU). Comprising anything between 1,500 and 3,000 personnel, an MEU comes complete with armour, artillery, aircraft, helicopters and stores.

The LPD-17 was first planned to be built in numbers, to operate particularly as an element of a flexible, three-ship LHA/LHD, LSD41/LSD-49, LPD/ARG combination. Economic realities reduced the programme, however, first to 12 ships, then to the current nine.

RIGHT: **The docking well on USS *San Antonio* (LPD-17) extends forward to a point just short of the hangar doors. Forward, there are three levels of vehicle decks which extend to beyond the forward funnel.**

In appearance, the LPD-17 is dominated by radar signature reduction measures which, with suppression of exposed detail and sharply sculpted oblique surfaces, makes the ship appear to radar smaller than true size. Masts have evolved into poly-sided, tower-like structures that contain electronics.

Unlike earlier LPDs, the LPD-17s incorporate covered facilities for the aviation element. Landing spots for two Sikorsky CH-53Es or equivalent type are provided but, as alternatives, four Sikorsky CH-46Es or two Bell Boeing V-22B Ospreys may be accommodated.

The flight deck is permanent and the docking well is sized to carry two LCACs, four LCM (8) or 20 AAVs. Up to 800 troops can be accommodated, some 100 less than in LPD-4s. Following a period when highly valuable amphibious warfare ships appeared to carry a minimum, defensive armament, the LPD-17s have not only two RAM launchers, space/weight margins for a 16-cell Vertical Launch System (VLS), two CIWS and two General Dynamics Mk 46 Mod 1 30mm cannon in a turret. A full air-defence sensor and weapon integration system is also fitted.

The VLS is primarily for the Sea Sparrow, which can be loaded at four to a cell, but it can also accept other weapons such as Tomahawk, Standard SM-2 or ASROC anti-submarine rocket.

Accounting for some of the high cost, the LPD-17 has three-dimensional air search radar (SPS-48E, which is due for replacement), contributing to a fully integrated air defence system (Akcita Control Element Environment) and Cooperative Engagement Capability (CEC), which permits data to be shared between ships, and which will be also fitted to later aircraft carriers and destroyers. As the system is in the late stages of development USS *San Diego* (LPD-22) will probably be the first of the class to be equipped with the full system. Earlier ships in the class will be retrofitted.

ABOVE: **Viewed from above, it is apparent that minor radar-reflective detail is screened by high bulwarks. For so bulky a vessel, USS *Green Bay* (LPD-20) has a commendably clean wave system.**

Landing Ship, Personnel, Dock (LPD), San Antonio class

Displacement: 25,300 tons (full load)
Length: 200m/655ft 9in (wl); 208.48m/683ft (oa)
Beam: 29.5m/96ft 9in (wl)
Draught: 7m/23ft (full load)
Armament (as fitted): 2 x 21-round RAM, VLS, CIWS and 2 x 30mm cannon
Machinery: 4 diesel engines, 2 shafts
Power: 31,037kW/41,600bhp for 22 knots
Fuel: Oil
Endurance: 18,400km/10,000nm at 20 knots
Protection: Not known
Complement: 361

Landing Craft, Control (LCC), Blue Ridge class

ABOVE: **Over time in service, the deck area has been greatly simplified as radio communications have been superseded by satellite links. USS *Blue Ridge* (LCC-19) is 40 years old.**

The merchant ship-type hulls of wartime-built AGCs could not be expected to survive beyond the 25-year "special survey" milestone, making early 1970s replacement urgent. Considerable debate was given to the specification for the new ships – a cruiser conversion could

retain much valued support firepower, a modified light carrier would provide the necessary internal volume, while a Mariner or P4 conversion would be cheaper. The first two, however, would be built on 25-year-old hulls, while the latter would only just meet the 20-knot requirement. The Iwo Jima-class LPH programme was nearing completion and, offering both space and the necessary speed, two further hulls were added for conversion.

To emphasize the amphibious status, the designator was changed from AGC (where "A" denoted "Auxiliary", not "Amphibious") to LCC, or Landing Craft, Control (rather misleading, and not to be confused with the British LCC of World War II). The AGC numbering sequence held, however, the ships becoming LCC-19 and 20.

The building of only two reflected the fact that computerization and, soon after, satellite communications, made it possible to distribute control of the amphibious group and task force commanders between other, increasingly better equipped ships. Although intended for amphibious warfare, both USS *Blue Ridge* (LCC-19) and USS *Mount Whitney*

(LCC-20) have been deployed in the role of 6th and 7th US Fleet flagship. Only the hull form and machinery from the Iwo Jima-class vessel was retained. A prominent sponson runs along each side of the ship, mainly to incorporate a larger boat complement. The overall length, particularly in earlier days was required to give necessary separation between a wide variety of communications antennas, for which the upper deck acted as groundplane.

There is a helicopter pad but no hangar facilities. After nearly 40 years in service, the two ships are designated to be fitted with RAM in addition to CIWS.

LEFT: **Wide side sponsons accommodating boats make for a spacious, unencumbered weather deck on USS *Mount Whitney* (LCC-20). Despite being steam-powered, the ship lacks a true funnel. Note the CIWS mounting at the bow.**

Landing Craft, Control (LCC), Blue Ridge class

Displacement: 12,750 tons (light), 19,300 tons (full load)
Length: 176.8m/579ft 8in (wl); 188.5m/618ft (oa)
Beam: 25.3m/82ft 11in (wl)
Draught: 8.2m/26ft 10in (full load)
Armament: 4 x 3in guns (2x2), 2 x 8 round Sea Sparrow BPDMS launchers (all since removed)
Machinery: Steam turbine, 2 boilers, single shaft
Power: 16,412kW/22,000shp for 21.5 knots
Fuel: Oil
Endurance: 23,920km/13,000nm at 16 knots
Protection: Kevlar plastic armour added later; extent unknown
Complement: 690

Maritime and Prepositioning Force (MPF), Bob Hope class

Today's much-changed strategic policy requires that essential heavy equipment is stored semi-permanently at a forward location, to be moved by sea to any trouble spot in the world while troops are flown in by transport aircraft.

Much of this material is loaded aboard ships of the Maritime Prepositioning Force (MPF). The force is maintained by specialist teams, the ships sailing regularly on exercise, not least to prevent them becoming an easy, high-value target for pre-emptive attack. Having discharged the vital first-wave support task, the MPF ships revert to "sealift", the general transport duties associated earlier with large numbers of AKAs.

World War II-built AKAs were standard cargo ships, relying upon cargo derricks to load and discharge over the side. Methods have since been revolutionized by the introduction of vessels such as Roll-on, Roll-off (Ro-Ro) ships and the use of cargo containers. Foreign merchant ship design being ahead of that of the USA caused the latter to purchase large ships mainly from European operators in order to expand the Rapid Reaction Force (RRF) during the 1980s. The ships were modified with the addition of heavy cranes and larger side openings to service the existing loading ramps.

Stemming from these conversions were the US-designed and built Watson and Bob Hope classes. All displace a massive 62,000 tons, and are classified T-AKR (i.e. Ro-Ro cargo ships operated by Military Sealift Command [MSC]). All have a small (by naval standards) crew of around 26 civilians. The vessels can carry 100 tracked and 900 wheeled vehicles. All have modularized pontoon sections, some self-powered, which can be used as a floating jetty, a temporary causeway or to transport vehicles. Non-trailerized heavy gear and containers are unloaded by the four 55-ton deck cranes.

ABOVE: **The Bob Hope-class USS *William S. Seay* (T-AKR 302). Note the cranes in paired lift mode and the use of the side door. The loading ramp is carried as deck cargo.**

Maritime and Prepositioning Force (MPF), Bob Hope class

Displacement: 34,410 tons (light); 62,100 tons (full load)
Length: 271.28m/889ft 5in (bp); 289.56m/949ft 4in (oa)
Beam: 32.3m/105ft 10in
Draught: 11.25m/36ft 10in (full load)
Armament: None in peacetime
Machinery: 4 diesel engines, 2 shafts
Power: 48,639kW/65,200bhp for 24.5 knots
Fuel: Oil
Endurance: Not known
Protection: Nominal
Complement: 27 (peace); up to 95 (war)

Landing Ship, Tank (LST), Maracaibo type

Early British amphibious operations showed that raids against defended locations were unlikely to succeed without armoured support. An urgent requirement developed for a seagoing tank carrier, to land 25- to 40-ton vehicles directly on to a beach, rather than using slow over-the-side loading into smaller craft. It was 1940 and, with no earlier experience of such a vessel, it was decided to convert three small oil tankers.

The ships had been designed for the Shell Oil Company to negotiate the shallow bar at Maracaibo, Venezula, when carrying crude to the company's Aruba refinery. The hull was consequently very wide and shallow.

To reduce wasted space and free surface area (the latter affected stability) the design incorporated a raised centreline trunk deck some two levels 5m/16ft in height. The bridge block was forward of amidships and the heavy steam machinery located aft.

In conversion, the trunk was extended to the sides of the ship creating two long vehicle spaces, the trunk provided further garaging, maintenance and accommodation area. Much of the original forward oil tankage was allocated for water ballast. Flooded at sea for stability and trim, the tanks were pumped out before grounding to reduce the forward draught to around 1.2m/4ft.

ABOVE: **Although improvised, the Maracaibo type was significant in that it proved the case for the LST. The vessels were selected for their shallow draught.**

Even so, this still required the design and incorporation into the modified bow of a two-part ramp, extendable to around 30.5m/100ft to allow tanks to be landed. Ten- and 25-ton cargo derricks were also provided. The original oil-cargo tanks were also utilized to extend fuel space.

All three ships proved invaluable at the Oran sector of the North African (Operation "Torch") landings. In practice, however, the vessels were too large for the task. The three Maracaibo-type vessels gave excellent experience for designing of what would soon become the Landing Ship Tank LST (1).

ABOVE: **HMS** *Bachaquero,* **one of the oil tankers converted to an LST, being unloaded at Bone harbour, Sicily, on March 16, 1943. Over 100 Bren Gun Carriers and crews were carried on the vessel.**

Landing Ship, Tank (LST), Maracaibo type	

Tonnage: 4,890 tons (gross); 5,710 tons (displacement)
Length: 19.52m/64ft
Beam: 10.98m/36ft
Draught (seagoing): 3.28m/10ft (mean)
Draught (beaching): 1.29m/4ft 3in (forward); 4.58m/15ft (aft)
Armament: 4 x 2pdr "Pom-Pom" (4x1), 6 x 20mm (6x1) smoke mortars
Machinery: 2 vertical triple expansion steam engines, twin shafts
Power: 2,238kW/3,000ihp for 10 knots
Endurance: 11,408km/6,200m at 10 knots
Complement: 98
Capacity: 18–22 tanks, 2 LCMs on deck, 210 troops

ABOVE: **HMS** *Bruiser*, one of the three vessels built. A sister ship, HMS *Boxer*, was converted to a navigational training ship after World War II and was later used for experimental radar trials. LEFT: **HMS** *Thruster*, the third vessel in the class, at sea. The 40-ton crane is in the raised position.

Landing Ship, Tank (LST), LST (1) class

Even as the experimental Maracaibo-type tankers were being converted, specialist ships were also being designed and built. Prime Minister Churchill's demand for an ocean-going tank-carrier capable of lifting the full 60-tank establishment of an armoured division proved impractical because of size and draught. In place of this a class of three 20-tank capacity ships was built. As the original project had, unofficially, been referred to as a "Winston", the smaller type became known as "Winettes". Classified as "Tank Assault Carriers", all were later recategorized as Landing Ships, Tank, Mk 1 (LST [1]) to differentiate from other LST types then in series production. Uniquely, all were named from the outset; HMS *Boxer*, HMS *Bruiser* and HMS *Thruster*.

Without earlier experience for guidance, designers had to make some presumptions. One was that a 17-knot speed was critical, a full six knots faster than later, mass-produced LSTs. This required a hull with a finer entry and a deeper draught. Thus able to beach but only on slopes of 1 in 37 or steeper (*cf*. 1 in 50 for later LSTs) a two-part, 36.25m/119ft forward ramp was still required. This could be lengthened with an 26m/85ft causeway extension. Clamshell-type bow doors maintained the external shape, protecting a vertically hinged watertight door.

The engine and boiler room were located (inconveniently) amidships, necessitating loading being offset to starboard to allow through access for vehicles. Although capacity was less than that of later LSTs, the class introduced an open upper deck, accessible by elevator from the enclosed tank deck. A 40-ton crane was supplied to handle the small landing craft carried

on deck. Elaborate by later standards, these relatively fast ships proved valuable for special operations.

Landing Ship, Tank, LST (1) class

Displacement: 3,616 tons (beaching); 5,410 tons (full load, seagoing)
Length: 118.95m/390ft (bp); 122m/400ft (oa)
Beam: 17.15m/49ft
Draught (beaching): 1.6m/5ft 6in (forward); 4.54m/14ft 10in (aft)
Armament: 4 x 2pdr "Pom-Pom" (4x1), 8 x 20mm (8x1), smoke mortars
Machinery: Steam turbines, 2 shafts
Power: 5,222kW/7,000shp for 17 knots
Fuel: 2,100 tons oil
Endurance: 14,270km/8,000nm at 14 knots
Protection: Nominal
Complement: 165
Capacity: 13 x 40-ton or 20 x 25-ton tanks, or 28 loaded trucks, plus 193 troops

LEFT: **The British LST (3) was larger and more powerful than the diesel-driven US-built LST (2). After the war all were retained in service. British-built L3044 was modified to carry one LCT and five LCAs on deck.**

Landing Ship, Tank, Mark 3 (LST [3])

With completions beginning at the end of 1942, the LST (2) programme in the US eventually ran to over 1,000 hulls. Of these, 114 were transferred to the British under the Lend-Lease Program and required for mainly Allied joint operations. But the British needed more to assist in the recovery of territories seized by the Japanese. The refusal by the US government was partly political, so the British built their own LSTs.

The resulting LST (3) makes an interesting comparison with the more familiar LST (2). Against an April 1945 delivery target, 45 were ordered from British yards and 35 (later 74) from Canadian. Off these, 35 and 26 respectively were completed before hostilities ended in August 1945.

US-built diesel engines were offered, but not auxiliaries, necessitating the installation of frigate-type steam reciprocating engines, one to each shaft.

Because of the distances involved in Pacific operations, a British Staff Requirement specified 15 knots (LST [2] was 10.8 knots). The penalties on hull design were such, however, that 13 knots was agreed. The result was a deeper beaching draught, caused by finer lines made heavier by a riveted hull. Riveting was necessary because neither British nor Canadian yards had yet adopted welding for ship building.

ABOVE: **HMS *Reggio* (L3511) was one of 16 further steam-driven LSTs modified to carry assault craft under davits. The vessel is entering Grand Harbour, Malta.**

Externally the LST (3) differed from the smaller LST (2) in having a larger funnel and two substantial kingposts mounted against the front of the bridge for handling LCAs.

The open upper deck was connected to the tank deck by a ramp. As an alternative to motor transport, the upper deck could accommodate five LCM (6) or causeway pontoon units, resting on skids and launched over the side. Further causeway units could be carried against the sides of the hull.

All US-supplied LST (2) were returned in 1945, the LST (3) remaining as the standard post-war British tank landing ships. British-built vessels were numbered LST 3001–3045 and those Canadian-built were numbered LST 3501–3574.

Landing Ship, Tank, LST (3)

Displacement: 4,980 tons (full load, seagoing); 3,065 tons (beaching)

Length: 100.53m/330ft (bp); 106m/347ft 6in

Beam: 16.83m/55ft 3in

Draught (beaching): 1.4m/4ft 7in (forward); 3.51m/11ft 6in (aft)

Armament: 10 x 20mm guns (4x2, 2x1)

Machinery: 2 vertical steam reciprocating engines, 2 shafts

Power: 4,103kW/5,500ihp for 13 knots

Fuel: Not known

Endurance: 14,720km/8,000nm at 11 knots at seagoing displacement

Protection: Some splinter protection

Complement: 104

Capacity: 15 x 40-ton or 27 x 25-ton tanks, plus 14 loaded trucks and 168 troops

Landing Ship, Emergency Repair (LSE)

The Operation "Torch" landings of November 1942 were staged at several differing locations. As the largest such operations to date, valuable lessons were learned, none more so than that the attrition rate in small assault craft was far higher than planners had anticipated. Landing Ships, Tank (LST) were not yet available, so the assaults were dependent on smaller craft off-loaded from attack transports (APA) and cargo ships (AKA). On the Atlantic coast of Morocco heavy surf was a problem. Inexperienced coxswains had to cope with darkness, unexpected sea currents, failing tides and, often,

strafing by aircraft or being targeted by artillery. Not surprisingly, craft collided when ranged together on landing. Others broached in the surf, stranded and became swamped through poor load distribution. Many salvageable craft were simply abandoned and left to break up. Total loss rates varied widely from around 20 per cent to an unsustainable 94.2 per cent.

In the same way that the US Marine Corps soon identified the need for dedicated teams to move stores quickly away from a beach, the US Navy moved to establish an organization for the salvage and repair of assault craft. Larger craft, such

ABOVE: **The function of the LSE was primarily to reduce the high attrition rate among small landing craft. Many were recoverable, but were often abandoned.**

as LCTs, were often docked in LSDs, for which the latter had been neither designed nor intended. For smaller craft, some 40 US-built LST (2) were earmarked for conversion to Auxiliary Repair Ships (ARL). Two vessels, ARL-5 and 6, were transferred to the Royal Navy, being referred to as Landing Ships, Emergency Repair, or LSE (1) and (2).

Conversions varied but on most the ramps were removed and bow doors permanently sealed. The elevator was removed, the opening becoming an access hatch. An A-frame could be stepped to the port-side deck edge to support a 50- (later 60-) ton derrick.

ABOVE: **Landing Ship, Emergency Repair (LSE) quickly became non-standard with the addition of more workshop and accommodation space. The heavily braced kingpost supports a 60-ton derrick.**

Landing Ship, Emergency Repair, LST (2) as ARL

Displacement: 1,490 tons (light)
Length: 96.4m/316ft (wl);
  100m/327ft 9in (oa)
Beam: 15.3m/50ft 2in
Draught: 3.35m/11ft (normal operating condition)
Armament: 1 x 3in gun, 8 x 40mm (2x4),
  8 x 20mm (8x1)
Machinery: 2 diesel engines, 2 shafts
Power: 1,343kW/1,800shp for 10.8 knots
Fuel: Not known
Endurance: 34,518km/18,760nm at 10 knots
Protection: 9.5mm/³⁄₈in plate for splinter
  protection
Complement: 108

Landing Ship, Infantry (LSI)

In British terminology, the function of a troopship was simply to transport a large number of troops from one point to another. The Landing Ship, Infantry (LSI), on the other hand, carried a military formation direct to the point of attack, to be embarked in assault craft for the landing. To suit the scale of various operations, the LSI was built in sizes classified as Large, LSI (L), Medium, LSI (M), or Small, LSI (S).

The concept of ships carrying both troops and assault craft had been considered pre-war. But a purpose-built vessel was rejected as being little superior to a converted merchant ship and too expensive. With the German capture of Norway in April 1940, the case for the LSI was made and three new Glen Line cargo liners (SS *Glenearn*, *Glengoyle* and *Glenroy*) were identified as suitable vessels for the transport of 1,000 troops and twelve LCAs. Weighing up to 14 tons loaded, the LCAs were designed to be carried under davits. The British were fortunate to have a company, Welin Maclachlan Davits Limited, with considerable design ingenuity, whose products were later fitted to all US-built APAs. Later in the war, the Glen-class ships were fitted with revised davits and stowage, enabling the transportation of 24 LCAs. Three LCMs were carried on deck, and handled by the ship's cargo gear.

In size and capacity a Glen class compared directly with the C3 conversions that became the US standard – slightly longer, a little narrower and with

ABOVE: **More powerfully armed than the US-built APAs, the Glen class had six 4in HA guns in three twin mountings, together with full director control. HMS *Glenearn* is shown here at anchor during an exercise.**

around 10 per cent less troop capacity (US troop formations differing in size from British equivalents). In general, designated cargo spaces were easily converted into compartments for messes and military stores other than vehicles. Not so obvious, perhaps, was that space needed to be created for the fuel tanks and the evaporators necessary for the production and storage of considerable quantities of fresh water. Space was also required for increased generator capacity and for fuel tanks to supply the LCAs. In addition, extra space (some refrigerated) was required for

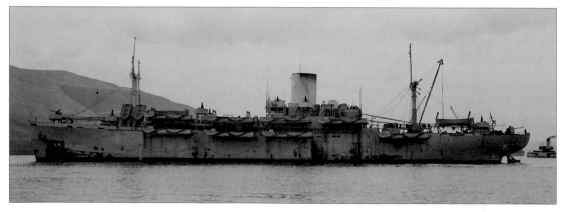

LEFT: **SS *Empire Javelin*, originally named SS *Cape Lobos*, was launched in 1944 for service with the US War Shipping Administration. The vessel was a bareboat chartered by the Transport Department of the British Ministry of War, and managed by the Blue Star Line.**

galleys, bakeries, ammunition magazines and a sick bay. Although built to the same high standards as commercial cargo vessels, the Glen class were now intended to be used in war, so subdivision and stability range had to be improved. Paradoxically, following all this work, the ships were still very much in the "light" condition, much valuable space being used to accommodate permanent solid ballast.

The Glen class were considered a valuable asset and used only for special operations. With the planning for the eventual invasion of Europe proceeding apace, however, further LSI (L) were obviously going to be required. With no further tonnage suitable for conversion, the British sought US assistance, acquiring 13 C1s during 1943. These smaller, single-shaft ships were slower

and more vulnerable than the Glen class, but were intended to carry 1,000 troops over only short distances. The vessels carried 18 LCAs under davits.

Operated by the Ministry of War Transport with civilian crews, the class was identified by the lead ship, HMS *Empire Broadsword*. Following the successful Normandy landings, planning attention was switched to the Far East. The surviving 11 ships were transferred to the White Ensign and renamed after famous racehorses. Nine were "tropicalized" and sent to the Pacific, but operated mainly in casualty evacuation.

Further down the scale, the difference between the LSI (M) and LSI (S) was mainly a matter of degree. Being converted from passenger ferries all were valuable as, despite limited range, being

ABOVE: **Following service as Armed Merchant Cruisers, the Royal Canadian Navy's HMCS *Prince Henry* and HMCS *Prince David* were reconverted to LSI (M). Both were used for the Normandy landings on June 6, 1944.**

capable of around 24 knots. Best were the two Ex-Canadian National Steamships (CNS) ferries, HMCS *Prince David* and HMCS *Prince Henry*, and the Dutch HMS *Princess Beatrix* and HMS *Queen Emma*. Carrying some 450 and 375 troops respectively, each carried two LCMs in addition to six LCAs. Similar in size and speed, but accommodating only 200–250 troops, were the nine mainly ex-Belgian State Railways LSI (S).

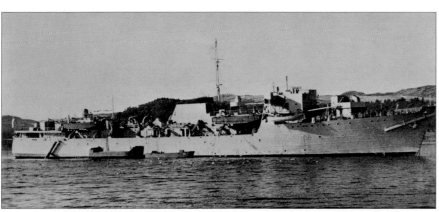

ABOVE: **Dutch-flagged, HMS *Princess Beatrix* (shown here) and HMS *Queen Emma* were built for the Harwich-Hook service. Much modified as LSI (M), they retained their distinctively shaped funnels.**

Landing Ship, Infantry, LSI (L), Glen class

Tonnage: 9,840 tons (gross); 15,500 tons (displacement, full load)
Length: 146.1m/479ft (bp); 155.86m/511ft (oa)
Beam: 20.28m/66ft 6in
Draught: 9.3m/30ft 6in (loaded)
Armament: 6 x 4in guns (3x2), 4 x 2pdr "Pom-Pom" (4x1), 8 x 20mm (8x1)
Machinery: 2 diesel engines, 2 shafts
Power: 8,952kW/12,000shp for 18 knots
Fuel: Not known
Endurance: 22,080km/12,000nm at 14.5 knots
Protection: Nominal
Complement: 523
Capacity: 3 LCMs, 24 LCAs, 1,098 troops

Landing Ship, Carrier, Derrick Hoisting/ Gantry/Stern-chute (LSC/LSG/LSS)

Landing Ships, Infantry (LSI) carried mainly LCAs, (i.e. troop-carrying craft); the ability to transport heavy equipment, and the LCMs with which to land it, was limited to what could be stowed on deck. For any landing larger than a raid, therefore, LSIs would require support by vessels dedicated to carrying cargo and LCMs. The latter were required in numbers sufficient to facilitate rapid ship-to-shore movement. To carry both heavy equipment and LCMs on the same ship appeared advantageous, but this was difficult in practice as a 35-ton loaded LCM (I) needed specialized means of launch and recovery.

A dedicated LCM carrier was the obvious answer but this, in 1940, was beyond Britain's resources to produce. Until such a vessel, ultimately the LSD, could be obtained from the USA (the first four not being delivered until September 1943), suitable examples would need to be modified from ships already in service.

ABOVE: **Three Dale-class tankers were equipped with gantries to handle 15 LCMs, stowed on deck and moved on rollers. The ships transported small craft, but were not used as assault ships. RFA *Derwentdale* lies at anchor in 1942.**
RIGHT: **Two railway-owned train ferries were requisitioned to carry 13 LCMs apiece. This is the stern ramp of HMS *Princess Iris*.**

The simplest means of shipping LCMs in numbers was to carry them as deck cargo, using heavy-lift derricks for launch and recovery. Sir W. G. Armstrong Whitworth & Company Limited had recently built a suitable vessel for Belship, a specialist Norwegian shipping company, and ten were ordered by the Ministry of War Transport (MoWT). Only the first two, HMS *Empire Charmian* and *Empire Elaine*, were designated Landing Ship, Carrier, Derrick Hoisting (LSC).The ships were built with machinery aft and the bridge forward of amidships. Three 120-ton lifting derricks were stepped against substantial posts. The large hatch covers were reinforced to support the distributed load of 21 pre-loaded LCM (I). Substantial ballasting and pumping capacity permitted the ships to maintain stability, while working heavily loaded.

Three tankers (RFA *Derwentdale*, *Dewdale* and *Ennerdale*) were modified to Landing Ship, Carrier, Gantry (LSG). Carrying liquid cargoes, the deck-piping was retained, which limited the LCM capacity to 15, six stowed forward of the bridge, nine behind. These were handled by massive lifting gantries on each side. Pre-loaded with a maximum of 9 tons, the LCMs were slid to the gantries.

Because the LSGs could at the same time carry some 7,000 tons of hazardous cargo (or, in the Far East, fresh water) the type were used to deliver LCMs to a front rather than to a specific operational location.

A third variety of interim LCM carrier came from the modification of two of London & North-Eastern Railway's (LNER) three train ferries to Landing Ships, Carrier, Stern-chute (LSS). These were old vessels dating from World War I. Beamy and slow (11 knots), the vessels had a low freeboard deck fronted by a bluff bow and flanked by narrow side decks. Over 80 per cent of the length was laid to four parallel tracks for railway rolling stock, which was loaded and discharged over the stern. When converted, the stern was reconfigured as a ramped slipway and, mainly on the existing rails, 13 LCM (I) were stowed on trolleys. At the forward end of the vehicle deck a traversing system was installed to align LCMs from the side tracks to the centre, from where the boats were launched.

The conversions were made during 1940 but age, lack of endurance and speed made the two ships unsuitable for front-line service, and they were used

ABOVE: **One of two of railway-owned ferries, HMS *Daffodil* had a train deck running almost her complete length. Thirteen loaded LCMs could be carried and trolley-launched over the stern ramp.**

only to transport LCMs. During 1943 both were converted back to transport railway rolling stock to the shattered European network, after the D-Day landings. From early 1942, LSDs built in the USA used the most simple and versatile means of launching small craft in numbers, that of float-on, float-off.

Landing Ship, Carrier (LSC), HMS *Empire Charmian*

Tonnage: 7,510 tons (gross);
　14,500 tons (displacement, full load)
Length: 126.88m/416ft (bp); 132.22m/433ft 6in (oa)
Beam: 20.36m/66ft 9in
Draught: 8.08m/26ft 6in (mean)
Armament: 1 x 4in gun, 1 x 12pdr,
　6 x 20mm (6x1)
Machinery: Diesel engine, single shaft
Power: 1,865kW/2,500bhp for 11 knots
Fuel: Not known
Endurance: 4,232km/2,300nm at 10 knots
Protection: Nominal
Complement: 40
Capacity: 21 LCM (I), 295 troops

Commando Carriers

To rapidly increase the number of available flight decks during World War II, the Admiralty embarked on the extensive series of "no-frills" Colossus/Majestic-class carriers, collectively termed the "Light Fleets". Rapid increase in aircraft size and weight, however, demanded a larger version. These, and the opportunities to improve speed by a full five knots, increased standard displacement from the "Light Fleets" 13,190 tons to 18,310. By completion of the first of what became known as the Centaur class, this had increased to 20,260 tons.

As the war progressed, so did the Royal Navy's priorities; carrier construction was being reduced. Few "Light Fleets" were completed by the end of the war and only four of a planned eight of the class had been laid down. Post-war, the hulls were slowly completed to launching condition, mainly to clear the shipyards. HMS *Albion*, HMS *Bulwark* and HMS *Centaur* were launched between 1947 and 1948, but HMS *Hermes* was not launched until 1953. On completion, the

first three were already obsolete, and HMS *Hermes* was completed in 1959 to a considerably updated specification.

British amphibious warfare specialists had been following with interest US Marine Corps trials in using carrier-borne helicopters to land spearhead troops. In 1955 they requested suitable aircraft and ships to develop the method in the Royal Navy. The Suez crisis occured shortly afterward. Here, with minimal rehearsal, two "Light Fleets" were able to validate the concept ("Vertical Envelopment") for the first time in combat.

The US Navy ordered the first dedicated Landing Ship, Personnel, Helicopter (LPH), USS *Iwo Jima*, in February 1959. The Royal Navy's three Centaur-class ships, only marginally effective in the strike role, were relatively new and available for conversion. Government funding permitted only two, HMS *Albion* and *Bulwark*, to be modified into what were designated as "Commando Carriers". Both ships were selected because, as yet, neither had received any modernization.

ABOVE: **Although stripped of aircraft handling equipment, HMS *Bulwark* (R08) here retains the original aircraft carrier configuration. The vessel is at US Naval Station, Mayport, Florida.**

Portsmouth Dockyard converted HMS *Bulwark* (1959–60), then HMS *Albion* (1961–62). The major alteration lay in the removal of equipment associated with "fixed-wing" operations – catapults and arrestor gear. Maintenance facilities were installed for each carrier's 16 helicopters, initially Westland S-55 Whirlwind but replaced by Westland Wessex HAS-1 on their introduction in 1961. Developed from the US-built Sikorsky S-58 Choctaw, the Wessex could lift 16 equipped Royal Marines. HMS *Albion* could accommodate 800 troops, HMS *Bulwark* around 730. Both ships were fitted to carry four LCVPs under davits, to allow the troops to be landed during non-flying weather conditions.

From early in 1966, government policy was to run down the Royal Navy carrier force, for which there would be no replacement. HMS *Hermes*, last of the class to be completed, was kept in front-line service until 1971, escaping disposal

by a two-year conversion to join the Commando Carriers. On her completion to this role in 1973, HMS *Albion* was, in fact, decommissioned.

Benefiting from the experience gained with earlier refits, that carried out on HMS *Hermes* was more effective. To maximize hangar and flight deck area, the forward elevator had been located on the port deck edge, US Navy-style. This formed, in the raised position, part of the overhang of the fully angled flight deck. This extra capacity allowed some 73 Royal Marines to be accommodated. A total of 16 Westland Wessex helicopters and four LCVPs, together with a flight of four Westland S-61 Sea King ASW helicopters were carried. A second full Commando could be accommodated in an emergency.

Conversion again involved the removal of "fixed-wing carrier" equipment, the large Type 984 three-dimensional radar being replaced by a "single bedstead" Type 965 air search unit.

With the introduction of V/STOL, HMS *Hermes* regained front-line status, operating both Hawker-Siddeley Sea Harrier FRS-1 and Sea King ASW/AEW while still retaining Commando capabilities. The ship was to demonstrate during the 1982 Falklands War the continuing relevance of the aircraft carrier. After the war the ship was sold to India. HMS *Albion* was scrapped in 1973 and HMS *Bulwark* in 1984.

ABOVE: **HMS *Albion* (R07) was built as a Centaur-class aircraft carrier in 1947 and converted into a "Commando Carrier" in 1962. The Westland Wessex HU-5 entered operational service in 1964. The type could carry up to 16 troops or, underslung, artillery or a light vehicle. Sixteen were carried by each "Commando Carrier", although, as can be seen, only eight could be spotted simultaneously. A complement of 800 Royal Marines was accommodated onboard.**
LEFT: **Although operating helicopters only, HMS *Hermes* (R12) retained the angled deck and "ski jump". Note the side elevator, set into the overhang.**

Commando Carrier, HMS *Hermes*

Displacement: 23,900 tons (standard); 28,700 tons (full load)
Length: 198.25m/650ft (bp); 227.02m/744ft 4in (oa)
Beam: 27.45m/90ft (wl)
Draught: 8.85m/29ft (mean)
Armament: 2 x quadruple Sea Cat PDMS
Machinery: Steam turbines, 4 boilers, 2 shafts
Power: 56,696kW/76,000shp for 28 knots
Fuel: 3,380 tons oil
Endurance: 8,832kW/4,800nm at 20 knots
Protection: Not known
Complement: 1,830 plus 733 troops
Capacity: 20 helicopters

LEFT: **HMS** *Manxman*, launched on September 5, 1940, was the last of six Abdiel-class fast minelayers built for the Royal Navy in World War II. In 1960 the vessel was converted to a Support Ship for minelayers. Two 4in gun mountings and two boiler rooms were removed to create space for workshops and accommodation.

Minesweeper Support Ship

ABOVE: **Designed as a minesweeper support ship, the layout of HMS** *Abdiel* **was similar to that of HMS** *Manxman.* LEFT: **HMS** *Abdiel* **also functioned as an Exercise Minelayer, but in wartime could be used to lay mines.**

Amphibious operations always need to be preceded by mine clearance. Minehunters/sweepers are small ships and are not intended to work alone. Submarines and destroyers have, in the past, been supported by large, purpose-designed tenders or depot ships.

Of only 360 tons, the Ton-class Coastal Minesweepers (CMS) for instance, were deployed in the Far East during the so-called "Indonesia-Malay Dispute" of 1963–66, often as patrol craft and only supported by HMS *Manxman*, a Fast Minelayer. Laid down in 1939, the ship was the last of six in the class. When new the vessel could make 36 knots (although invariably credited with over 40 knots). Later two of the four boilers were removed to create new space for extra generator and evaporator capacity. The design featured two long mining decks,

terminating in doors set into an almost flat transom. These galleries (a weak point from the survivability aspect) were ideal for storage of spare equipment to support CMS. This experience probably influenced the decision to build the 1,375-ton HMS *Abdiel*. Launched in 1967, the vessel was diesel-driven and functioned as an Exercise Minelayer, with minesweeper support duties. For this the ship was built with unusually spacious facilities for a small warship. As an Exercise Minelayer, the task was to lay all types of modern mine for Minehunters/sweepers to find, classify and neutralize (or recover). The capacity of 44 mines was also useful offensively, but in this context the lack of speed was a limiting factor.

HMS *Abdiel* was used between 1974 and 1975 in support of CMS deployed to clear mines and unexploded

ordnance from the Suez Canal, which had been closed following the Yom Kippur War (also the October/Ramadan War), October 6–25, 1973.

Minesweeper Support Ship, HMS *Abdiel*

Displacement: 1,375 tons (standard); 1,500 tons (full load)
Length: 74,57m/244ft 6in (bp); 80.83m/265ft (oa)
Beam: 11.74m/38ft 6in
Draught: 3.05m/10ft (mean)
Armament: Light automatic weapons, normally unarmed
Machinery: 2 diesel engines, 2 shafts
Power: 2,014kW/2,700bhp for 16 knots
Fuel: Not known
Endurance: Not known
Protection: Not known
Complement: 123

LEFT: **The replacement RFA *Sir Galahad* was of an uprated design that was nearly 13m/42ft 8in greater in length. She and the modernized *Sir Bedivere* were recognizable by their distinctive mast and funnel.**

Landing Ship, Logistic (LSL), Sir Lancelot class

Suez highlighted the parlous condition of the Royal Navy's amphibious capability. Commencing in 1960, new vessels began to replace the older vessels from World War II. Launched early in 1964, RFA *Sir Lancelot* was the first of six versatile 17-knot landing ships. All were built to commercial standards and, until transfer to the Royal Fleet Auxiliary (RFA) in 1970, were operated under charter.

All had a raised forecastle and afterdeck, designed for "drive-through" operation with doors and ramps at either end. The tank deck, accommodating 16 main battle tanks, was connected by ramp to the open upper deck amidships, where there was stowage for 34 large vehicles. Cranes served the upper deck and, via a hatch, the tank deck. Aft was a helicopter landing platform, but no hangar. Accommodation was for over 400 troops.

Not designed to beach, except in an emergency, the ships carried powered "Mexeflote" pontoons against each side of the hull in place of small landing craft. Designed to have considerable range, the type could operate worldwide.

The original RFA *Sir Galahad* was lost in the Falklands, being replaced by a new ship of the same name in 1987. At 145m/480ft and displacing over 8,500 tons, the ship was considerably larger than other LSLs. The ship had arranged two interconnected internal decks, linked to the upper deck by both ramps and a scissor-type lift. While having much the same vehicle capacity, alternatively, it was possible to stow up to six large helicopters on the vehicle dock. These were lifted to the two landing spots on the upper deck by elevator. Both types of LSL were used very effectively as mine forces support ships in the Arabian Gulf. For these duties a fully containerized Forward Support Unit, completely fitted-out for rapid deployment, was carried.

ABOVE: **RFA *Sir Bedivere*, as built. The half-lowered stern ramp was for the use of vehicles only; there was no stern docking well.**

LEFT: **RFA *Sir Geraint* shows the class appearance as built in the 1960s. Note how the helicopter deck was one level higher than that of the later design.**

Landing Ship, Logistic (LSL), Sir Lancelot class

Tonnage: 4,475 tons (gross); 3,270 tons (displacement, light); 5,675 tons (displacement, full load)
Length: 111.72m/366ft 4in (bp) 125.66m/412ft (oa)
Beam: 18.24m/59ft 10in
Draught: 4m/13ft (mean, seagoing)
Armament: Light automatic weapons only
Machinery: 2 diesel engines, 2 shafts
Power: 6,956kW/9,400bhp for 17 knots
Fuel: 816 tons oil
Endurance: 14,270km/8,000nm at 15 knots
Protection: Nominal
Complement: 68

Landing Platform, Dock (LPD), Fearless class

Having returned the four Lend-Lease, Casa Grande class LSDs at the end of World War II, the Royal Navy operated none of the type for the next 20 years. The US Navy continued development and, between 1962 and 1963, commissioned two Raleigh-class LPDs, a more versatile type that exchanged some docking well space for extra garaging and stowage. When, following Suez, the British replaced the outdated Amphibious Warfare

Squadron, the Raleigh-class design was acquired as the basis for two LPDs of almost-identical dimensions. The ships were not designed to beach.

Fitted to act as Headquarters Ships for brigade-size operations, HMS *Fearless* and HMS *Intrepid* could each accommodate 400 troops on a long passage, and up to 700 on a short passage. Four LCA (later LCVP), each carrying 30-plus platoon, were stowed

under davits. Above the docking well the helicopter deck was large enough to handle four to six assault helicopters. No hangar was provided. The original ship was designed around the then main battle tank, the Centurion (52 tons), two of which could be carried by each of the six LCMs. With the larger Chieftain (54 tons) and later, the Challenger (62 tons), however, the capacity of both ship and embarked LCM was reduced. Only four LCM (9) were carried in later days. Never armed with anything heavier than point-defence weapons, the two ships were in service for 40 years and were superseded by the Ocean and Albion class.

ABOVE: **Despite having a layout similar to the US-built Raleigh-class LPD, HMS *Fearless* (shown here) and HMS *Intrepid* were instantly recognizable by the tall mainmast.**
LEFT: **The ship's LCM (9) preparing to form up prior to moving to the beach. Two Westland Sea King helicopters are stowed on the flight deck, as no hangar space was provided.**

Landing Platform, Dock (LPD), Fearless class

Displacement: 11,060 tons (standard); 12,120 tons (full load); 16,950 tons (ballasted)
Length: 152.5m/500ft (wl); 158.6m/520ft (oa)
Beam: 24.4m/80ft
Draught (seagoing): 6.25m/29ft 6in (mean)
Draught (ballasted down): 7.02m/23ft (forward); 9.76m/32ft (aft)
Armament: 4 x quadruple Sea Cat PDMS, 2 x 40mm (2x1)
Machinery: Steam turbines, 2 boilers, 2 shafts
Power: 16,412kW/32,000shp for 21 knots
Fuel: 2,040 tons oil
Endurance: 9,200km/5,000nm at 20 knots
Protection: Not known
Complement: 556

Landing Ship, Medium (LSM), Ardennes class

Further to military-manned (RN) and civilian-manned (RFA) amphibious warfare ships, there is also the "navy" operated by the Royal Logistics Corps (RLC). Not intended for offensive use except in an emergency, the vessels are used for training and in the supply of various garrisons.

The two "flagships" were the *Ardennes* and *Arakan* which, although classed as LSMs, had little in common with LSMs of World War II, not least in being appreciably larger. Speed was sacrificed for a wider beam and shallow draught, deck dimensions being tailored to carry five 54-ton Chieftain main battle tanks and for 24 TEU containers. As the latter were stacked, two 3-ton derricks were fitted for cargo handling.

For offensive use, the design looked vulnerable. The clamshell bows and the folded internal ramp dictated a very high forecastle making for dry seakeeping but necessitating a wheelhouse at an even higher level. Both wheelhouse and accommodation (34 troops in addition to 35 crew) were thus raised one level, allowing the deck below to be extended.

ABOVE: **On the Ardennes class, the vehicle deck extends to the after end of the bridge structure. Although head-on to the beach, the stern anchor has not been dropped.**

A surprisingly large afterdeck suggested that the whole superstructure could, with advantage, have been located further aft.

The RLC has adopted the practice of naming craft after campaigns and battles commencing with the letter "A" (Army). No distinction, however, is made between class or size, so that the nine 290-ton Landing Craft, Utility (LCU), although far smaller than the Ardennes class, are named similarly from *Arromanches* to *Arezzo*. Also known as Ramped Powered Lighters (RPL), several of the vessels remain in service.

ABOVE: **The considerably high bow is required to accommodate a usefully sized rigid loading ramp. The height also improves dryness but makes for poor visibility forward from the bridge. The large spaces under the side decks are kept empty or used to ballast the ship.**

Landing Ship, Medium (LSM), Ardennes class

Displacement: 870 tons (light); 1,660 tons (full load)
Length: 70.15m/230ft (wl); 73.2m/240ft (oa)
Beam: 14m/45ft 10in
Draught: 17.7m/5ft 9in (maximum)
Armament: None
Machinery: 2 diesel engines, 2 shafts
Power: 1,492kW/2,000bhp for 10 knots
Fuel: 150 tons oil
Endurance: 5,980km/3,250nm at 10 knots
Protection: Nominal
Complement: 35 plus 34 troops

LEFT: **Like most modern merchant vessels – car carriers, container or cruise ships – HMS *Ocean* is volume-critical, resulting in an efficient underwater form and angular topsides. Note the Vulcan Phalanx CIWS mounting at the bow.**

Landing Ship, Personnel, Helicopter (LPH), HMS *Ocean*

Design parameters for large amphibious warfare vessels are virtually limitless, balancing the conflicting demands of troop-carrying with both the heavy equipment and means of delivery. The simple approach is to include everything, but this results in ships the same size as the LHD in US Navy service. Such vessels can be unaffordable or unjustified by smaller navies, hence the requirement to make compromises. For the British this was to return to the original "Commando Carrier" concept as central to a battalion-sized operation and dependent on dock landing ships to provide heavy cargo capacity, the necessary landing craft and further troop accommodation.

Britain's capability to design and build large ships has contracted dramatically over recent years. Savings were clearly apparent in adopting the existing hull design of HMS *Invincible* as a starting point. The resulting HMS *Ocean* is an impressive ship but makes no concessions to elegance. The ship

incorporates commercial standards wherever appropriate. The bold union between the volume-maximized upper hull and the finer hull about the waterline is much like those of container ships or Pure Car Carriers (PCC). Both types set similar design problems. Some account has also been

taken of the need to reduce radar signature. The extreme flare beneath the ship's quarter overhangs required subsequent modification as being hazardous to the lowering of the LCVP (5) slung under the davits. These were then recessed into very large rectangular apertures in the side of the hull.

ABOVE: **HMS *Ocean* does not have a docking well. The ramp mounted on the stern is to allow light vehicles to be transferred to and from the four LCVP (5) carried on the ship.**

LEFT: **The extending stern ramp on the ship is used to link with a "Mexeflote" pontoon to off-load light vehicles. The unobstructed flight deck is long enough (130m/427ft) for the operation of Harrier V/STOL aircraft.**

Up to 500 troops can be carried on an extended passage, plus 300 more in an emergency. Light vehicles and 105mm artillery are off-loaded into landing craft via an off-centre ramp set into the wide stern. Each LCVP can accommodate a platoon, together with two light vehicles. A second ramp accessing the vehicle deck is located on the starboard side, below the bridge.

HMS Ocean has a full-length flight deck with a large, starboard-side island. There are, of course, no catapults or arrestor gear, the non-carrier status being further emphasized by the lack of a "ski jump" for V/STOL aircraft.

The hangar space is thought to be the largest ever incorporated into a Royal Navy ship, with headroom and area sufficient to accommodate 12 Merlin helicopters (which are too large for the elevators on HMS Invincible). As an alternative, 12 Sea King and six Lynx could be stowed below. The flight deck is stressed for occasional use by Chinook helicopters or Harrier V/STOL aircraft, for which a 130m/427ft take-off

run is possible. HMS Ocean has also operated Apache attack helicopters, but no provision appears to have been made for any future acquisition of the tilt-rotor Bell Boeing MV-22 Osprey. Although fitted with state of the art command and control facilities, HMS Ocean is not fitted as a flagship, nor can the level of military staff required for a brigade-scale operation be carried.

Main propulsion is by two commercial-type, medium-speed diesel engines, located in separate compartments. Both engines are fitted with a gearbox for reversing due to the relatively high output speed. Considerable criticism has been made over the choice of comparatively low-power units which limit the ship's sustained speed to a modest 18 knots. For quiet operation, the ship can be propelled by shaft-mounted electric motors.

Current thinking appears to continue to favour the LPH-style ship which optimizes helicopter-borne assault at the expense of a docking well and a large garaging area. Although of twice the

displacement, the planned replacements for the Tarawa-class in the US Navy are reported to lack a docking well. The size and design of HMS Ocean appears to have been followed closely by South Korea for two Dokdo-class ships which, reportedly, can accommodate ten Merlin helicopters and some 700 troops.

Landing Ship, Personnel, Helicopter (LPH), HMS *Ocean*

Displacement: 21,580 tons (full load)
Length: 193m/633ft 6in (bp); 203.4m/667ft 8in (oa)
Beam: 28.5m/93ft 6in (wl); 36.1m/118ft 6in (extreme width)
Draught: 6.65m/21ft 10in (mean)
Armament: 3 x Vulcan Phalanx CIWS, some smaller
Machinery: 2 diesel engines, 2 shafts
Power: 13,726kW/18,400bhp for 19 knots (maximum)
Fuel: 1,500 tons oil
Endurance: 14,720km/8,000nm at 15 knots
Protection: Not known
Complement: 497 including aircrew, plus 12 Merlins

LEFT: **Large British amphibious ships have a more "mercantile" appearance than US Navy counterparts. Note the funnels on the starboard side, two machinery uptakes, the open access door amidships and the size of the gantry davits for handling the four LCVPs carried.**

Landing Platform, Dock (LPD), Albion class

As early as 1985 the Royal Navy began preparations for the replacement of the two Fearless-class LPDs, after some 20 years service. Problems arose because the British shipbuilding industry had been reduced to the size where only one company could build ships of the required size. The perfectly competent Admiralty design organization was passed over in favour of a commercially produced design. Nine years and five design studies eventually produced the basis of a proposal which was then modified until an acceptable contract figure could be met. By the time that the two Albion-class ships entered service, HMS *Fearless* and HMS *Intrepid* had not been combat-capable for a considerable period.

That said, the Albion class has proved to be useful. Somewhat smaller than HMS *Ocean*, and accommodating fewer troops (305 against 500 or in emergency 710 against 803) both ships in the class have superior command and control facilities.

The ships carry both the naval task group and the army/marine landing force commanders (CATG and CLF) and staffs. Real-time information on the battle situation is enhanced by radar-equipped and unmanned drones.

The Albion class each carries four LCUs in a docking well accessed by a large stern gate. In the lowered position, but with the ship not flooded down, the gate is used as a loading ramp for the LCUs. Garaging is provided for six tanks

LEFT: **Despite the end of the Cold War, British amphibious forces still exercise in a full range of climatic conditions. A Griffon 2000 TDX (M) assault hovercraft is manoeuvred toward the open docking well.**

and up to 16 large or 36 smaller vehicles. The vehicle decks are interconnected by ramps which also link with the flight deck and docking well. Note, the dimensions of four LCU (10), are the same as those of two US-pattern LCACs stowed in tandem. In addition, four LCVP (5) are carried topside under davits.

Construction and fittings greatly reflect current commercial practice. The vehicle decks are also accessible via a starboard-side door and ramp. The cargo spaces are accessed by doors in the hull on each side. The latter are fitted for rapid stores transfer by the use of pallets.

Flooded down, there is an average 3m/9.8ft water depth in the docking well which equates to some 2,500 tons of water. The influence of this on stability is monitored by a dedicated computer system but ship movement in an anchorage can, nonetheless, create "sloshing", which can cause damage to closely berthed landing craft. A slow speed combination of bow thrusters and main engines may serve to keep the ship steady in most sea conditions. A further option in poor conditions is to flood down and release the LCUs while the ship is moving.

Diesel-electric propulsion has great advantages in being very responsive to demand and requiring few skilled personnel for operation and maintenance. The diesel-generator sets can be located with consideration to both quieteness and convenience, while the electric propulsion motors are located aft, shortening propeller shafts and reducing vulnerability.

With a full-width superstructure of considerable length, the Albion class has a helicopter landing deck at the aft end. Space is provided for two Westland Merlin or Sea King helicopters and space for a further, parked aircraft. One CH-47 Chinook may be operated as an alternative. Refuelling facilities are available, but there is no hangar.

ABOVE: **HMS *Bulwark* (L15) shows how modern warships, with dimensions driven by volume requirements, increasingly follow the design of current merchant vessels.**

Landing Platform, Dock, HMS *Albion* (L14) and HMS *Bulwark* (L15)

Displacement: 14,600 tons (standard); 16,980 tons (loaded); 18,500 tons (flooded)
Length: 162m/531ft 9in (bp); 178m/584ft 3in (oa)
Beam: 28.9m/94ft 10in
Draught: 6.1m/20ft (mean, seagoing)
Armament: 2 x Goalkeeper CIWS, some smaller
Machinery: Diesel-electric, 2 shafts
Power: 12,000kW/16,100bhp for 18 knots (maximum)
Fuel: Not known
Endurance: 14,720 km/8,000nm at 15 knots
Protection: Not known
Complement: 325 plus 305 Marines

LEFT: **The Dutch and Spanish influence on the design of the Bay class extended even to the first use in Royal Fleet Auxiliary service of the very high holding capacity Pool TW anchor. RFA L***yme Bay* **(L3007) was the last in the series to be built.**

Landing Ship, Dock (LSD), Bay class

Supporting HMS *Ocean* and the two Albion class are the four Bay-class vessels in RFA service. The ships are replacements for the Sir Lancelot class, but there the comparison ends for all are built to an entirely different concept, greatly influenced by the Dutch Rotterdam and Spanish Galicia designs which entered service 1998–2000.

The British types are larger and, indeed, almost the same displacement as the Albion class. Visually, the type is unmistakable with a large seven-deck accommodation and bridge superstructure located forward. A funnel is not required as the propulsion and auxiliary diesel engines exhaust below the waterline. Not designed to be beached, the class are equipped with "Mexeflote" powered pontoons, stowed on the sides of the hull. Internally there is a docking well, large enough to accommodate a single LCU (10) or two LCVPs. No LCVPs are carried. The ships have facilities to transport some 350 troops or 700 on short voyages.

The clear afterdeck can operate two Westland Merlin or Sea King helicopters, or a single Chinook. There is no hangar. Two 30-ton cranes are mounted at the forward end of the helicopter landing deck.

A permanent gantry with a capacity of 200 tons is used for transferring cargo and stores from the deck.

The class have over twice the vehicle capacity of an LSL, reportedly with room for up to 32 Challenger 2 battle tanks or 150 light trucks.

The class is the first in RFA service to be propelled by podded propulsers. Known as "Azipod" thrusters, these combine propeller and electric propulsion motor in a unit which may be rotated through 360 degrees and remove the requirement for rudders or propeller and shafts.

LEFT: **RFA *Cardigan Bay* (L3009) can maintain a precise alignment and position using two "Azipod" azimuth propulsion units in combination with bow thrusters.**

Landing Ship, Dock (LSD), Bay class

Displacement: 16,150 tons (loaded)
Length: 176.6m/579ft (oa)
Beam: 26.4m/86ft 7in
Draught: 5.8m/19ft
Armament: For, but not with, 2 x Vulcan Phalanx CIWS
Machinery: Diesel electrics, 2 podded propulsors
Power: Not known
Fuel: Not known
Endurance: 14,720km/8,000nm at 15 knots
Protection: Not known
Complement: 60 plus 356 marines

Sealift Ship, Point class

The final component of what is termed the Joint Rapid Deployment Force (JRDF) are the Hartland Point class vehicle carriers. Like T-AKRs, all are built to current commercial standards, with full Roll-on, Roll-off (Ro-Ro) access. The ships are not drive-through, but the full width stern door (which also acts as a loading ramp) and unobstructed vehicle decks permit on-board turning space. There are three interconnected internal vehicle decks, with further stowage on the upper deck and beneath the bridge block. This space is protected by deep bulwarks and a distinctive apron over the forward end.

A 40-ton pedestal-type crane is located on the starboard side, facilitating the handling of containerized cargo.

Further to the usual armoured vehicles, transport and artillery the ships (as with any commercial Ro-Ro) carry considerable freight pre-loaded on trailers. The need for such adaptability was amply demonstrated during the 1982 Falklands campaign, when the MV *Atlantic Conveyor* was lost.

Building of what is a commercial design was contracted to a German shipyard who built four. The other two ships were built by Harland & Wolff, Belfast. One addition is a passive,

flume-type stablization system which, unlike an active fin system, can be effective with the ship at anchor.

The ships are twin-screw, with the diesel engines exhausting through a funnel offset to port. Propulsive power was considerably increased in the last three built, with a corresponding improvement in speed. The Ministry of Defence (MoD) has purchased a 22-year charter from Forland Shipping, which owns, operates and crews all six ships in the class.

LEFT: **Very suitable for palletized, trailer-carried freight, MV *Longstone* is under commercial charter to Transfennica who operate a Ro-Ro cargo ferry service in the Baltic. All ships are available to the MoD at short notice.**

Sealift Ship, Point class	

Displacement: 22,000 tons (loaded)
Length: 182.39m/598ft (bp); 193m/632ft 9in (oa)
Beam: 26m/85ft 3in (wl)
Draught: 7.4m/24ft 3in (full load)
Armament: Unarmed
Machinery: 2 diesel engines, 2 shafts
Power: 13,055kW/17,500bhp for 18 knots (first three); 16,188kW/21,700bhp for 21.5 knots (last three)
Fuel: 1,100 tons oil
Endurance: 22,080km/12,000nm at 17 knots
Protection: Not known
Complement: 18

Landing Ship, Dock (LSD), Ouragan class

With a view to operations in the Indian Ocean, South-east Asia and the Pacific, France created a small but effective amphibious force as soon as post-war circumstances permitted. The LSD, capable of ocean voyages yet able to land a force directly "over the beach", was well proven during World War II. The French Navy designed and built two ships which were somewhat smaller than the other LSDs.

The bridge structure is set to starboard on the elevated helicopter deck that occupies the amidships area. Enclosed by a stern gate, the docking well is 120m/394ft in length, accommodating either two EDIC-type LCTs or eight LCM (8). All may be pre-loaded.

Flooded-down, the docking well has a depth of 3m/9ft 10in, sufficient to prevent large landing craft fouling the sill when undocking. Floating off, the larger landing craft requires the raising of the movable deck over the docking well. This deck, in whole or in part, may be used for an extra helicopter landing spot or for the stowage of vehicles or stores. For the latter,

two 35-ton cranes are provided. There is no helicopter hangar. Up to 470 troops may be accommodated and, as an alternative to landing craft, up to 1,500 tons of general cargo can be carried.

Intended for worldwide independent operation, the two ships in the class are equipped with comprehensive repair facilities and a command centre equpoied to control a complete amphibious operation. Both ships have also proved to be valuable when used for disaster relief.

Following 40 years in service, the ships were sold to Argentina.

ABOVE: **Only two of the class were built: FS** *Ouragan* **(L9021) and FS** *Orage* **(L9022). Both were withdrawn from service in 2007.**
LEFT: **The design of the ship is interesting in that by locating the island to the side and by using diesel propulsion, thus eliminating the requirement for a funnel, a large flight deck area has been created.**

Landing Ship, Dock (LSD), Ouragan class

Displacement: 5,965 tons (light); 8,500 tons (loaded); 15,000 tons (flooded)
Length: 144.5m/473ft 9in (bp); 149m/488ft 6in (oa)
Beam: 21.5m/70ft 6in (wl)
Draught: 5.4m/17ft 9in (mean, seagoing); 8.7m/28ft 5in (mean, flooded)
Armament: 2 x twin Simbad PDMS, 2 x 40mm guns (2x1), 2 x 30mm guns (2x1)
Machinery: 2 diesel engines, 2 shafts
Power: 6,714km/9,000bhp at 15 knots
Fuel: Not known
Endurance: 16,560km/9,000nm at 15 knots
Protection: Not known
Complement: 205 plus; 470 troops

Landing Ship, Medium (LSM), Champlain class

In service with the French Navy, the Champlain class are known as *Batiment de Transport Léger* (BATRAL) light ferry ships. The elegantly shaped hull was not designed to assist with quantity nor inexpensive production, but did result in a respectable vessel speed of 16 knots.

The class was built over a 12-year period, and individual ships show variations as the design developed. All have a box-shaped superstructure block topped by a small funnel. In the last three ships, the superstructure is one deck higher, with troop accommodation increased from 138 to 180. Capacity below is large enough to carry up to 12 vehicles and 330 tons of stores. The bow ramp can support 40 tons, more than sufficient for light tanks or armoured personnel carriers.

The last three built also carry an LCVP and an LCP on deck, ahead of the bridge. To handle these, a 35-ton hydraulic crane is carried. On the first two ships there is a cargo derrick supported by a substantial frame on the bridge.

All were completed with an elevated helicopter deck, capable of handling an Aérospatiale *Alouette* (Lark) light helicopter, but there is no hangar. The last in the series, FS *La Grandière*, was built speculatively and only later acquired by the French Navy. The ship has differences in detail, notably an enlarged helicopter deck.

The design has attracted export orders from friendly states – Gabon, Ivory Coast and Morocco. Chile built two under licence. The vessels have proved to be effective station ships, serving from New Caledonia to French Guiana.

ABOVE: **One of the two earlier ships, FS *Francis Garnier* (L9031) has a superstructure one level fewer than that of the greater-capacity FS *Dumont d'Urville* (L9032) shown in the photograph at the top of the page.**

Landing Ship, Medium (LSM), Champlain class

Displacement: 820 tons (standard); 1,385 tons (loaded)
Length: 68m/223ft (bp); 80m/262ft 3in (oa)
Beam: 13m/42ft 8in
Draught: 3m/9ft 10in (maximum, seagoing)
Armament: 2 x 81mm mortars, 2 x 20mm guns (2x1)
Machinery: 2 diesel engines, 2 shafts
Power: 2,686kW/3,600bhp for 16 knots
Fuel: Not known
Endurance: 6,440km/3,500nm at 13 knots
Protection: Nominal
Complement: 52 plus 180 troops

Landing Ship, Dock (LSD), Foudre class

Designed by the same bureau of DCN, Brest, a Foudre-class vessel may be mistaken in profile for a smaller Ouragan-class vessel. Neither has an obvious funnel but, in proportion, the larger ship has a larger bridge structure and longer flight deck amidships. From any other angle, it will be apparent that, where an Ouragan's bridge block is offset to starboard, that of a Foudre class is full width. Although larger, the class is designed similarly around a "regiment" of some 380 troops. The description "Rapid

Reaction Force" (RRE) is supported by the improved ability to land and support the troops. The docking well is of similar dimensions but accommodates a later type of LCU, the height of which may be reduced so as not to inhibit the use of the movable deck overhead.

The latter point is significant in that this deck provides a helicopter landing spot additional to the two on the permanent flight deck. All are dimensioned for Super Pumas, four of which can be hangared under the bridge structure.

Extending operational options are two LCVPs and side access doors in the hull. A neat arrangement lies in the moveable deck comprising five buoyant pontoon sections which can function similarly to the British "Mexeflote". The sections, together with any cargo carried on them, are handled by two side-mounted 37-ton capacity cranes.

ABOVE: **FS *Sciroco* (L9012) at the French naval base of Toulon. The second of the class, built four years after FS *Foudre* (L9011), it differs only in minor details.**

A Foudre class has a very large vehicle/cargo capacity, with a cumulative load of 1,880 tons. She is equipped with a 52-ton capacity elevating platform, with power to lift an AMX-10RC heavy armoured car (15 tons) and Leclerc main battle tank (40 tons), although light tanks are more usually carried.

FS *Foudre* had been in service for over four years before her sister ship was even laid down. As the FS *Sciroco* was thus built to an improved specification, FS *Foudre* has subsequently been updated.

Landing Ship, Dock (LSD), Foudre class

Displacement: 8,230 tons (standard); 12,010 tons (loaded); 17,200 tons (flooded)
Length: 160m/524ft 6in (bp); 168m/550ft 10in (oa)
Beam: 22m/71ft 2in
Draught: 5.6m/18ft 4in (seagoing); 9.1m/29ft 10in (maximum, flooded)
Armament: 2/3 twin Simbad PDMS, 3 x 30mm guns (3x1)
Machinery: 2 diesel engines, 2 shafts, bow thrusters
Power: 15,517kW/20,800 bhp for 21 knots
Fuel: Not known
Endurance: 20,240km/11,000nm at 15 knots
Protection: Splinter-proof
Complement: 224 plus 470 troops (maximum)

ABOVE LEFT: **An LCU approaches the stern gate to the flooded docking well on FS *Siroco* during operations in the Lebanon.**
LEFT: **FS *Foudre* (L9011) at Toulon naval base. Note how the *Sciroco* (above left) has fewer permanent apertures in the upper hull than *Foudre*. This, presumably, is to further reduce the radar signature.**

LEFT: The design presents a compact appearance, without the heavily sculpted changes in the hull plating. The somewhat over-elaborate funnel would appear to present an unnecessary and undesirable infra-red hot spot.

Landing Ship, Helicopter (LH), Mistral class

The two Mistral-class ships were originally ordered as Foudre class, but the specification was considerably uprated to multi-purpose landing and command ship, similar to but smaller than the US Navy's LHAs. Both have a full-length flight deck, with two elevators to the hangar space below. Unlike the similarly sized HMS Ocean, this is above a 57.5m/189ft docking well with a stern gate. The docking well is only half the length of that in the smaller Foudre class but is wider, enabling two US-pattern LCACs to be stowed as an alternative to the more usual four LCM (8).

On a moderate displacement, these volume demands translate to ships with an unusually high freeboard. The resulting advantage of a dry flight deck is offset by increased transverse accelerations countered by active fin stablizers.

In profile, the counter and stern gate are vertical, while the bow form is very similar to that of a maritime car carrier, or PCC. The angled funnel casing has exposed smoke pipes, currently the style in the commercial maritime world but, on a warship, likely to provide hot spots, detectable by infra-red equipment.

The hangar can accommodate 20 helicopters, either the Super Puma, Super Frelon or Eurocopter NH-90. Although only 27 of the latter are currently being acquired, more than half are to be configured as the ASW replacement for the Westland Lynx. Six deck spots are available for aircraft up to the size of Sikorsky CH-53E Super

Stallion or Bell-Boeing MV-22 Osprey. Accommodation is provided for 450 troops, 900 in an emergency. FS Mistral will also act as a replacement for the cadet training ship FS Jeanne d'Arc.

The two ships are the first major French warships to be fitted with "Azipod" azimuth propulsors, eliminating shafts and rudders. Both ships are equipped with extensive command and medical facilities.

LEFT AND ABOVE: **FS Mistral is seen here both complete (left) and in an advanced state of fitting out but lacking electronic systems (above). Not the centreline helicopter lift, on the stern, in the lowered position.**

Landing Ship, Helicopter (LH), Mistral class

Displacement: 16,500 tons (standard); 21,500 tons (loaded)
Length: 199m/625ft 6in (wl); 210m/688ft 6in (oa)
Beam: 28m/91ft 10in (wl); 32m/104ft 11in (extreme)
Draught: 6.2m/20ft 4in (mean, seagoing)
Armament: 3 x Simbad PDMS, 3 x 30mm guns (3x1)
Machinery: Diesel-electric, podded propellers and bow thruster
Power: 14,174kW/19,000shp for 19 knots
Fuel: Not known
Endurance: 11,040km/6,000nm at 18 knots
Protection: Not known
Complement: 160 plus 450 troops

Landing Craft Carrier, *Shinshu Maru*

In modern amphibious warfare, the *Shinshu Maru* is deserving of recognition in that the vessel was the first-ever ship to be designed for the purpose of transporting loaded landing craft. Japanese landing craft of the time were the various types of Daihatsu, the largest, when loaded with a light tank, displacing around 37 tons.

The concept of the ship, and funding, stemmed from the Imperial Army, which explains the over-ambitious design. Built with a false identity and operating under a mercantile name, *Shinshu Maru* was surrounded by such secrecy that even today much detail is unclear.

Twenty landing craft of unknown size were accommodated in two long side galleries, being launched down a slip through large doors set in the wide stern. The craft appear to have been lifted aboard by the large crane stepped from the massive tripod at the forward end. This served as a hatch in the foredeck and permitted craft to be placed directly on launching rails. Access to the galleries was provided by side doors amidships, which probably facilitated the loading of armour via ramps or the handling of more general cargo, as an alternative to landing craft. An open afterdeck was served by a single heavy cargo derrick, rigged from a second substantial tripod mast. The superstructure was bulky, as it enclosed a large floatplane hangar, with aircraft catapults on the foredeck.

The hull was low, and the gallery deck was almost certainly the freeboard deck. With completion overseen by the Imperial Navy, it was recognized that the ship's stability range was very limited. A "torpedo bulkhead" was therefore added.

ABOVE: **An artist's impression of *Shinshu Maru*. There are only two photographs in existence.**

LEFT AND BELOW: **Daihatsu craft are visible aft and forward, adjacent to doors accessing the superstructure. Smaller craft are operated via the many davits.**

Landing Craft Carrier, *Shinshu Maru*

Displacement: 9,000 tons (standard); 11,780 tons (full load)
Length: 150m/492ft 2in
Beam: 22m/72ft 2in
Draught: 8.2m/26ft 9in
Armament: 5–8 x 75mm guns (5/8 x 1)
Machinery: Steam turbines, 2 shafts
Power: 5,968kW/8,000shp for 19 knots
Fuel: Not known
Endurance: Not known
Protection: Not known
Complement: Not known

LEFT: **Japan began the war with a large number of fine cargo ships. Reckless use in action was a contributory cause of the nation's defeat. Discharge of cargo and troops by Daihatsu craft, as seen here, was laborious and possible only through the initial lack of Allied air power.**

Attack Cargo Ship, *Kibitsu Maru*

During the 1930s, when Japanese forces faced the technically backward Chinese, the Imperial Navy was presented with few problems. War with the USA, however, was a different matter. The widespread area of Japanese occupation would make this a maritime-based war against an opponent who, with time, could only become stronger.

The Pacific Ocean became a theatre of manoeuvre warfare on a grand scale, where the side with superior amphibious capabilities had the initiative and the greater number of options of where to strike next. Like US forces at the outset, the Japanese were lacking specialized ships and drew on an extensive merchant fleet for vessels which could be rapidly converted. In the Japanese military organization, the Army was the dominant authority and it was the Army that requisitioned merchant ships used as attack transport and cargo ships.

The success of the *Shinshu Maru* against almost non-existent Chinese opposition encouraged the Army to convert more merchant ships to landing craft carriers. These could carry up to 20 Daihatsu craft on rails for launching through stern doors. The conversions were complex and redefined the internal layout, greatly reducing access and capacity for cargo or accommodation.

Ships such as the *Kibitsu Maru*, typical of those requisitioned, compared poorly with equivalent US Navy ships. The conversions did not impinge on troop space below, although it should be appreciated that Japanese troops were more accustomed to enduring long sea passages on the open decks.

Although loading facilities were sometimes split to accommodate a Daihatsu trackway, the ships retained cargo-lifting gear. Increasingly the ships were used for cargo carrying as the attrition of the merchant fleet from submarines, aircraft and surface vessels of the US 7th Fleet increased.

ABOVE: **Japanese troops were resilient and undemanding, and were prepared to travel on open, crowded upper decks with a minimum of facilities. In the East Indian archipelago, however, the distances travelled were usually relatively short.**

Attack Cargo Ship, *Kibitsu Maru*

Tonnage: 8,000 tons (gross);
9,650 tons (deadweight),
12,000 tons (displacement, loaded)
Length: 142m/466ft (wl)
152.5m/500ft (oa)
Beam: 20m/64ft 3in
Draught: 7m/23ft (mean, loaded)
Armament: 8 x 75mm guns (8x1), 2 x 81mm
mortars, up to 60 x 25mm guns
Machinery: Steam turbines, 2 boilers, 2 shafts
Power: 7,460kW/10,000shp for 19 knots
Fuel: Not known
Endurance: Not known
Protection: Nominal
Complement: Not known

Landing Ship, Tank (LST), Type 1

ABOVE: **The distinguishing feature of the Type 1 was the long, sloping after end for the carriage and launching of various landing. The barriers across the rails may be to prevent the afterdeck from being swamped by a following sea.**

As 1943 progressed, Japan's requirements were not so much for amphibious warships designed for further conquest but for specialized vessels built to support and supply garrisons in the Solomon Islands. US air power was dominant by day, so the Japanese needed ships fast enough to operate overnight, taking minimum time to turn around. The solution was typically innovative, relying in no way on outside influence. Known generally as a Type 1, or Class 1, the vessel was of under 2,000 tons (loaded) displacement, although it appeared much larger. Designed to be built rapidly, the Type 1 incorporated plating that was either flat or had no more than simple curvature. The hull lacked sheer or camber and, although flush-decked, had freeboard that diminished forward to aft. Indeed, freeboard aft

was zero, the clear afterdeck acting as a slipway for four pre-loaded and trolley mounted Daihatsu craft.

Amidships were cargo holds of some 250 tons capacity, served by conventional cargo-lifting gear. The ships were capable of 22 knots and, in an emergency, could launch the landing craft at speeds up to 16 knots.

By late 1943, orders are believed to have been for 46 but, despite build simplicity, only 21 were actually completed. The type was used to transport alternative launchable deck loads, such as midget submarines, human torpedoes or amphibious tanks, but was equally used to transport troops and equipment.

By May 1944, when the Type 1 entered service, US forces dominated the area and, despite a reasonable armament for their size, progressively boosted by radar,

sonar and even depth charges, the class suffered greatly, with only five ships surviving to serve as repatriation transports after the surrender of Japan.

Landing Ship, Tank (LST), Type 1

Displacement: 1,500 tons (standard); 1,750 tons (loaded)
Length: 89.06m/292ft bp; 96.08m/315ft (oa)
Beam: 10.22m/33ft 6in
Draught: 3.58m/11ft 9in
Armament: 2 x 5in DP guns (2x1), 15 x 25mm guns (3x3, 1x2, 4x1)
Machinery: Steam turbine, 2 boilers, single screw
Power: 7,087kW/9,500shp for 22 knots (maximum)
Fuel: Not known
Endurance: 6,810km/3,700nm at 18 knots
Protection: Nominal
Complement: Not known

ABOVE: **The Daihatsu Type A was the largest built. Unlike other Daihatsu types, this vessel was relatively heavily armed.**
LEFT: **Two Daihatsu Type B landing craft abandoned on a beach in the Pacific.**

Daihatsu Landing Craft

Unique among small landing craft, the Daihatsu design dated from the late 1920s and, serving Japanese requirements very well, the type continued in production for almost two decades. Daihatsu was the adopted Allied term embracing different Japanese sub-types, measuring between 10 and 17m/33 and 56ft overall. Of these, the 14m/46ft type was the most common.

Although displacing anything between 6 and 37 tons, the general design features were similar. Based on a traditional fishing boat, the craft were of a "sampan-shaped" in appearance, with a continuous sheer line. The stern was either rounded or had a curved transom. Strength and longitudinal stability was by two built-on, parallel and protruding keels, terminating forward as two pronounced skegs. The bow was fitted with a ramp.

Designed for loading and discharge while laying alongside a larger ship in open anchorages, the Daihatsu had heavy, braced rubbing strakes, incorporated into the structure of the craft to improve overall stiffness on what was an open and shallow hull.

The type was built in the thousands, options including an open vehicle deck, protected helmsman's position or light steel canopy and protective, hinged side plates. The type does not appear to have been adapted for lifting by davits.

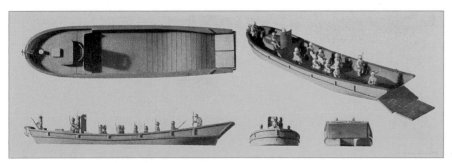

ABOVE: **The Daihatsu Type B was mainly used to transport troops or supplies. The full-width loading ramp was adopted by the US Navy for use on the Higgins boat.**

Daihatsu Landing Craft (Type B)

Displacement: 21 tons
Length: 14.57m/47ft 10in
Beam: 3.35m/11ft
Draught: 0.76m/2ft 6in (mean)
Armament: 2/3 x 25mm guns, 2 x machine-guns
Machinery: 1/2 petrol or diesel engines, single shaft
Power: 44.8–111.9kW/60–150hp for 7.5–8.5 knots
Endurance: 80–160km/50–100nm at 7.5 knots
Protection: None
Complement: Up to 12, depending on duty

Coastal Minesweeper (CMS), Kasado/ Takami class and Support Ship, *Hayase*

The Korean War of the early 1950s alerted the world to the dangers of Communism and re-awakened the menace of seaways being mined. Japan was still very much under US military protection and, despite a firm non-aggressive stance, the country was strategically important due to the geographical location between China and the USSR.

Japan still possessed a minimal naval capability but the rapid expansion in mine warfare craft being primarily defensive followed the programmes undertaken, post-Korean War by her allies. Historically, these programmes were the last to use wood for the building of warships.

The 21 Kasado-class minesweepers, commissioned between 1958 and 1967, closely paralleled the design of US-built MSC and MS that were already in

service. Size and displacement were much the same but, in appearance, the Japanese craft did not have a funnel, while the heavy rubbing strake terminated below the bridge.

The 19 Takami class built between 1969 and 1978 retained the same hull but now had a funnel and lower bridge, more closely resembling the many "NATO-standard" CMS, such as the British-built Ton class. The Takami class was effectively an updated version of the Kasado class, designed for minehunting, with new sonars and facilities for clearance divers.

Japan's first post-war-built minelayer, *Souya*, was commissioned in 1971. The 2,150-ton ship was used not only as an Exercise Minelayer but also as a command ship for a mine countermeasures group. The *Hayase* was built to act as a general support and repair ship, replacing the ageing US-built LST *Hayatomo*, which had been used in that role. In parallel with the Takami class, the Japanese built inshore

LEFT: **Although only 46m/150ft in length, the 20 Yakami-class vessels (*Awaji* shown here) were classed by the Japanese as "coastal" rather than "inshore".**

ABOVE: **The shape of the *Hayase* is very similar to JMSDF frigates of the period. The after hull is deep, with two flush doors in the square transom, which may have been used for a secondary minelaying role. Note the crane, mounted on a pedestal, and the large drums of heavy minesweeping cable. A second ship, *Souya*, had a considerably wider beam.**

minesweepers. These, at just 53 tons displacement, were smaller than Western equivalents and were classed as Minesweeping Boats (MSB). Older units of the Kasado class were modified for support in harbour clearance.

Coastal Minesweeper (CMS), Takami class

Displacement: 380 tons (standard); 450 tons (full load)
Length: 52.34m/171ft 7in (oa)
Beam: 8.81m/28ft 10in
Draught: 2.41m/7ft 10in
Armament: 1 x 20mm gun
Machinery: 2 diesel engines, 2 shafts
Power: 1,074kW/1,440bhp for 14 knots
Fuel: Not known
Endurance: Not known
Protection: None
Complement: 47

Landing Ship, Tank (LST), Miura class

Japan's post-war amphibious capability began simply with the transfer of smaller craft such as LSMs and LCUs. Only in 1960–61 were four LST (2) acquired. These World War II vessels gave a decade of service before the Japanese Maritime Self-Defence Force (JMSDF) built replacements. The three Atsumi class were commissioned between 1972 and 1977 and the three Miura class between 1975 and 1977.

Post-war, US-built LSTs became larger, mainly to achieve higher speeds. With different priorities, the JMSDF did not follow this trend. The Japan archipelago is made up of many islands, and the frequency and severity of volcanic activity emphasized the suitability of amphibious warfare ships for use in disaster relief. Built with this role in mind, the Atsumi class were actually smaller than the US-built LST (2), measuring only 89m/292ft against

100m/328ft overall. Despite the smaller size, superior peacetime building methods allowed a top speed of over 13 knots. Except for a low funnel, the vessel closely resembled an LST (2). An LCVP was carried under davits on each side aft, with a third on deck, forward of the bridge. This was handled by crane or derrick. Twenty vehicles could be accommodated, along with 120 troops. A useful 400 tons of cargo could be carried as an alternative.

The three Miura-class ships, built in a parallel programme, were more military. Of much the same length as the LST (2), the type was more slender and had more than twice the engine power to sustain 14 knots. In addition to the LCVPs, two LCM (6) were carried on deck, handled by a transverse gantry crane. Ten heavy battle tanks plus 200 troops or, alternatively, 1,800 tons of cargo could be carried.

ABOVE: **Unusually fast at 14 knots, the Miura-class ships had a transverse gantry crane to handle the two LCM (6) carried on deck. Two LCVPs are carried abaft the funnel on davits. Number 4152, shown here, is *Ojika*.**

Landing Ship, Tank (LST), Miura class

Displacement: 2,000 tons (standard),
3,800 tons (loaded)
Length: 98m/321ft 4in (oa)
Beam: 14m/45ft 10in
Draught: 3m/9ft 9in (mean, seagoing)
Armament: 2 x 3in guns (1x2),
2 x 40mm guns (1x2)
Machinery: 2 diesel engines, 2 shafts
Power: 3,282kW/4,400bhp for 14 knots
Fuel: Not known
Endurance: Not known
Protection: Nominal
Complement: 116

LEFT: **Although much smaller, an Osumi-class vessel resembles a US Navy LHA. The afterdeck has landing spots for Boeing CH-47 Chinook helicopters. The docking well can accommodate two US-built LCACs.**

Landing Ship, Tank (LST), Osumi class

The exact rationale behind the Osumi design is not easy to define. With flat and unobstructed upper deck areas, island superstructure, enclosed vehicle storage and accommodation, together with a docking well closed by a wide stern gate, an Osumi class vessel is, in all but type, an LSD.

In the Japanese Maritime Self-Defence Force (JMSDF), however, the Osumi class is a Landing Ship, Tank (LST) and they are thus numbered. This is despite LSTs, as generally understood, being designed to load and discharge over the beach.

Even as designed, however, the class is scarcely conventional, except in that the docking well is sized to carry two US-built LCACs. The island superstructure to starboard is relatively wide, leaving only vehicle access between the forward and after areas of the upper deck.

Both areas of the upper deck have an elevator, linking to a common garage space below. Neither elevator is large enough to carry a helicopter. At the after end there are landing spots for two Boeing CH-47 Chinook-sized aircraft. There is no hangar accommodation.

Fourteen main battle tanks (or 1,400 tons of cargo) may be stowed below, with access to the docking well deck. The forward part of the upper deck is another designated area for vehicles, which are exposed to the weather despite the high freeboard. The extreme bow section is reduced one level, similar to a British Invincible-class vessel as built.

On the port side is a large 70-ton-capacity hydraulically operated crane. Unusually, minor landing craft other than the LCACs do not appear to be carried, except as deckloads.

Accommodation is provided for 330 troops, or 1,000 in an emergency.

ABOVE: **As on the British-built Invincible class, the short forecastle deck appears to be poorly utilized space. The deck area forward of the bridge is not used by helicopters.**

Landing Ship, Tank (LST), Osumi class	

Displacement: 8,900 tons (standard); 12,000 tons (full load)
Length: 170m/557ft 4in (wl); 178m/583ft 7in (oa)
Beam: 25.8m/84ft 7in
Draught: 6m/19ft 8in
Armament: 2 x Vulcan Phalanx CIWS
Machinery: 2 diesel engines, 2 shafts
Power: 19,396kW/26,000bhp for 22 knots
Fuel: Not known
Endurance: Not known
Complement: 135 plus 330 troops

LEFT: *Aishima,* a Sugashima-class minesweeper, is built of wood rather than glass-reinforced plastic (GRP). Note the 20mm Sea Vulcan Gatling-type cannon mounted on the forward deck.

Coastal Minesweeper (CMS), Sugashima class

At 58m/190ft overall, Sugashima-class vessels of the JMSDF are shorter than the Hunt class in Royal Navy service. During the Normandy landings on June 6, 1944, such vessels were vital for the clearance of the approaches to the beaches. The shallow waters were cleared of mines by a total of 98 fleet and 149 coastal minesweepers. A further 40 were held in reserve.

The hull design of the type follows that of most European-built coastal minesweepers, with a long, full-height forecastle and a short afterdeck The continuous flare of the lower hull acts to increase the waterplane, improving stability with increasing angles of heel. A major departure is the use of wood for construction, and this is common to all current Japanese mine-wartare craft. Apparently it is considered that the perceived advantages of GRP do not warrant the expense of creating a purpose-built production facility.

The forward end of the afterdeck forms a covered stowage for ROV/AUVs and extends between the two large funnel casings, which is a major recognition feature.

A comprehensive range of both positional and plotting electronics is carried, mainly of licence-built European origin. Up to eight clearance divers may be accommodated.

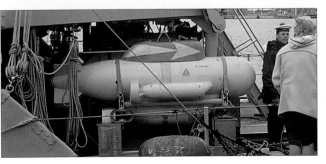

ABOVE: **Two of the fleet of Sugashima-class vessels in Japanese naval service. Note the distinctively large funnel casings.** LEFT: **The PAP-104 Mk 5 Remote Operating Vehicle (ROV) is standard equipment on all Sugashima-class vessels.**

Coastal Minesweeper (CMS), Sugashima class

Displacement: 510 tons (standard); 620 tons (loaded)
Length: 58m/190ft 4in (oa)
Beam: 9.5m/31ft 2in
Draught: 2.5m/8ft 3in
Armament: 1 x 20mm Sea Vulcan cannon
Machinery: 2 diesel engines, 2 shafts with CP propellers, 2 electric creep motors
Power: 1343kW/1800bhp (diesels), 261kW/350hp (electric)
Endurance: 4600km/2500nm at 10 knots
Protection: None
Complement: 37+8

Landing Ship, Tank (LST), Alligator class

This series of 14 ships was built at Kaliningrad, on the Baltic coast, over a period of some 14 years. While representing a considerable increase in size over the standard World War II-built LST (2), all were far smaller than the contemporary US-built equivalent. The more modest size limited speed to an extent (an Alligator class could still make 18 knots), but improved versatility by widening accessibility to landing beaches.

The drive-through design included bow and stern ramps, the former being enclosed by clamshell doors. The class could carry an estimated 24 heavy tanks, together with vehicles on the open upper deck. For beaching, payload was limited to around 600 tons, but this could be increased to 1,500 tons for freighting. The cargo-handling equipment varied from a single 5-ton crane forward to a 5-ton crane both forward and aft. An additional larger 15-ton crane could be mounted forward.

The superstructure was typical of a 1960s merchant ship – curved bridgefront, combined mast and funnel, and sweeping curves to the curtain plating. The size resulted from the need to carry 300 troops accommodated above the tank deck. Defensive fire was by an automatic reloading 40-tube 140mm rocket launcher mounted in a small deckhouse. All were fitted with 57mm cannon

ABOVE: **Although first appearing in the early 1970s, the Alligator class has not yet been entirely withdrawn from service.**

in a dual-purpose twin mounting forward of the bridge. Up to four 25mm cannon were mounted aft. Quadruple mountings for light point-defence SAMs, either the SA-N-5 (NATO name: *Grail*) or SA-N-8 (NATO name: *Gremlin*) could also be mounted. By the end of a long period in servce, the Alligator class was superseded from 1975 by the Ropucha class.

ABOVE: **The well-designed hull shape of the Alligator class permits a speed of 18 knots. The bow doors and stern ramp allow a drive-through configuration for the tank deck.**

Landing Ship, Tank (LST), Alligator class

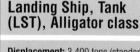

Displacement: 3,400 tons (standard); 4,500 tons (loaded)
Length: 114.07m/374ft (oa)
Beam: 15.5m/50ft 10in
Draught: 4.5m/14ft 9in
Armament: 2 x 57mm guns (1x2), 1 x 140mm multiple rocket launcher, 4 x 25mm guns (2x2), PDMS on occasion
Machinery: 2 diesel engines, 2 shafts
Power: 6,714kW/9,000bhp for 18 knots
Fuel: Not known
Endurance: 20,240km/11,000nm at 15 knots
Protection: Nominal
Complement: 92 plus 300 troops

Landing Ship, Medium (LSM), Polnochny class

More than 50 Polnochny-class vessels were built in Poland between 1961 and 1973. Although many were retained under both the Polish and Soviet flags, there were frequent transfers to friendly states and they could consequently serve anywhere from Algeria to Vietnam.

In profile, a Polnochny-class vessel resembled a large LCT, but had the upper deck and interconnecting ramp of an LST. The tank deck was accessible only through the bow doors, and could accommodate six heavy tanks. As usual, vehicles and cargo could be stowed on the upper deck, accessed by the ramp.

In order to realize the much-demanded 18-knot speed, designers had to compromise with the hull shape. The bow is "ship-shaped", with earlier vessels having a fuller, convex flare. Later vessels had a more seakindly concave flare. The

finer-hulled craft could be loaded with an 180 tons of cargo; the earlier version carried 250 tons.

Again, for a vessel required to be at the forefront of an amphibious attack, the large superstructure appeared vulnerable, with a long, full-width deckhouse. This feature is longer again in the later, wider beam type. Accommodation was for 180 troops, compared to 100 in the earlier vessel.

Early ships were distinctive in having recesses along either deck edge for the stowage of live charges. These were towed by two remotely controlled motor boats to the beach area for mine clearance. Many of the later vessels were modified as anti-aircraft support craft, with the addition of improved electronics equipment and up to four quadruple launchers for SA-N-5 or SA-N-8 point defence missiles. Some of the class mounted a 30mm Gatling-type cannon at the stern.

ABOVE LEFT: **Probably anchored in a shallow area of the Mediterranean Sea, these two Polnochny vessels are of the early A type with short superstructure and straight stern.**
ABOVE: **A later Polnochny C type with extended superstructure. What appears to be a ramp is in fact a hatch to facilitate crane-loading of vehicles down to the tank deck.**

Landing Ship, Medium (LSM), Polnochny C type

Displacement: 720 tons (standard); 1,150 tons (loaded)
Length: 81.6m/267ft 6in (oa)
Beam: 10.1m/33ft 2in
Draught: 1.9m/6ft 3in
Armament: 2–4 x 30mm guns (1/2 x 2), 1 x 140mm multiple rail rocket launcher (in some), 2–4 x PDMS
Machinery: 2 diesel engines, 2 shafts
Power: 5,000bhp for 18 knots
Fuel: Not known
Endurance: 5,520km/3,000nm at 14 knots
Protection: Nominal
Complement: 40 plus 180 troops

Landing Ship, Tank (LST), Ropucha class

To replace the Alligator-class LSTs, around 24 Ropucha class LSTs were built in Poland. This resulted in a close resemblance to the smaller Polnochny class. From a quarter-bow view, the transition from the constant-freeboard after end to the severe, straight-line sheer of the bow section is very marked. What appears to be a ramp, located on the forward end, is, in fact, a hatch. Vehicles are not carried on the foredeck, and hatch loading is by crane where ramp facilities are not available.

The tank deck is "drive-through", with doors and ramps fitted at each end. Accommodation for up to 225 troops is located topside, in a long, full-width deckhouse comprising most of the lowest level of the four-deck superstructure. The bows are extremely raked and flared, the extreme forward end being squared off and overhanging the bow doors.

For a diesel-powered ship, the funnel casing is a massive angular structure.

Forward and aft of the main superstructure are twin-mounted 57mm cannon with dedicated fire control radar mounted on a pedestal immediately abaft the funnel. As with the Polnochny class, a number have been converted, in some cases temporarily, as anti-aircraft support craft and fitted with up to four

ABOVE: **Around 12 Ropucha-type vessels were built. The tank deck is drive-through but, when the ship is used for cargo, freight is loaded by crane through the large hatch in the foredeck.**

small point-defence missile launchers. Some have also carried a later type of the 40-barrelled 122mm barrage rocket launcher. An apparent innovation was to fit temporary mine-launching rails on the tank deck. As an alternative to ten medium tanks or a variety of smaller vehicles, a total of 92 mines could reportedly be carried and laid presumably via the stern door. A further option was 480 tons of freight.

ABOVE: **Only three Ropucha vessels are known to have been converted for anti-aircraft support. Note the air/surface search radar dome and the single 76mm gun which replaced the earlier twin 57mm cannon.**

Landing Ship, Tank (LST), Ropucha class

Displacement: 2,770 tons (standard); 4,100 tons (full load)
Length: 105m/344ft 3in (wl); 112.5m/368ft 10in (oa)
Beam: 15m/49ft 2in
Draught: 3.7m/12ft 2in (maximum, loaded)
Armament: 4 x 57mm guns (2x2), 1/2 x 122mm multiple rail rocket launchers (in some), 2/4 x PDMS (in some)
Machinery: 2 diesel engines, 2 shafts
Power: 14,323kW/19,200bhp for 17+ knots
Fuel: Not known
Endurance: 6,440km/3,500nm at 16 knots
Protection: Nominal
Complement: 95 plus 225 troops

Landing Ship, Dock (LSD), Ivan Rogov class

Four of these massive ships were planned, but only three were ever built. Despite costs and complexity, the lead ship was scrapped following only 20 years in service (the Alligator class was still in use after 40 years, and the Ropucha class over 30 years). The second vessel, *Aleksandr Nikolayev*, was unsuccessfully offered for sale after 17 years in service and apparently remains on the market. A planned fourth ship was cancelled. The whole programme gives the impression of being undertaken primarily to gain experience in what is a difficult area of ship design.

The specification was driven by the requirement to accommodate, transport and land a 500-plus battalion of naval infantry, together with vehicles and equipment. The solution contrasts interestingly with US-built equivalents, of approximately the same size.

In the latter, the superstructure is positioned forward and all helicopter operations are conducted aft, the flight deck covering the docking well. The Ivan Rogov class, in contrast, has the superstructure three-quarters aft and over the docking well. Helicopter operations are, therefore, split between the fore and aft decks. Unlike US vessels, the Ivan Rogov class is designed to carry four helicopters with hangars on each deck.

The foredeck, one level lower than the aft deck, can also be used to carry vehicles. These can directly access, via a hoistable ramp, the bow doors

ABOVE: **The open foredeck is connected by a shallow ramp and doors with a vehicle garaging area inside the superstructure.**

and ramp. The doors are level with the tank deck, which can accommodate up to 25 heavy tanks,

The docking well can house six Ondatra-class landing craft, similar in size to an LCM (8). This would suggest a size of approximately 75 x 11.5m/ 246 x 37ft 9in, which would allow three Lebed-type LCAC craft to be carried. Being enclosed, the Lebed-type can transport up to 120 troops – a considerable advantage over the US-built LCAC. Unusually for such large ships, vessels in the Rogov class are gas turbine-powered.

LEFT: **Folding doors enclose the main helicopter hangar. The vehicles and helicopters area is located in the central area of the superstructure, with accommodation on each side. Note the 30mm Gatling-type guns in twin mountings, with directors.**

Landing Ship, Dock (LSD), Ivan Rogov class

Displacement: 11,600 tons (standard); 14,100 tons (loaded)
Length: 149.9m/491ft 6in (wl); 157.5m/516ft 4in (oa)
Beam: 22m/72ft 2in (wl)
Draught: 4.2m/13ft 9in
Armament: 2 x 6mm guns (1x2), 4 x 30mm Gatling-type guns (4x1), 1 x SA-N-4 (Gecko) SAM system, 2 x SA-N-8 (Gremlin) PDMS, 1 x multi-rail 122mm barrage rocket projector
Machinery: Gas turbines (COGAG configuration), 2 shafts
Power: 26,856kW/36,000shp for 21 knots
Fuel: Not known
Endurance: 7,360km/4,000nm at 18 knots
Protection: Not known
Complement: 239 plus 565 troops

ABOVE: **A company of troops leaves a Yudao-class vessel. Note that the ramp is made up of two folding sections.** LEFT: **Two Yudao-class vessels are here berthed alongside a frigate.**

Landing Ship, Medium (LSM), Yudao class

China has historical claims to offshore land from the size of Taiwan to reefs once considered insignificant. The amphibious means to enforce such claims was by little more than war-built ships. By the 1960s, the vessels were in urgent need of replacement. With no previous experience upon which to draw, the Chinese began modestly, producing perfectly serviceable, updated versions of the LCU and LCM.

More ambitious designs were built in the 1980s including eight Yudao-class 1,500-ton LSMs that appeared to combine the main features of the LSM (1) and LST (2). Earlier ships had been modified over the years, with the superstructure extended from only the starboard side to full width, spanning the vehicle deck. Side spaces aft had also been adapted for minelaying. The Yudao class combined such features with larger size and

ramped forward and after ends. The tank deck was covered with an upper deck and not intended for wheeled transport. All accommodation was above, built over the through tank deck and, as a result, very bulky for the size of craft.

Having the weak feature of an exposed bow ramp, not protected by doors, and the blunt entry, the class, despite its size, was both slow and incapable of safely being used for an extended sea passage. Better described as a large LCU, the Yudao class was not a success in service.

An apparent derivative was the one-off *Yudeng* of 1994, also rated an LSM. The ship resembled a slightly enlarged French-built Champlain class. With an improved forward entry, and bow doors enclosing the ramp, it had a speed of 17 knots.

LEFT: **Only one Yudeng-class vessel was built in 1994. Categorized as an LSM, the substantial build quality contrasts with the general utility of amphibious ships.**

Landing Ship, Medium (LSM), Yudao class

Displacement: 1,460 tons (loaded)
Length: 78m/255ft 9in (bp)
Beam: 12.6m/41ft 4in
Draught: 3.1m/10ft 2in (maximum, seagoing)
Armament: 8 x 25mm guns (4x2)
Machinery: 2 diesel engines, 2 shafts
Power: Not known
Fuel: Not known
Endurance: Not known
Protection: Nominal
Complement: About 65

Landing Ship, Tank (LST), Yukan/Yuting class

ABOVE: The Type 072-II (Yuting II class) can discharge up to 12 tanks directly through the bow doors, or float an LCU from a floodable docking well. Note the LCAs carried in davits.

Built as a replacement for China's remaining war-built LSTs, the Yukan class differed in having a drive-through configuration. To achieve this, all accommodation was moved topside, resulting in a bulkier superstructure. The term "drive-through" also needs to be qualified, as only the forward ramp had a 50-ton rating. With the after ramp reportedly being able to support only 20 tons, heavy armour thus needed to be both loaded and disembarked through the bows. The beaching payload of 500 tons also limited the number of heavy vehicles carried. The Yukan class was fitted with the SEMT-Pielstick medium-speed

diesel engine. This lightweight unit was compact enough to fit in the space below the tank deck.

Following the building of seven Yukan-class vessels, an improved version, designated Yuting, was introduced. Both types were relatively small, some 20m/66ft longer than an LST (2). As the ships can carry two LCA/LCVPs, the small docking well would appear to be an expensive complication. Two deck cranes were added and the under-utilized space aft remodelled as a helicopter pad, although without a hangar. Hull dimensions remained unchanged. Some 12 Yuting-class vessels were built between 1991 and 2001.

Reported capacity for both the Yukan and Yuting classes was 250 troops and 10 tanks. This was increased to 300 and 12 when a Yuting II was introduced in 2002. This was 10m/33ft longer but retained the same beam measurement. To compensate for reduced stability, the helicopter deck was lowered one level. Space for the extra accommodation saw the superstructure block extended to the full width of the ship.

The extra length enabled the dimensions of the docking well to be extended to hold two small air-cushion vehicles (ACV) but these, each with a troop capacity of only ten, are of limited use.

ABOVE: The Yuting II class is thought to be capable of 18 knots, the hull being nicely faired. Note the access tunnel connecting the foredeck with the helicopter deck, and twin 37mm cannon on the forecastle.

Landing Ship, Tank (LST), Yuting I class

Displacement: 3,430 tons (loaded)
Length: 119.5m/391ft 10in (oa)
Beam: 164m/53ft 9in
Draught: 2.8m/9ft 2in
Armament: 6 x 37mm guns (3x2)
Machinery: 2 diesel engines, 2 shafts
Power: 7,087kW/9,500bhp for 18 knots
Fuel: Not known
Endurance: 5,520km/3,000nm at 14 knots
Protection: Not known
Complement: 104 plus 250 troops

LEFT: **A single 76mm gun is mounted forward for defensive armament on the Yuzhao class. Four 30mm Gatling-type cannon are mounted ahead and to the rear of the funnels on the upper deck.**

Landing Ship, Personnel, Dock (LPD), Yuzhao class

China's astonishing progress, from being a client state for ex-Soviet era vessels to a builder of large, sophisticated warships, brings to mind the similar route taken by Japan in the early 20th century.

At possibly 18,000 tons standard, and an estimated 210m/689ft in length, the first of the Yuzhao class, reportedly named *Kunlun Shan*, is around the same size as USS *San Antonio* (LPD-17) but more closely resembles the much-smaller Dutch-built Rotterdam type.

LEFT: **The vast well deck of the Yuzhao class. On board are Payi-class air cushion vehicles (ACV), each capable of carrying a maximum of 10 troops.**

Commissioned at the end of 2007, the vessel has a relatively longer superstructure, with accommodation for a marine battalion of 800 men. Two heavy helicopters are also hangared in a space extending forward between the large funnel casings. A wide, clear landing deck extends to the stern.

A full-width, single-piece stern gate serves the docking well, which is probably large enough to accommodate four LCAC-type craft, or up to six LCUs. These can load and discharge directly on to ramps connecting the forward end of the docking well with two vehicle decks. A starboard-sided deck crane facilitates over-the-side loading of landing craft.

The ship is powered by four, licence-built SEMT-Pielstick diesel engines, driving to two shafts. Following the

general trend, the ship is relatively lightly armed, with a single 76mm gun forward and four 30mm Gatling-type cannon on the upper superstructure, allowing a wide arc of defensive fire.

Although the type is being offered for export, it is likely that the ship will remain a one-off until fully evaluated.

Landing Ship, Personnel, Dock (LPD), Yuzhao class

Displacement: 18,000 tons (standard); 21,000 tons (loaded)
Length: 689ft/210m (oa)
Beam: 28m/91ft 10in
Draught: 7m/23ft
Armament: 1 x 76mm gun, 4 x 30mm Gatling
Machinery: 4 diesel engines, 2 shafts
Power: 35,210kW/47,200bhp for 21 knots
Endurance: 10,000km/6,250nm at 18 knots
Protection: Nominal
Complement: 175 plus 600–800 Marines

Amphibious Transport Ship (LPD), MV *Rotterdam* and MV *Johan de Witt*

International cooperation to develop common ship designs has an unfortunate tendency to become unravelled, but an exception was the Spanish-Dutch project for a large amphibious transport. Results so far include the Dutch ships MV *Rotterdam* (1998) and MV *Johan de Witt* (2007), the Spanish ships MV *Galicia* (1998) and MV *Castilla* (2000), and the four British Bay class. The ships planned to be built in Germany have been delayed by budget cuts, while Belgium has plans to build a smaller version of the type. The MV *Rotterdam*'s sister ship was to have been identical, but the design was lengthened and the ship named MV *Amsterdam*.

Except for topside detail, the Dutch and Spanish ships are effectively identical. The high freeboard of the hull and the large block superstructure are relieved only by subtle changes of plane to reduce their radar cross section, and openings for a considerable number of encapsulated life rafts. Unlike the British variant, all have a short but large funnel casing.

Three doors per side serve storage and transport areas while facilitating disembarkation to small craft alongside. Thirty main battle tanks can be carried, while the docking well is large enough to accept Dutch, US or British LCUs, and LCMs. There are two large helicopter landing spots and two cranes. Six helicopters may be hangared.

Motor transport is transferred to the helicopter deck by elevator. Over 600 marines can be accommodated, with 150 more carried in an emergency.

The MV *Johan de Witt* is 10m/33ft longer than MV *Rotterdam*, with an even larger superstructure block to house a complete marine battalion. Externally, she differs in having masts and funnel significantly reduced in size. The addition of side stowage aft to accommodate landing craft under davits aids identification.

The docking well is shorter but wider, and able to accommodate a standard 29.8m/98ft British LCU (10).

Amphibious Transport Ship (LPD), MV *Rotterdam*

Displacement: 10,800 tons (standard); 12,750 tons (loaded)
Length: 142.4m/466ft 10in (wl); 166.2m/544ft 11in (oa)
Beam: 23.3m/76ft 3in
Draught: 5.23m/17ft 2in
Armament: 2 x 30mm Goalkeeper CIWS
Machinery: 4 diesel-generators powering 2 electric propulsion motors, 2 shafts
Power: 12,384kW/16,600shp for 19 knots
Fuel: 830 tons
Endurance: 11,040km/6,000nm at 12 knots
Protection: Not known
Complement: 113 plus around 600 marines

ABOVE: **The two-tone paint scheme on the MV *Johan de Witt* is proficient in reducing the effect of the vessel's large bulk. Note the access doors to the large helicopter hangar.**

Landing Ship, Dock (LPD), San Giorgio class

These two interesting ships of the Italian Navy could only be fully funded by configuring the second, MM *San Marco* (L9893), for disaster relief. As built, however, too much was attempted on a limited displacement. The full-length flightdeck was divided by the starboard side island. The forward end terminated in a forecastle deck one level lower. A 20.5 x 7m/62 x 23ft docking well was large enough for one of a new class of 18.5 x 5.1m/61 x 17ft LCM. Three LCVP were carried on deck and handled by crane. Surprisingly, in

view of the large, merchant ship-type bow bulb, the class was expected to beach, being equipped with a ramp, enclosed by faired-in clamshell doors.

Below the flight deck, and connected to it by an elevator, was a 100 x 20.5m/ 328 x 67ft vehicle stowage area. Due to the lack of height, helicopters were carried on deck. Design limitations quickly became apparent, both ships being substantially altered between 1999 and 2001. A very deep sponson was added on the port side. This was 5m/16ft wide, and provided landing

ABOVE: **MM *San Giorgio* (L9892). Too much was designed into a limited displacement, so the two ships have undergone considerable modification.**

spots for two helicopters. Two Westland SH-3D Sea Kings or five Agusta Bell AB-22s can be carried. The forward flight area was enlarged and improved by extending the upper deck over the forecastle area and squared off, carrier-style. The bow doors were permanently sealed, all transport now being put ashore by landing craft. Some 350 troops could be accommodated. Unusually, the ships have a water-transfer, passive stabilization system fitted.

ABOVE: **Both LCVPs have to be accommodated on the outside of the hull of the San Giorgio class. A very large sponson to accommodate these vessels was constructed on the port side of the ship, prone to slamming.**

Landing Ship, Dock (LPD), San Giorgio class

Displacement: 7,665 tons (loaded)
Length: 118m/386ft 11in (bp);
133.3m/437ft 1in (oa)
Beam: 20.5m/67ft 3in
Draught: 5.25m/17ft 3in
6.5m/21ft 4in (flooded down)
Armament: 2 x 20mm guns (2x1),
PDMS to be fitted
Machinery: 2 diesel engines, 2 shafts
Power: 12,533kW/16,800bhp for 20+ knots
Fuel: Not known
Endurance: 13,800km/7,500nm at 16 knots
Protection: Not known
Complement: 163 plus 350 troops

Landing Ship, Dock (LPD), MM *San Giusto*

Effectively the third unit of the San Giorgio class, MM *San Giusto* (L9894) was not commenced until the other ships had been in service for several years. The ship therefore incorporates some improvements, based on experience and underwent mid-life modernization in 2010, so further changes may be expected.

The hull is almost identical except that the vessel was never designed to take the ground and was not fitted with bow doors or a ramp. MM *San Giusto* was slightly longer as built, but this will increase if the forward flight area is extended. Before modernization, the foredeck carried the same low structure as earlier ships, for mounting a later type of 76mm OTO-Melara cannon.

From the port side, the vessel appears very similar, carrying three LCVPs under heavy gantry davits on a long sponson running just one level below the upper deck. The starboard-side island superstructure is even wider than that on the earlier ships, the "taxiway" connecting forward and after flight decks is both narrow and restricted by the upper parts of the LCVP davits. This will certainly be changed to the San Giorgio-type deep sponson with recesses for LCVPs. This will enable a CH-47 Chinook-type

ABOVE: **Three LCPs are stowed under gantries on the port-side platform to be replaced by a San Giorgio-type sponson. Note the "bumper" protection on each side of the open stern gate.**

helicopter to be operated at both ends of the ship. Two light helicopters can be operated simultaneously amidships. All three ships are equipped for night operations. Although not fitted with sonar equipment, any of the class will be able to support a specialist anti-submarine group by providing a base for five helicopters.

Post-modernization, MM *San Giusto* will doubtless closely resemble the earlier ships but may be immediately identified by the square tower base to the mast.

The role of the vessel in peacetime is as a training ship for cadets of the Italian Naval Academy.

Landing Ship, Dock (LPD), MM *San Giusto* (pre-modernization)

Displacement: 5,600 tons (standard); 7,950 tons (loaded)
Length: 118m/386ft 11in (bp); 137m/449ft 2in (oa)
Beam: 20.5m/67ft 3in (wl)
Draught: 6m/19ft 8in (mean, seagoing)
Armament: 2 x 76mm gun, 2 x 20mm guns (2x1)
Machinery: 2 diesel engines, 2 shafts
Power: 12,533kW/16,800bhp for 20 knots
Fuel: Not known
Endurance: 13,800km/7,500nm at 16 knots
Protection: Not known
Complement: 198 plus 266 training or 350 troops

Minesweeping Drones

Modern mines are sophisticated in design, and this requires suspicious areas to be investigated by remotely controlled craft. Shallow coastal waters have required German naval planners to develop a high level of expertise in mine countermeasures.

An innovation of the late 1970s was Troika, groups of three drone craft remotely controlled from a specially equipped minehunter, designated a Type 351. Six sets of three drones, known as *Seehunde* (Seals), were built, configured primarily to counter magnetic mines, although conventional sweep gear could also be used. This, however, was essentially area minesweeping (equivalent to the use of helicopter-towed sleds used

by the US Navy), while investigation of a beach approach demands special minehunting techniques.

Over the years the *Seehunde*, which are designed to be explosion-resistant, have been continuously updated and are now able to deploy Remotely Operated Vehicles (ROV). Bottom coverage by the average vehicle is limited, and requires input guidance to where the mines are located. Towed sidescan sonar is invaluable, identifying "minelike objects", even if barely buried in the sand.

Such sonars are built into "towfish" which are required to be towed by an ROV where the data is stored or transmitted in real time to the control ship. Classification and evaluation of objects located is possibly followed by close visual examination by remote TV. The mine can be exploded by an expendable "one-shot" device which has to be precisely targeted. This level of capability currently demands a new generation of craft and ROVs.

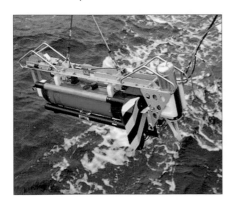

LEFT: **A Seafox C being launched from its handling cradle. The type is described as a One-Shot Mine Identification and Disposal (OSMID) vehicle, and is guided to the target by signals through a fibre-optic cable linked to a controller on a minesweeper.**

ABOVE: **Three of the 18 Troika vessels built for the German Navy moored alongside a quay. The *Seehunde* (Seals) are operated in "threes" under remote control from a Type 351 minehunter.**

A SWATH-hulled control vessel will provide a more stable command platform. *Seehund* will be replaced by *Seepferd* (Seahorse), designed to deploy towed sonar and sensors. Used with the above will be "intelligent" sacrificial one-shot devices known as *Seewolf* and *Seefuchs* (Seafox).

Minesweeping Drone, *Seehund*

Displacement: 91 tons (light); 96.5 tons (loaded)
Length: 24.92m/81ft 9in (oa)
Beam: 4.46m/14ft 7in
Draught: 1.8m/5ft 11in
Armament: None
Machinery: 1 diesel driving a Schottel directional propulsor
Power: 332kW/445bhp for 9.5 knots
Fuel: Not known
Endurance (for transit): 957km/520nm at 8.8 knots
Protection: Explosion-resistant mountings for machinery
Complement: 3 for transit; none while operational

Landing Ship, Tank (LST), Frosch class

Built for the navy of the German Democratic Republic (East Germany) the 12 Frosch-class vessels were based on the Soviet-built Ropucha class but were smaller for operations in the Baltic Sea.

Few, if any, appear to have been fitted with stern doors for access to the tank deck, all movement thus being through the bows. As with the Ropucha class, the forecastle was not raised, but had a prominent sheer to increase forward freeboard. Much of the ramp was exposed, only the lower half being enclosed within the bow doors. The doors were not watertight, acting both to protect the ramp from impact with the sea and to present a less bluff entry. The forward run had a prominent knuckle at the junction of the wide upper hull and the relatively fine lines of the underwater hull. As the class had a speed of 18 knots, the correct compromise appears to have been reached.

The Ropucha class featured a long superstructure based on a single-level deckhouse. In contrast, the Frosch superstructure had a two-level house over most of the length. As was customary, the foredeck was largely unobstructed for stowage of motor vehicles. Around 12 heavy battle tanks could be accommodated.

As a cargo carrier, a Frosch could lift some 600 tons. Indeed, a further two were built around 1980 with cargo hatches and an 8-ton capacity crane. Designated as Amphibious Warfare Support Ships (AWSS), these were known as the Frosch II. The earlier vessels now became Frosch I.

As with the Ropucha class, twin 57mm cannon were mounted ahead and aft of the bridge structure. Forward of the bridge were two 40-tube, 122mm barrage rocket launchers. Mines could be laid over either quarter. The class was quickly disposed of following German reunification.

ABOVE: **A Frosch II, the cargo-carrying variant of the basic design. The bows have a unique design in that the ramp is largely exposed, protected by only two small bow doors.**

Landing Ship, Tank (LST), Frosch I class

Displacement: 1,745 tons (standard); 2,150 tons (loaded)
Length: 90.7m/297ft 4in (bp); 98m/321ft 4in (oa)
Beam: 11.2m/36ft 9in
Draught: 2.8m/9ft 2in
Armament: 4 x 57mm guns (2x2), 4 x 30mm guns (2x2), 2 x 40-tube 122mm barrage rocket launchers
Machinery: 2 diesel engines, 2 shafts
Power: 8,952kW/12,000bhp for 18 knots
Fuel: Not known
Endurance: Not known
Protection: Nominal
Complement: Not known, plus one company of troops

A Directory of Landing Craft

It would be very simple if amphibious vessels could be divided into landing ships, for shore-to-shore passages, and landing craft, designed for ship-to-shore movement. In general, such definitions work well but, as ever, there are exceptions, not least because "shore-to-shore" might mean an ocean passage or a short-sea crossing. Larger types, such as the LCT and LCI (L), were often used on limited open-sea crossings.

Developed to meet evolving needs, landing craft came in many forms, from the large Landing Craft, Tank (LCT) to the smaller Landing Craft, Personnel (LCP). Austere wartime conditions concealed a vast amount of skilled and innovative design. Craft, for instance, needed to be trimmed in order to be grounded in the shallowest waters, then be refloated. Vehicle/cargo decks needed to be spacious and accessible, yet the craft had to remain stable despite carrying all types of military equipment and personnel.

Modern-day amphibious landings require a different mode of operation, hence the entry into service of the Landing Craft, Air Cushion (LCAC). This type allows Over The Horizon (OTH) operations away from the danger of shore-based artillery and missile batteries.

This chapter documents the development of the landing craft from 1921 to the present day.

LEFT: **A Zubr-class LCAC approaching the landing zone during *Zapad* 2009 (West 2009) military exercises held by Russian and Belarusian forces at the training centre for the Baltic Fleet near Baltiysk, Kaliningrad.**

LEFT: **Early craft built to the requirements of the US Marine Corps were based heavily on the design of the British "X-lighters" used at Gallipoli. When the removable bullet-proof canopy was fitted, the type were known as "Beetles".**

Early Landing Craft, 1921–41

Before 1934 the US Navy lacked a commitment to amphibious warfare, and early developments must be credited to the US Marine Corps (USMC). This force was in the process of transformation from something akin to a static police force to a seaborne assault force resolved on defining and developing the techniques of amphibious assault. With Japan identified as the most likely future enemy, the US war plan (Plan Orange) detailed the requirement to seize islands in the Pacific for advanced bases. This would involve opposed landings, for which the USMC was largely remodelled.

From the outset, funding was desperately short, but the early 1920s saw the first innovations. For landing personnel, a standard ships' boat proved unsuitable. Underpowered, they handled poorly in surf. The V-shaped bottoms dug into sand, causing the craft to broach and tip. Refloating was difficult. Above all, the type provided little protection for the marines.

Known officially as a barge, but popularly as a "Beetle", the first personnel landing craft appeared in 1924. Designed to carry a full 110-man USMC company, it was fitted with a rounded, bullet-proof steel canopy. Alternatively, a 75mm field gun or, with canopy removed, an artillery tractor could be carried. At 15m/50ft long and weighing 24 tons, it could be handled only by heavy ships' cranes. It proved to handle poorly in surf and had too great a draught. Efforts to improve it were finally abandoned around 1930.

The 1920s also saw USMC experiments with amphibious tanks, able to support personnel landing on an open beach. Prototypes were developed by the influential designer J. Walter Christie. At this stage, the technology lacked the maturity to be successful, but the concept remained dormant, eventually to resurface as the Landing Vehicle, Tracked (LVT), which was used in a significant a role in the Pacific War.

Also in service was the 45ft Artillery Lighter, with a shallow draught but unpowered. It had to be towed to a point just beyond the surf line before being turned and winched to the beach stern-first. Wheeled equipment was rolled ashore over short folding ramps. The weight of the lighter proved to be too heavy for standard cargo lifting gear.

Only in 1934 could sufficient funds to be allocated to reconsider specialist landing craft for personnel. Amphibious assault thinking at this stage dictated two sizes of craft. The "X-Boat" would carry a 12-man USMC "squad", together with a crew of six. This included two gunners to lay down covering fire. The speed was to be a high 15 knots and the type would comprise the first wave. The "X-Boats" would be followed by "Y-Boats" of the second wave, each carrying a two-squad "section" of marines.

ABOVE: **The LCP (R), or Landing Craft, Personnel (Ramp), was similar to the LCP (L), but was fitted with a bow ramp for more rapid disembarkation.**

ABOVE: **The LCP (L), or Landing Craft, Personnel (Large), was built in both the UK and the USA. It could accommodate a platoon, but did not have bow doors.**

LEFT: **Carried under davits, the LCP (R) could be set afloat fully loaded. It was carried widely by APA, AKA and APL, and was powered by either diesel or petrol engines. The gun tubs allowed covering fire but formed a bottleneck short of the ramp.**

bow, and heavy skegs to protect propellers and rudders. The type had a useful top speed of 20 knots.

The US Navy acquired a Eureka in May 1937, in addition to other types, including some of its own design. Some were built of wood, some were of steel and the specification was changed continuously. A basic requirement emerged for an 18-troop capacity, a length not exceeding 9m/30ft (to be accommodated under davits) and a maximum loaded launch weight not exceeding 15,000lb.

A final decision was made when, in July 1940, the British military identified the 36ft Eureka as a 15-knot improvement over the existing 10-knot ALCs, and ordered 50.

With a war also looming for the USA, the US Marine Corps was authorized to acquire 335. With modifications, the design eventually became the ubiquitous LCP (L).

This programme, if it ever began, was quickly outdated by the approach of Andrew J. Higgins to the relevant authorities. Higgins ran a towage and construction company in New Orleans, and hoped to interest the US Navy in his Eureka craft. Designed to cope with the snags and shallows of Louisiana swamp country, the vessel had a continuously curved spoon-shaped

ABOVE: **Two Canadian coastal passenger ships, HMCS _Prince David_ and _Prince Henry_, were modified to Landing Ships, Infantry (LSI), carrying LCAs under davits.**

ABOVE: **LCAs are guided to shore by a converted Vosper 70ft launch. Note the loud-hailer and the chemical smoke generator.**

ABOVE: **US Rangers in LCAs manned by Royal Navy personnel leaving harbour to join HMS _Prince Charles_ (the letters PC on the side of the vessel denoting this) in preparation for the D-Day landings.**

Early Landing Craft, Eureka

Displacement: 12,500lb (light); payload about 5,000lb
Length: 9.3m/30ft 6in (oa)
Beam: 3.31m/10ft 10.5in
Draught: 0.61m/2ft (forward); 0.9m/3ft (aft, light)
Armament: 1 x 0.30in machine-gun
Machinery: Petrol engine, single shaft
Power: 38kW/50hp for 9 knots
Fuel: 454 litres/120 gallons (US)
Endurance: 239km/130nm at 8 knots
Protection: None
Complement: 3 crew plus 18 troops

Landing Craft, Tank, LCT (5) and (6)

Early British planning for the invasion and conquest of occupied Europe required huge numbers of craft to land armoured vehicles. The programme was so large that the still-neutral USA was approached for assistance. A drawback was that, in order to be able to cross the Atlantic safely, the resulting craft would be of too great a size and draught to beach satisfactorily.

The British had already developed a tank landing craft, known as a TLC. This would be modified frequently and become known as LCT (1) to (4). In talks with the US military, the British proposed an "Atlantic TLC" (which later became the LST) and a "Tank Ferry", small enough to be carried as deck cargo on an LST delivery passage. Having ordered 200 LST

and 400 "Tank Ferries", the British left the US Navy Bureau of Ships (BuShip) to prepare the detailed design.

Once agreed, the specification for the LST governed the size of the LCT. It was decided that the latter would be craned aboard, chocked and secured to the deck of an LST. On arrival, the smaller craft would be launched sideways by the simple expedient of tilting the LST, using the vessel's considerable built-in water ballast capacity.

Initially classed as a Yard Tank Lighter (YTL), the craft was recognized as a new type of LCT from July 1942 and recategorized as LCT (5). The vessel was built in three sections which could be shipped over separately and bolted together while afloat.

Where earlier British LCTs were intended for extended passages, the LCT (5), limited by size, usually needed to be towed over similar distances. Governed by beaching draught, the hull was broad and shallow. A loaded speed of 7 knots reduced to 3.5 knots when operating in a short head sea. The hull would flex alarmingly in these conditions.

The LCT (5) had neither rise of floor nor turn of bilge. The bottom of the hull aft curved upward to meet the base of the counter near the load waterline. This allowed the three small-diameter propellers (each with a rudder) to be raised above the keel line. The loading ramp had a distinctively curved front face. On a beach of shallow slope, the ramp could prove to be too short.

ABOVE: **A line of LCT (5) discharging on a beach of ideal slope, enabling transport to land without causeways. Vulnerability to air attack is obvious.**
LEFT: **Superseding the LCT (5), the LCT (6) had a sided superstructure to facilitate a drive-through capability. The beach is steep, so the vessels' engines are being used to maintain position.**

LEFT: **USS LST-228, wrecked in the vicinity of Bahia Angra Island, off Tercina, Azores. The vessel went ashore on January 19, 1944. Note that LCT (6) 582 is about to be washed off the deck of the vessel. Both were lost in this incident.**

A short, raised afterdeck housed basic accommodation for the crew of 13. Outboard of the deep comings that flanked the tank deck were narrow side docks, which allowed rapid fore-and-aft access for personnel. At loaded draught, the tank deck was above the waterline, but scuppers were provided to discharge water. It water accumulated the stability of the vessel could be affected.

From April 1943, some were completed as a drive-through design. These were termed LCT (6) and were intended to dock with a ramp on an LST to speed up the transfer of vehicles. In this mode, the LST (6) could even act as a bridge, connecting a deeper-draught LST to the beach. This type of craft had the accommodation divided along each side of the after end of the tank deck. The small pilot house was mounted on the starboard side. Details and capacity were, otherwise, very similar.

First deployed in the Pacific toward the end of 1942, in time for the climax of the Gudalcanal campaign, LCTs would go on to make a huge contribution to US forces' success. In total, 1,435 were built and usually operated as very large flotillas. The senior officer of a flotilla was a lieutenant commander who, typically, controlled three "groups" of 12 LCTs. Commissioned officers were in short supply so a group, organized in two "divisions", became the responsibility of a lieutenant, often a reserve officer. LCTs were not commissioned ships in the US Navy, the commander being called Officer in Charge.

ABOVE: **USS LCT (6) 1362, a 143-ton Landing Craft Tank, underway, probably soon after completion in October 1944. Note the sprayed-on pattern camouflage.**

Landing Craft, Tank, LCT (5)

Displacement: 134 tons (light); 285 tons (beaching)
Length: 32.03m/105ft (wl); 35.38m/116ft (oa)
Beam: 9.76m/32ft
Draught (light): 0.47m/1ft 6in (forward); 1.14m/3ft 9in (aft)
Draught (beaching): 0.86m/2ft 10in (forward); 1.27m/4ft 2in (aft)
Armament: 2 x 20mm guns (2x1)
Machinery: 3 diesel engines, 3 shafts
Power: 504kW/675bhp for 8 knots
Fuel: 11.1 tons oil
Endurance: 1,288km/700nm (loaded) or 2,2208km/1,200nm (light) at 7 knots
Protection: 63.5mm/2.5in plastic armour to pilot house, 7.50mm/2in to gun tubs
Complement: 13–15
Capacity: 5 x 30-ton, 4 x 40-ton or 3 x 50-ton tanks, or alternatively 9 lorries or 150 tons (maximum) cargo; no troop accommodation

Landing Craft, Mechanized, LCM (2), (3) and (6)

The unpowered Artillery Lighter proposed for the USMC during the late 1920s was hopelessly impractical, even though artillery was not required during the assault phase. What was wanted, however, was light armour to be put ashore rapidly to support the first attack. Early amphibious tanks had failed so, in 1930, the USMC requested a specialized craft, capable of putting a light tank ashore or, alternatively and with minimum modification, artillery or personnel.

Funding, as ever, was limited, and time was lost in the USMC having difficulty in defining an ideal small

tank. Finally, in 1935, a requirement was made for BuShips to design a 13-knot craft that could transport a 12,000lb vehicle.

The British Army had been experimenting with what was termed an MLC (Mechanized Landing Craft, or sometimes Motor Landing Craft) for over a decade and, by 1938, had produced the prototype for what would later become the LCM (1). A first US-designed craft appeared in the same year and was of a different design concept. Where the British craft retained buoyancy within a very deep, pontoon-type double bottom, with side

ABOVE: **Two LCM (3) from the attack cargo ship USS *Almaack* (AKA-10) unloading armoured bulldozers after the initial landing. Note the pedestal-mounted heavy machine-gun on KA10-7.**

bulwarks, the US craft had a shallow double bottom with added buoyancy dependent upon wide side walls. This difference was significant for, where the British design had far more usable space, the load was carried very high and could become unstable if carelessly loaded. The US craft carried the cargo lower and had greater in-built stability. The side walls were intrusive, making the cargo deck narrow, and

RIGHT: **The sharply raked coamings on the LCM gave full support for the ramp in the housed position, while allowing improved seakeeping in a head sea. The helmsman could steer from a lower, protected position.**

hazardous to load at sea. Opinion was that the craft was unnecessarily large to carry only a 5-ton tank.

Then, in 1940, the USMC was ordered to use standard US Army tanks of which the then-smallest was the M5A1 Stuart of around 18 tons. Being designed at the time, however, was the M4 Sherman, starting at 30 tons. Fortunately, the creative mind of Andrew J. Higgins had already been applied in this direction, somewhat in competition with BuShips. The Higgins' "Tank Lighter" was a 13.7m/45ft vessel weighing 18.75 tons, allowing it to be handled by cargo derricks. It could accommodate a 27-ton M3A1 Grant but would prove to be too narrow for a Sherman. With the design available and the requirement urgent, two orders for 50 each were placed in mid-1941.

The alternative BuShip design, also 13.7m/45ft, was officially favoured and 147 were built as LCM (2). The craft was unusual in having a rounded stern but could safely load only 30,000lb. With a M3A1 Grant aboard, the Higgins boat was felt to be at the safe limit, so work began to find a suitable 15.25m/50ft craft for new and larger vehicles.

Inadvertently, the British now influenced events in favouring existing Higgins' craft, ordering 250 of what was designated Mark 2 MLC. This craft was duly lenghtened by Higgins and, in May 1942, was used in comparative landing tests against a 15.25m/50ft BuShips design. In conditions of heavy surf the type proved to be far superior and was adopted for production (from July 1942) as the LCM (3).

First used in Operation "Torch", November 1942, the LCM (3) appeared everywhere, more often ferrying 60 troops rather than tanks. The type was too large to be carried under davits, and had to be handled by a cargo derrick. It could not be pre-loaded and had to be lifted empty. The relatively shallow bottom meant that engines had to be located in a stern compartment, further reducing cargo space.

Nevertheless, LCM (3) production eventually ran to over 8,600. Still officially limited to a 30-ton tank or 60,000lb of distributed cargo, however, it was dangerous to carry heavier vehicles. This was remedied by adding an extra 1.8m/6ft of length in the mid-body, creating the LCM (6). A total of some 2,700 were delivered.

ABOVE LEFT: **Ugly and slow, the LCM (1), originally known as an MLC, was nonetheless a well-designed craft.** ABOVE: **The LCM remained in British military service after World War II. Note the raised helmsman position at the stern.**

Landing Craft, Mechanized, LCM (3)

Displacement: 23.21 tons (light); 52 tons (loaded)
Length: 15.25m/50ft (oa)
Beam: 4.3m/14ft 1in
Draught (light): 0.76m/2ft 6in (forward); 1m/3ft 3in (aft)
Draught (loaded): 1.37m/4ft 6in (forward); 1.68m/5ft 5in (aft)
Armament: 2 x 50in heavy machine-guns
Machinery: 2 diesel engines, 2 shafts
Power: 164–336kW/220–450bhp for 8 to 11 knots
Fuel: Not known
Endurance: 1,012km/550nm at 7 knots
Protection: 6.4mm/¼in plating around helm position
Complement: 4
Capacity: 1 medium (30-ton) tank, or 60,000lb cargo, or 60 troops

Landing Craft, Infantry (Large), LCI (L)

One of the key types of landing craft in World War II, the LCI (L) was designed purely for the transport and rapid disembarkation of infantry.

Again this began as a British requirement, early in 1942, for a "giant raiding craft". The specification was for a vessel to carry a 200-man company at over 17 knots with an endurance of up to 48 hours. Preliminary calculations indicated that the craft would be of at least 45.7m/150ft overall length.

With British war production at maximum capacity the USA was requested to finalize a design and then build 300 craft. Such numbers went well beyond raiding requirements and indicate early planning for the eventual invasion of Europe in 1944.

The outcome definition required a forward beaching draught of only 0.61m/2ft, which had to be reconciled with hull characteristics seaworthy enough to make an Atlantic crossing. With raiding still in mind, quiet machinery, good manoeuvrability and a low silhouette were specified. Troops would disembark rapidly via two gangways, which extended from either side. At this point in landing, troops were perceived to be most vulnerable.

Politically astute, the British interested the US Army in the proposed craft, thus elevating priority in a country already busy with emergency war programmes. A suggestion to give Higgins a free hand in the craft's production was, however,

vetoed as his manufacturing facilities were already fully occupied with essential work for the US Navy.

BuShips thus translated the requirements into a practical design. This was not easy, the difficult dimensions/draught combination having a detrimental effect on speed, with only around 15 knots being predicted. Despite this, power and propellers were specified for at least 17 knots. Three diesel engines and three shafts were proposed, but shortages dictated two shafts driving larger-diameter propellers.

Four automotive diesel engines powered each shaft, coupled ingeniously by means of an inflatable collar that

removed the requirement for gearing. As the engines were not reversible, the craft were fitted with variable-pitch and reversible propellers.

The short, high forecastle was extended toward the bridge by high protective bulwarks, flanked by narrow and partly sponsoned side decks upon which were mounted the 8.5m/28ft (later 11m/36ft) gangways. These were slid forward and lowered by means of a transverse beam termed a "cathead". Troops leaving their accommodation, immediately below, were screened by the high bulwarks until the gangways were lowered. A low centreline superstructure was provided for

ABOVE: **LCI (L) 351 was the lead craft of a revised design which featured a higher, round-sectioned bridge structure. The side gangway ramps were retained. Note the high protective bulwarks.**
LEFT: **Crude but effective, although vulnerable to damage, the side gangways were later superseded – in LCI (L) 641 onward – by bow doors and ramp.**

ABOVE: **The poor design of the gangway is evident here. It was difficult to access at the inboard end, and too steep for fully equipped infantry.**

ABOVE: **Infantry reinforcements being delivered to "Gold" beach by LSIs of the Royal Navy on D-Day "Plus One", June 7, 1944.**

British-designated craft. US craft were to be built with a higher bridge.

LCI (L) were built in non-shipbuilding facilities that simply assembled and fitted out steel modules trucked-in from subcontractors. As much complex curvature as possible was designed out. Craft delivered to Britain travelled in convoys accompanied by larger craft or tugs. In general, they were good vessels at sea but required careful ballasting for ocean voyages as well as an alert helmsman prepared for the vessels' tendency to yaw heavily prior to broaching.

From LCI (L) 351 (mid-1943), the superstructure was widened to the sides of the hull to allow rapid exit by troops from below. Accommodation facilities were upgraded as it had been found that the craft were capable of longer sea passages than those originally envisaged.

A year later, and commencing with LCI (L) 691, the somewhat vulnerable and exposed gangways were removed in favour of bow doors and an extendable landing ramp.

US-operated LCIs were better protected than British vessels, carrying heavier defence. The extra weight came at the cost of significantly increasing beaching draught and a knot of speed when loaded. Externally, the US type differed in having a rounded pilot house/compass platform. A total of some 940 LCI (L) were completed as personnel carriers.

Over 330 more became Landing Craft, Support (Large), rocket craft or small headquarters ships.

ABOVE RIGHT: **Later craft mounted five 20mm cannon in single mountings, one at each corner of the superstructure and one on the forecastle. The tubular guard is to limit the firing arc.**
LEFT: **Troops here are embarking via the side gangways and passing through the protective bulwark to the access to the accommodation deck.**

Landing Craft, Infantry, LCI (L), 351 type

Displacement: 246 tons (light);
  250 tons (beaching);
  390 tons (loaded)
Length: 46.67m/153ft (wl);
  48.34m/158ft 6in (oa)
Beam: 7.09m/23ft 3in
Draught (beaching): 0.91m/3ft (forward);
  1.52 m/5ft (aft)
Draught (loaded): 1.73m/5ft 8in (forward and aft)
Armament: 4/5 x 20mm guns (4/5 x 1)
Machinery: 8 diesel engines, 2 shafts
Power: 1,194kW/1,600bhp for 14 knots (sustained),
  or 16 knots (maximum)
Fuel: 110 tons oil
Endurance: 14,720 km/8,000nm at 12 knots
Protection: 70mm plastic armour to pilot houses
  and gun tubs
Complement: 28 plus 205 troops

ABOVE: **Built in vast numbers, the LCVP was the most basic and widely used assault craft. Aboard a transport, an LCVP would fit inside an LCM.** RIGHT: **LCVPs being used as liberty boats for the crew of USS** *Hyde* **(APA 173). The designation "21" gives some indication of the number of craft carried.**

Landing Craft, Vehicle, Personnel (LCVP)

The LCVP was a combination of the LCV (Landing Craft, Vehicle), and the LCP (Landing Craft, Personnel).

From late 1940, the 36ft Eureka or Higgins boat was adopted as the standard US assault craft, although not being officially labelled an LCP (l) until July 1942. Although seaworthy, troops on the Eureka had to leap from the side on landing, risking injury, even drowning.

During the late 1930s, the Japanese had been observed using ramped Daihatsu craft in landing. BuShips refused a similar arrangement for the Eureka, but this was changed when Higgins built speculative prototypes. From May 1941 the BuShips experimented with the layout for a craft

that, with a ramp, had the versatility to carry a small vehicle or artillery just as easily as personnel. As a second-echelon craft, it was not armoured. Later termed an LCV, the type had an open cargo deck 5.87m/19ft 3in in length.

In parallel, otherwise unaltered LCP (L) equipped with ramps became known as LCP (R). The ramp was flanked by two forward-firing positions for 0.30in Browning machine-guns.

Both types began to be used together and, of the two, the versatile LCV proved by far the more useful. The open design lacked stiffness, which did not allow the boat to be loaded before launching. The raised helmsman's position also made it

impossible to be stacked under davits, fewer thus being carried. Over 2,600 LCP (R) had been built by the end of 1942, when it was superseded by the LCVP, essentially an improved LCV. With positions for the helmsman and gunners recessed into a stiffened hull, the vessel could be stacked and lowered fully loaded. The LCVP had a wider ramp and could accommodate 36 troops. By 1945, a staggering 23,350 had been produced.

Landing Craft, Vehicle, Personnel (LCVP)

Displacement: 8 tons (light); 12 tons (maximum, loaded)
Length: 11.25m/36ft 10in (oa)
Beam: 31.7m/10ft 5in
Draught: 0.66m/2ft 2in (forward); 0.91m/3ft (aft, loaded)
Armament: 2 x 0.30in machine-guns
Machinery: 1 diesel or petrol engine, single shaft
Power: 168kW/225bhp diesel or 187kW/250hp petrol engine for 9 knots
Fuel: Not known
Endurance: 188km/102nm at 8 knots
Protection: 6.35mm/0.25in plate to ramp and sides
Complement: 3
Capacity: 36 troops, or 1 x 6,000lb vehicle, or 8,100lb distributed cargo

---

ABOVE: **In an LCV, forerunner of the LCVP, the elevated steering position in the stern made the helmsman vulnerable to enemy fire, or even being swept overboard.**

Landing Craft, Support (Small)/(Large), LCS (S)/(L)

Although naval fire support was effective in the pre-assault phase, it had been recognized, even before the war, that the early waves of assault craft would require close support to suppress any surviving beach defences. The Higgins boat carried two forward-firing machine-guns for this purpose. Further similar hulls, compatible with davit stowage on APAs, were completed for the support role. Later designated LCS (S), they differed in being decked, except for a rectangular cockpit area. On some this was open, on others covered by a steel canopy, open at the rear.

Davit capacity limited weight to 9 tons, so the open cockpit version was preferred, with an armament of a 0.30in and 0.50in machine-guns and

4.5in rocket launchers. A useful addition was chemical smoke generator equipment. The petrol engines made the type unpopular with APA captains.

While valuable, the LCS (S) lacked the firepower necessary to silence Japanese strongpoints. Destroyers were too valuable to be risked inshore, leading to conversion of the 48m/158ft LCI to "LCI Gunboats", later LCS (L). A local Pacific Fleet initiative saw 48 LCIs undergo conversion with added protection and a variety of 40mm and 20mm cannon plus 0.50in heavy machine-guns.

The "official" version, the Mark 3 – LCS (L) (3) – appeared late in 1944. Completely rearranged internally, it had a 3in general-purpose gun firing over protective bulwarks forward. Twin 40mm

ABOVE: **The LCS (L) (3) was well-armed. Note the 3in gun forward, below a twin 40mm mounting. There is a second twin 40mm mounting aft and four single 20mm cannon.**

cannon were carried on a high mounting. A second twin 40mm cannon was mounted aft, and four single 20mm on mountings around the superstructure. Some variants had mortars as the main armament, others rockets.

The craft were large enough to undertake sea passages, act as escorts, or even patrol offensively in the popular nocturnal pastime of "barge-busting", intercepting Japanese inshore supply barge traffic.

In addition to the 130 standard LCS (L) (3) conversions may be added 172 gun-armed LCI (G), 59 mortar-armed LCI (M) and 52 rocket-armed LCI (R).

ABOVE: **Hard-hitting miniature warships in their own right, the LCS (L) were viewed as expendable. This type of vessel was used to operate close inshore to support the landing forces.**

Landing Craft, Support, LCS (L) (3)

Displacement: 250 tons (light); 387 tons (full load)
Length: 46.67m/153ft (wl); 48.19m/158ft (oa)
Beam: 7.09m/23ft 3in
Draught: 1.45m/4ft 9in (forward); 1.98m/6ft 6in (aft, full load)
Armament (typical): 1 x 3in gun, 4 x 40mm (2x2), 4 x 20mm (4x1)
Machinery: 8 diesel engines, 2 shafts
Power: 1,194kW/1,600bhp for 15 knots
Fuel: 76 tons oil
Endurance: 10,120km/5,500nm at 12 knots
Protection: 6.35mm/0.25in steel to pilot house and gun positions
Complement: 70

Landing Vehicle, Tracked, LVT (1) to (7)

In amphibious warfare, the beach presents a difficult interface between the sea and land phases. In the late 1930s, the USMC sought a solution and approached Donald Roebling, who had developed an amphibious tractor to work in the Florida Everglades. Called an Alligator, it ran on tracks fitted with curved metal cleats. With the pontoon body afloat, the cleats acted as miniature paddles.

in 1941 despite two years of discussion with Roebling, the USMC could only fund two prototypes. Extensive trials resulted in an initial order for 200 of what would become the LVT (1). First appearing in mid-1941, the vehicle was unarmoured and had an open well for personnel or stores. The driver's position forward was fitted with a metal cab, open to the rear. The LVT was around 3m/10ft high, making it difficult for fully equipped troops to enter or leave via footholds recessed into the sides.

Usually transported in an LST, the LVT were often set afloat too far offshore. Capable of only 4 knots, they frequently suffered from swamped petrol engines. The vehicle's shortcomings were addressed by the end of 1943 with the introduction of the lightly armed LVT (2), which had 30 per cent more power and a more accessible cargo bay.

Coral atolls were frequent USMC objectives. These were fringed by reefs enclosing a shallow lagoon, a combination that could defeat conventional assault craft. The LVT was driven over the reef, across the lagoon to the beach, and then inland.

An obvious next step was to produce a fighting version to escort the troop carriers and to provide initial support ashore. The LVT (A) (1) ("A" for Armored) was better protected, with the turret and

ABOVE: **The LVT (1) entered service in 1941 and could travel at 4 knots in water and 19kph/12mph on land. The vehicle carried 24 fully equipped troops from transport ship to shore.**

37mm gun from the M5A1 tank, and two machine-guns. Based on the LVT (2), it entered service in August 1943. Early 1944 saw the arrival of the confusingly numbered LVT (4) which, with the engine mounted in front, now had a larger cargo well and a watertight rear ramp. As LVTs were used extensively to unload from cargo ships (AKA), this made for easier unloading ashore.

RIGHT: **The LVT (A) (1) was an LVT (2) modified with a 37mm gun turret and two 0.30in machine-guns. The function of the type was to come ashore with the troop-carrying LVTs and render immediate light armoured support.**

LEFT: **The LVT (2), known to the British as "Buffalo", was used during the Walcheren operation and on other river crossings in World War II.**

The delayed LVT (3) appeared later in 1944. Again, the cargo well was enlarged, this time by the use of two smaller engines, mounted in the side walls. Although petrol engines increased fire hazard, they were preferred due to an excellent power-to-weight ratio.

Battle experience demanded further improvement. The 37mm-armed LVT (A) (1) had little effect against enemy strongpoints and so, following infantry-suppression variants armed only with machine-guns, the LVT (A) (4) emerged, late in the war, mounting a short-barreled 75mm howitzer. Total production of LVTs was some 18,000 units, of which almost half were LVT (4).

LVT development slowed following World War II but was revived by the Korean War. During 1955–56, the massive LVTP (5) headed a new family of variants, including the LVTH (6) fire-support version.

Used widely in Korea and later in Vietnam, LVTs did not perform particularly satisfactorily. By the early 1960s, a replacement was required.

The LVTP (7) family (including command and recovery vehicles but none specifically for fire support) began to enter service in early 1972. Auxiliary water jet propulsion allowed an increase in speed when afloat, while track design was optimized for speed over land. Diesel engines and an aluminium armoured body were further advantages.

Landing Vehicle, Tracked, LVT (1) to (7)

	Weight		Capacity		Speed		Power
	Empty	Loaded	Cargo	Troops	Water	Land	(hp)
LVT (1)	8.65	10.9	2.25	20	4 knots	24kph/15mph	150
LVT (2)	12.2	15.45	3.25	24	5.5 knots	40kph/25mph	200
LVT (3)	15.3	19	4	24	5 knots	40kph/25mph	450
LVT (4)	13.7	16.7	3.25	24	5.5 knots	24kph/15mph	200
LVP (5)	32.1	40.9	6	34	7 knots	48kph/30mph	800
LVTP (7)	18.5	25	5	25	7.5 knots	48kph/30mph+	400

Note: Weights are expressed in US tons of 2,000lb

ABOVE: **An LVTP (5) about to land at Da Nang during the Vietnam War. The type was designed by Borg Warner Inc., and entered service in 1956.**

ABOVE: **The LVTP (7) was introduced in 1972, and underwent several upgrades. This example has reactive armour and a bow vane to improve seaworthiness.**

Minesweeping Boats (MSB)

From the 100-fathom line to the high water mark, an amphibious force commander needs to be aware of the danger of mines and improvised explosive devices. Deep-water moored mines menace major vessels, the loss of any one of which can severely disrupt a well-executed plan. The designated anchorage needs to be guaranteed mine-free, and the necessary checks and minesweeping activities are often the first indication to an enemy of a pending invasion.

Progressing shoreward from the anchorages and embarkation areas, small craft move into increasingly shallow water, the area for bottom-laid "ground mines". From their inception, mines incorporated the highest degree of sophistication available with the technology of the time. Not adept in this direction during World War II, the Japanese generally preferred improvised devices, attached to obstructions or to coral heads located in the obvious approaches. These were removed by Underwater Demolition Teams (UDT).

The Germans, in contrast, were technically adept and ingenious, making shallow-water mine countermeasures a challenging task. By 1945, particularly in and around

ports, ship minesweeping operations had become merged with, or subordinated to, teams of skilled naval clearance divers.

In European waters the US Navy was, by 1944, experimenting with radio-controlled drone minesweepers to precede the first attack wave. Linked to a suitably equipped LCC, they were followed closely by rocket-firing LCM (3), known as "Woofus", which laid a carpet

ABOVE: First a large minelayer, then a troop transport, then a vehicle carrier (LSV), USS *Ozark* and USS *Catskill* were converted to Mine Countermeasures and Support Ships (MCS) in the 1950s. The ships had a force of 20 minesweeping launches and carried two Sikorsky helicopters.

of bombs across the beach to detonate ground mines and improvised devices.

The end of World War II saw a rapid rundown of Allied naval fleets. Mine warfare was neglected, military planners perceiving it as unimportant, prioritising the building of the carriers

ABOVE: The Korean War provided a salutary reminder that inshore mine clearance was a necessary precursor to an amphibious landing. This US Navy LCV, built in 1953, has been refitted as Minesweeping Boat, MSB-2.

and submarines. The Korean War suddenly reminded planners that large-scale amphibious operations were, as much as ever, dependent upon state-of-the-art mine countermeasures. War-built veteran ships were already inadequate and too few in number.

Along with its NATO partners, the USA embarked as a consequence upon building a series of wooden coastal and inshore minecraft during the 1950s. The programme produced several minor types which were to prove valuable in Vietnam.

This war was waged largely in swampy delta areas where, in the absence of roads, the highways were a tangle of sluggish, silt-laden river tributaries edged, for the most part, by dense jungle. By necessity, US troops conducted a low-level amphibious campaign in these areas.

Mines, mostly of Chinese origin, were used extensively by the enemy. Of the 57ft and 82ft Minesweeping Boats (MSB) operated by the US Navy, the smaller type was most suitable for the task.

Designated as "assault sweepers" an MSB might have preceded a column of armoured river craft. Vulnerable to ambush at close-range, however, these duties were usually subordinated to sweep-equipped LCM (6). These were equipped with excellent defensive firepower but, being steel-built, were more vulnerable to mines.

MSBs were designed to be used worldwide, often transported by ship, but they were too heavy to be handled by standard cargo lifting gear, necessitating heavy cranage. For this reason, LSDs were usually used as transport. Although diesel-propelled, many MSBs were fitted with an auxiliary gas turbine engine to generate power for the sweeps. One late hull was built from glass-reinforced plastic (GRP).

Compact, high-definition sonar was available for shallow-water mine detection while drag gear was a portable item that could be deployed by Minesweeping Launches (MSL) or even LCVPs. A 7m/23ft GRP-hulled Minesweeping Drone (MSD) was also

In service, controlled from a sweep-equipped patrol craft known as a River Minesweeper (MSR). As with so much high-technology equipment in Vietnam, however, it proved disappointing in service.

Vietnam was the severest test for inshore mine clearance. It was a war of improvisation. Territory was not held, and rivers cleared of mines one day could be re-mined by the next.

Minesweeping Boat (MSB), 57ft type

Displacement: 30 tons (light); 42 tons (loaded)
Length: 17.42m/57ft 2in (oa)
Beam: 4.72m/15ft 6in
Draught: 1.22m/4ft
Armament: Officially 1 x 20mm gun; usually carried more
Machinery: 2 diesel engines, 2 shafts
Power: 448kW/6,00bhp for 10 knots
Fuel: Not known
Endurance: Not known
Protection: Nominal
Complement: 8

LEFT: **A Swift Boat, of which over 100 were abandoned when US forces withdrew from Vietnam. Note the 81mm mortar on the aft machine-gun mounting and the scrambling net for access to and from the banks of creeks and rivers.**

Patrol Craft, Fast (PCF), Swift Boat

The United States campaign in Vietnam between 1965 and mid-1975 was conducted largely around inland waterways, for which the US Navy built up a range of specialist craft for what was probably the largest-ever "Brown Water Navy". The structure and composition of this navy have been likened to a regular, balanced fleet. The heavily armed and armoured monitors and landing craft served as capital ships and cruisers. The PCFs and PBRs (Patrol Boats, River) acted as destroyers.

PCFs, together with the WPBs (Patrol Craft, Coastguard), were deployed in October 1965, soon after the beginning of "Market Time", the blockade of the South

Vietnam coast to counter infiltration from the North. Eventually the number of PCFs deployed was over 100.

Capable of a sustained speed of 25 knots (28 maximum), they were known universally as Swift Boats, as they were called by Gulf of Mexico oil rig crews, for which the craft were originally designed as workboats. They were rugged but, being built of welded aluminium, were vulnerable to underwater obstacles.

At 15.2m/50ft in length, a PCF had a considerable draft of over 1.2m/4ft, but was sufficiently small to negotiate restricted waterways. The type was frequently used to ferry troops for

offensive shore incursions. On such operations, 20 or more fully equipped troops might be carried topside, greatly inhibiting the boat's armament.

The usual complement was one officer and four enlisted men (ratings). Standard armament comprised twin 0.50in machine-guns in a tub mounting over the wheelhouse. Aft there was a single 0.50in machine-gun with an 81mm mortar in the same mounting.

Built in Louisiana by Sewart Seacraft, the Swift Boats were completed in two large batches. The first, later termed a Mark I, had a larger superstructure than the subsequent Mark II.

ABOVE: **Formations of the "Brown Water Navy" operated in the same manner as the regular fleet. PCFs are shown here acting as a forward screen for armoured Monitors on a river in Vietnam.**

Patrol Craft, Fast (PCF), Swift Boat	

Displacement: 22 tons
Length: 15.23m/50ft
Beam: 4.57m/15ft (oa)
Draught: 1.22m/4ft
Armament: 3 x 0.50in machine-guns (1x2, 1x1), 1 x 81mm mortar
Machinery: 2 diesel engines, 2 shafts
Power: 723kW/960bhp for 28 knots (maximum)
Fuel: Not known
Endurance: Not known
Protection: Nominal
Complement: 5

Patrol Craft, Coast Guard (WPB)

Only in the unique situation of Vietnam could the small Coast Guard cutter be included in a force that, in the widest sense, was "amphibious". That the US Coast Guard was there at all was due to Clause Five of its mission statement, i.e. that "in time of national emergency, or when the President so directs, the Coast Guard operates as part of the Navy".

In 1965, at the outset of the campaign, the US Army believed (incorrectly) that the major part of supplies supporting the North Vietnamese military activities was arriving by sea, either by local craft following the normal coastal traffic or by transfer-type vessels anchored offshore to unload weapons.

The resulting "Market Time" blockade divided the 1,448km/900-mile coast from 17 degrees north to the border with Cambodia into four coastal zones. These were broken down into nine patrol areas (Coast Guard), each of which controlled three to six inshore zones (Swift Boats).

The Coast Guard operated two types of small, steel-built cutter (WPB). Those chosen were the smaller 82ft Point class. Eight arrived in July 1965, and were quickly reinforced to 26.

ABOVE: USCGV *Point Highland* **in its earlier paint scheme. Those serving in Vietnam were painted grey, and mounted a variety of armament. Their availability relieved ships of the US Fleet from everyday surveillance duties.**

In addition to routine-patrol and surveillance duties, the WPBs gave seaward flank support to military search and destroy operations.

The 70-strong Point-class programme ran from 1960 to 1967, with stage improvements resulting in the three main groups, known as "A", "B" and "C" classes. The only major variation was in the "C" class (the final 39 craft) having engine power increased from 1,200 to 1,600bhp, with maximum speed raised from 17 to over 20 knots. Most of those assigned to Vietnam were of the slower "A" and "B" classes. All retained Coast Guard insignia.

Patrol Craft, Coast Guard (WPB), "A" and "B" classes

Displacement: 67 tons (loaded)
Length: 23.82m/78ft 2in (wl); 25.32m/83ft (oa)
Beam: 5.25m/17ft 3in
Draught: 1.77m/5ft 10in
Armament: 1 x 0.50in machine-gun,
　　1 x 81mm mortar
Machinery: 2 diesel engines, 2 shafts
Power: 895kW/1,200bhp for 17 knots
Fuel: Not known
Endurance: Not known
Protection: Nominal
Complement: 8–10
Capacity: Up to 1,900 tons distributed load
　　on tank deck

LEFT: The Armored Troop Carrier (ATC) was built on the hull of an LCM (6). This is the basic version with the troop-carrying compartment covered by a protective roof.

Armored Troop Carrier (ATC)

The 56ft LCM (6) was designed during World War II, but proved to be of considerable subsequent value and continued in production until 1980. Available in numbers, it was an important vessel in the Vietnam War, where it was used in a variety of roles. It was shallow in draught, manoeuvrable and had a forward ramp, qualities eminently suitable for use in the creeks of the Mekong Delta. A great disadvantage was the lack of speed, rarely better than 6 knots when loaded. When used on waterways, where the adverse current might be some 5 knots, this caused some problems.

Although also modified for the command and fire support roles, as well as "refuellers", LCM (6) were usually deployed as Armored Troop Carriers

(ATC). For this role, the tank deck was covered with a pitched metal roof. Alternatively, a flat, overhead platform was sometimes fitted, to land a helicopter for rapid evacuation of wounded troops.

Basic accommodation was for a 40-strong platoon. Three sections, each of three ATCs, were required for a company-strength operation. The superstructure was extended further forward, and featured tubs and drum-shaped turrets for a variety of defensive armament.

Some were equipped with a powerful water cannon which, in this land of mud and reed, could simply wash away an enemy position or destroy the "spider holes" that concealed Viet Cong troops.

A River Assault Squadron (RAS) had an establishment of two command craft (CCB), five fire support monitors, a refueller to extend endurance, and 26 ATCs. All were LCM (6) conversions. In support were 16 Assault Support Patrol Boats (ASPB), developed purely for service in Vietnam. These 50-footers could make 15 knots and carried an armament formidable enough for the type to be used as escort to a Riverine column and to guard the flanks.

Armored Troop Carrier (ATC)

Displacement: 56 tons (loaded)
Length: 17.07m/56ft (oa)
Beam: 4.37m/14ft 4in
Draught: 1.2m/4ft (aft)
Armament: 2 x 20mm guns (2x1), 2 x 0.50in and 2 x 0.30in machine-guns
Machinery: 2 diesel engines, 2 shafts
Power: 246kW/330bhp for 10 knots
Fuel: Not known
Endurance (designed): 239km/130mm at 10 knots
Protection: Bullet-proof overall, Appliqué gratings to defeat shaped charges
Complement: 9–10
Capacity: 40 equipped troops, or about 4 tons cargo

ABOVE: **Some ATC vessels were fitted with a landing pad for helicopter operations.** LEFT: **ATCs of the "Brown Water Navy" alongside a headquarters ship in the Mekong Delta.**

ABOVE: **A Monitor proceeding slowly in the very shallow water of a river creek. The turret mounts a 40mm cannon and a machine-gun.** LEFT: **A "Zippo" Monitor with two flamethrowers in turret mountings. Note the blanked-off gun turret ring on the foredeck and the conventional bow replacing the ramp.**

Monitor (MON)

The "capital ship" of the Mobile Riverine Force (MRF) was the Monitor (MON), the title of which was close in the traditional sense to those of the American Civil War – relatively heavily armed for size, well protected in an improvised way, largely modified from suitable shallow draught craft, and intended to operate on a disputed river system.

Again, an LCM (6) provided the basic hull, but as the vessel did not act as a transport, the ramp was replaced by a conventional bow, with a flat overhang as seen on lighters. The freeboard of the hull was low, seaworthiness depending on the

coaming, now continued forward where, in earlier craft, this was faired into the base ring of the forward turret. In an effort to increase speed, later craft had a spoon bow. Earlier examples had a short superstructure, leaving a section of the original tank deck, either open or roofed over. With increasing firepower the superstructure became more massive, supporting armoured vehicle-type turrets.

The original bow gun was a 40mm, in an angular mounting open at the back. This was developed to a taller gunhouse with a rear door. Late craft had a light tank turret mounting a short-barrelled 105mm

howitzer. Alternatively, some were fitted with flamethrowers, which projected a napalm stream for 150m/492ft. With grim humour, these were called "Zippo" boats.

Monitors armed with a 40mm cannon also usually carried a 20mm cannon, an 81mm mortar, two 0.50in and two 0.30in machine-guns. The 105mm variant normally carried two 20mm cannon in a single mount as secondary armament. All were fitted with both high- and low-velocity grenade launchers. All were fitted with external grills to defeat the rocket-propelled grenades (RPG).

ABOVE: **Capital ship of the "Brown Water Navy", the Monitor was heavily armed. This example has a 105mm tank turret forward and two 20mm cannon. The appliqué protection was necessary as defence against short-range weapons used by the Viet Cong.**

Monitor (MON)

Displacement: 90 tons (loaded)
Length: 18,45m/60ft 6in (oa)
Beam: 5.34m/17ft 6in
Draught: 1.07m/3ft 6in
Armament: 1 x 105mm gun, 2 x 20mm guns (2x1), 2/3 x 0.30in machine-guns (2/3x1), Grenade launchers
Machinery: 2 diesel engines, 2 shafts
Power: 246kW/330bhp for 10 knots
Fuel: Not known
Endurance: Not known
Protection: Bullet-proof overall; Appliqué gratings to defeat shaped charges
Complement: 11–12

Landing Craft, Utility (LCU)

ABOVE: **The LCT (6) was the first drive-through design of World War II. The after ramp has the appearance of a fixed transom.**

Designed for simplicity, capacity and economy, World War II landing craft were unavoidably slow. The Cold War saw large amphibious groupings threatened by nuclear attack, and faster craft were required. The key amphibious warfare ships were the recently completed LSDs, whose docking wells had been designed to accommodate large numbers of existing craft. Redesign would have to take this into account.

In support of an all-20-knot force, a new LST was being developed during the 1950s and, to be carried topside as in the war, a new LCT was also required. To highlight the latter's greater versatility, it became known from 1952 as a Landing Craft, Utility (LCU).

Rather confusingly, surviving war-built LCT (6) had also been recategorized LCU, the highest hull number being LCU 1465. The prototype of the new class, completed in 1953 was, therefore, numbered LCU 1466. Production of the class was completed in 1956 with LCU vessel number 4609.

The 1466 type had the same dimensions as the preceding LCTs but, oddly, was configured as a closed-stern LCU (5) rather than a drive-through LCU (6). The latter was not only for convenience in loading and discharge but also to allow the LCT to act as an in-line causeway to assist LSTs to discharge over beaches with a very shallow slope.

The reversion may have been due to load distribution associated with the exceptional lift capability of the 1466. Although the craft's displacement was only 180 tons, three 49-ton M48 Patton main battle tanks could be carried. Alternatively, there was space to carry six M41 Walker Bulldog light tanks, totalling 140 tons.

Height restrictions within an LSD demanded that a 1466 type had minimum air draught (height), the low wheelhouse accordingly being no higher than the two 20mm cannon mountings on each side. The single pole mast, with radar, had to be lowered. However, except for improved

LEFT: **The US-built LCU 1610 type reduces the landing craft to the basics: a diesel-propelled raft with high coamings, a ramp at each end, and a side position for the helmsman to permit drive-through.**

ABOVE: **On a relatively steep beach, this 1610 type has grounded at the water's edge, permitting a dry landing for the articulated store carrier.**

lines, little had been done to increase speed, the craft having the same engine power and triple shafts (to minimize propeller diameter) as war-built craft.

Lack of speed and drive-through capability soon became identified as a problem and, on some later hulls, propulsive efficiency was improved by fitting propeller ducts, known as Kort nozzles. By straightening the flow over the propeller these ducts augmented the thrust. In a bid to improve manoeuvrability and to reduce the tendency to broach in surf, others

were fitted with vertical-drive propellers. The latter machinery was intended to turn the craft rapidly in order to beach stern-first. The design objective was to produce a faster hull by having an after ramp and a ship-type bow section.

As the requirement for a drive-through facility remained, however, a new LCU 1610 type was developed. With length increased by 6m/20ft and beam decreased by no less than 1.5m/5ft, the type also had a 50 per cent increase in engine power, allowing a respectable 11 knots. Lift capacity was also marginally improved.

The 1610 type did have a split superstructure, however, and this was retained in the "LCU 1626" design, which

reverted to the same dimensions as the earlier 1466 type. Hull depth was increased, adding stiffness and buoyancy, improved cargo area layout and permitting the use of twin-shaft propulsion. Short, blunt hulls such as this show a distinct "hump" in the speed/power curve. Beyond this, no amount of power will show significant increase in speed. As the craft was already powered for its maximum "natural" speed, the machinery also reverted to that of a 1466 type.

For this basic design, a lower speed simply had to be accepted. Nonetheless useful, the 1626 continued to be built until the mid-1980s, terminating at LCU 1681. Alternative high-speed craft were being designed and evaluated in parallel. The air cushion type proved the most promising, leading to the design of the LCAC.

ABOVE: **An LCU 1610 type had a forward beaching draught of 1.07m/3.5ft. A 50 per cent increase in engine power allowed the top speed of the vessel to be increased to 11 knots.**

Landing Craft, Utility (LCU) 1626 type

Displacement: 380 tons (beaching); 395 tons (loaded)
Length: 35.53m/116ft 6in (oa)
Beam: 10.37m/34ft
Draught (beaching): 1.07m/3ft 6in (forward); 1.98m/6ft 6in (aft)
Draught (seagoing): 2.06m/6ft 9in
Armament: 2 x 0.50in machine-guns
Machinery: 4 diesel engines, 2 shafts
Power: 507kW/680bhp for 8 knots
Fuel: Not known
Endurance: 2,208km/1,200nm at 6 knots
Protection: Nominal
Complement: 14

Landing Craft, Mechanized, LCM (6) (Mods) and LCM (8)

As mentioned earlier, the original LCM (6) was an LCM (3) with 1.8m/6ft added in the mid-hull. The purpose was to carry heavier tanks – the 27-ton M3A2 Grant, then the 32-ton M4A3 General Sherman. The lengthening raised the vehicle weight limit from 30 to 34 tons, and the cargo load, some 30 tons, required care when loading. Where an armoured vehicle represented a relatively concentrated weight which could be positioned to give the LCM a favourable trim, the distribution of general cargo, although no greater, could, without due care, result in considerable seakeeping problems, including the risk of swamping. The extra length precluded the craft from being loaded on to some earlier transports and cargo ships. The LCM (6) first appeared during 1943 and, by the end of the war, over 2,700 had been built.

Under the Lend-Lease Program, the British received over 600 LCM (2) and (3), but none of the LCM (6), as they had developed a stretched version of the LCM (3).

Known as the LCM (7), and not limited by a required compatability with transports, it had larger dimensions of 17.63 x 4.9m/57ft 10in x 16ft. The extra beam width gave the stability and extra buoyancy to carry a 35-ton tank (sufficient for a 27.5-ton Cromwell but not for a 40-ton Churchill).

Post-war, the LCM (6) remained in service but, perhaps influenced by the huge armoured fighting vehicles developed late in the war by Germany, the US Army wanted a new 50-ton limit for the capacity. BuShips was keen to improve the basic war-built LCM (6), and was looking at ways to improve beaching conditions in surf. The hull was virtually rectangular in plan, flat-bottomed but with a curved rise forward and aft. In the hands of an inexperienced coxswain, it was a difficult vessel to reverse off a beach. The LCM (6) had a tendency to broach, becoming stranded against the beach and, frequently, being wrecked. Loss rates were high.

When modified, the same 17.1m/56ft overall length had to be observed for stowage aboard AKA and APA. Beam was also limited by a requirement that the vessel be rail-transportable.

LEFT: **The LCM (8) has a lift capacity of 60 tons. Note the engines are running to keep the craft firmly head-to-beach. Only just visible is a Newport-class LST on the horizon.**

To cater for the larger dimensions of the projected 50-ton military vehicle, the cargo space was widened by reducing the width of the side walls. This narrowed the side decks outside the coamings to little more than a ledge to carry essential fittings. It also considerably reduced reserve buoyancy in the event of the cargo deck being flooded.

The ramp was increased in length, from 2.79m/9ft 2in to 3.35m/11ft. The grid-type extension enabled the new Mod. 1 to be distinguished from the earlier type. Experiments with different bottom configurations showed little advantage, and the existing arrangement was largely retained.

Series production of the LCM (6) Mod. 1 began in 1952. A later Mod. 2 was built and had reduced hoist weight from which a "high-performance" version

was developed. It had been assumed that the basic laws of hydrodynamics could be bypassed by installing sufficient power. It was expected that a 9-knot craft would make 13, if existing 450bhp engine power was increased to 1,200 bhp. The result was 10 knots and a craft so weighted down by engines that it trimmed very stern down. Nonetheless, around 100 were built.

Ever larger loads carried in craft of fixed dimensions had the inevitable consequence of requiring a deeper beaching draught. This resulted in a larger craft, transportable on some later transport ships but most easily by LSD. This craft, the LCM (8), was built from the 1950s until 1992 for both the US Army and the US Navy. Obviously larger, the LCM (8) had a one-piece ramp mounted at a far shallower angle.

Like the LCM (6), the LCM (8) had a completely parallel cargo area, and this extra space permitted the alternative load of 150 troops, compared with 80 in the LCM (6).

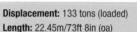

Landing Craft, Mechanized, LCM (8)

Displacement: 133 tons (loaded)
Length: 22.45m/73ft 8in (oa)
Beam: 6.4m/21ft
Draught (beaching): 1.35m/4ft 5in (forward); 1.47m/4ft 10in (aft)
Armament: None
Machinery: 2/4 diesel engines, 2 shafts
Power: Up to 806kW/1,080bhp for 9 knots (loaded)
Fuel: 5 tons oil
Endurance: 350km/190nm at 9 knots (loaded)
Complement: 4–5
Capacity: 53.6 tons (60 US tons) of vehicles, or distributed cargo weight

ABOVE: **Heavy armour now demands landing craft that are too large and heavy to be carried as deckloads on all but a few attack cargo ships.** LEFT: **Docking wells can become subject to water surge when the ship is at an open anchorage.**

LEFT: **An LCAC loaded with troops of the 11th Marine Expeditionary Unit during exercise "Eager Mace", September 24, 2002.**

Landing Craft, Air Cushion (LCAC)

As already noted, the beach forms a difficult barrier between the seaborne assault force and objectives. Personnel, being adaptable, fit reasonably into a wide variety of craft. To survive an opposed landing, however, prompt, on-the-spot support and resupply is required. LVTs satisfied these various roles to a point, lifting personnel and supplies and, in armoured types, used as light tanks. The vehicle's strength was in the ability to cross the beach without trans-shipment, proceeding directly from the transport offshore to the landing area. Their capacity was, nonetheless, small and,

with the nuclear age, there came the desirability of high-speed approach from beyond the horizon. Whatever the type of craft adopted, it had to be large enough to cope with conditions over a long approach while being capable of carrying tanks and heavy equipment as well as stores which, for speed of handling, were increasingly palletized.

Studies began in the mid-1960s to define a range of high-speed craft to replace, in order of size, the LCVP, LCM (6) and LCM (8). The LCVP was effectively replaced by the helicopter. Again, the other types developed into

a proposed single design of planing craft, to be propelled at 35 knots by waterjets. The vessel would carry two 60-ton M1 Abrams main battle tanks, which had entered service in 1980. Designated the LCM (9), the craft would have been of around 37m/122ft long, drive-through and designed to fit docking wells. The craft never entered production but, in view of the high

BELOW: **The two swivelling ducts (one of which is visible above the tank) each provide 10 per cent of forward thrust and most of the directional thrust. Turning radius at speed is over 1.6km/1 mile.**

ABOVE: **The noise of an LCAC entering an empty docking well is so great that access galleries are cleared. Note the narrow clearance.** RIGHT: **The JMSDF Osumi-class LSD is designed to carry two US-built LCACs in the docking well.**

capital and through-life costs of the preferred craft, it remains a candidate as a further replacement for the LCU.

British-built hovercraft used in Vietnam, although not judged particularly successful, had demonstrated the ability to negotiate a wide variety of otherwise impassable terrain. The air cushion made the type truly amphibious and, as the tiresome laws of hydrodynamics no longer applied, it was (by vessel standards) fast. From the US Marine Corps perspective, the craft made a greater range of beaches accessible. From a holding area, some 40km/25 miles offshore, they could threaten around 161km/100 miles of coastline, thereby diluting the enemy's capacity of defence.

The size of the prototype selected for development as the LCAC needed to be around twice as long as it was wide. An M1 Abrams set the lift capacity at some 60 tons, a 25 per cent overload being

permissible. The resulting cargo deck was sufficiently spacious, at 21 x 8m/ 67 x 27ft, to allow numerous lighter vehicles to be carried.

In essence, the LCAC is built as a deep, aluminium alloy raft, bounded by flexible skirting to contain the air cushion. Flanking the cargo deck are narrow superstructures housing four gas turbine engines, of which two drive the lift fans, and two power large, ducted propellers for propulsion. The cargo deck is open, with short ramps forward and aft.

Personnel aboard are usually limited to the five operators and up to 24 vehicle crew. Heat and noise from the engines, together with the safety aspects of riding a breaking sea at 40-plus knots, makes troop-carrying dangerous. When used for this purpose (the US Marine Corps still prefer LVTs for higher on-shore mobility), a prefabricated Personnel Transport

Module (PTM) is mounted on the vehicle deck, with capacity for just 145 fully equipped troops.

Air cushion craft have a low signature for mines, and a high resistance to the explosive effects. Towed mine counter-measures sleds have been developed for leading an assault. To the US Marine Corps, the LCAC is a vital vehicle carrier. Due to the wide beam, only one could be carried on earlier LPDs and LHAs. Later-designed LHD vessels can carry three, and two are carried on an LPD-41 type.

Corrosion in the aluminium structure and high maintenance levels have caused modernization programmes to be brought forward, the opportunity also being taken to upgrade the propulsion units.

LEFT: **The noise levels and acceleration experienced aboard an LCAC are so extreme that personnel may be transported only when housed in a bolt-on-module.**

Landing Craft, Air Cushion (LCAC)

Displacement: 91 tons (light); 167 tons (loaded); 182 tons (overload)
Length: 24.69m/81ft (wl); 26.8m/87ft 10 (oa)
Beam: 13.31m/43ft 8in (wl); 14.33m/47ft (oa)
Draught: 0.78m/2ft 6in
Armament: None
Machinery: 4 gas turbines; 2 for lift, 2 for propulsion
Power: 11,190kW/15,000hp total for 54 knots (light), or 40 knots (loaded)
Fuel: 6.2 tons kerosene
Endurance: 414km/225nm at 48 knots (light); 368km/200nm at 40 knots (loaded)
Protection: None
Complement: 5+ 24 vehicle crew
Capacity: About 70 tons of vehicles/cargo, or 145 troops

LEFT: **USS *Gunston Hall* (LSD-5) has not been flooded down, the PACV being able to exit over the lowered stern gate from a dry docking well.**

Patrol Air Cushion Vehicle (PACV)

During the Vietnam War, the "Plain of Reeds" in the Mekong Delta was something of a "no-go" area. Vast lagoons of shallow water were covered with thickly growing short reed and, as in the Bayou country in the USA, the few dry tracks and habitable locations were known only to the local population. The area quickly became a haven to the Viet Cong, as US forces experienced mobility problems. The propellers of conventional craft and the tracks of LVTs were quickly fouled by reed, which also presented a physical barrier to waterjet craft. With helicopters always in short supply, the US Army and US Navy both experimented with hovercraft, which could float over the reed without any limitations.

These vehicles, procured in the mid-1960s, were the Bell SK-5, a licence-built version of the British Hovercraft Corporation SRN-5 Warden class. While only half as fast as a helicopter, they were able to stop anywhere in the "raft" mode, and were virtually mine-proof.

In more open waters, the light aluminium structure was prone to slamming damage. The airscrew propulsion made the type extremely noisy. In the damp and humid conditions of the delta, the craft required considerable maintenance. The peripheral skirt, essential in containing the lifting air cushion, could be damaged by shingle abrasion or in the negotiation of rocky areas. (Similar experience was

encountered in Arctic exercises, where ice was the problem. Canadian forces, however, are actively pursuing the possibilities of ACVs for Arctic use.)

The US Navy's PACVs were of standard configuration, a cabin with side decks all round, and were modified to carry a heavy machine-gun position and a grenade launcher. The US Army's craft were of a flat-bed type, intended for moving equipment.

Always considered "experimental", the vehicle nonetheless inspired Bell to produce a larger type, the SK-10, which proved to be the forerunner of the LCAC now in service.

RIGHT: **In calm conditions, the air cushion vehicles have a considerable speed advantage, but this is rapidly reduced in choppy to rough sea conditions.**

Patrol Air Cushion Vehicle (PACV), SRN-5	

Weight: 5 tons (loaded)
Length: 12.2m/40ft (oa)
Breadth: 5.79m/19ft
Draught: 0 (under weigh); 0.31m/1ft (stationary)
Armament: 1 x 0.50in machine-gun, 1 x grenade launcher
Machinery: Rolls-Royce Marine Gnome
Power: 597kW/800hp for 55 knots (maximum)
Fuel: Not known
Endurance: About 322km/200 miles
Protection: Minimal
Complement: 4–5
Capacity: 20 troops, or 2 tons cargo

ABOVE AND LEFT: **Although shallow draught might be an asset in inshore waters, the high-speed wave-piercer is actually less effective than the USS *Inchon* (MCS-12) type that it replaced.**

Mine Countermeasures Support Ship (MCS)

Amphibious warfare vessels are "volume-critical" or, in other words, dimensions and configuration are governed by considerations of space rather than weight. For those craft that need not incorporate a docking well, a twin-hulled catamaran has much to commend it in terms of stability, seakeeping and spacious deck plan.

A conventional catamaran type has the drawback of greater wetted area and of consequent greater resistance. The Small Waterplane Area, Twin Hull (SWATH) has the same disadvantage, but offset by increased stability in a seaway. Both require considerable propulsive power and, where speed

is an important consideration, a wave piercing catamaran has a clear advantage. The wave-piercer has become a particular speciality of Australian shipyards, where Incat designed and built USS *Swift* (HSV-2). The vessel has two slender outer hulls that are designed to slice through waves rather than rise in the conventional manner. A deep V-form centreline hull provides the necessary reactive buoyancy in contacting the surface on any tendency to plunging. Waterjet propulsion obviates the requirement for conventional propellers, shafts or rudders, while reducing draught and vulnerability. Nonetheless, the choice of this vessel to replace the USS *Inchon* (MCS-12) as

support ship to mine countermeasures craft has been criticized. USS *Inchon* could operate a squadron of Sikorsky MH-53E minesweeping helicopters with six deck-landing spots, while USS *Swift* can house just two Sikorsky HH-60 Seahawks, with a single landing spot.

USS *Swift* is basically a high-speed commercial car ferry, modified for naval service. The relatively shallow draught is thought to be an asset in the MCS role. The wide stern ramp is strengthened for heavy armoured vehicles, and it is very likely that the vessel will be evaluated in a variety of alternative roles, despite its poor tolerance to damage.

LEFT: **The HSV is a slightly modified commercial ferry. It is in the high-speed vehicle transport role that the vessel will probably find the best usage when deployed with the amphibious fleet.**

Mine Countermeasures Support Ship (MCS), USS *Swift*, HSV-2

Displacement: 1,870 tons (loaded)
Length: 92m/30ft 8in (wl); 318ft 9in/97.22m (oa)
Beam: 87ft3in/26.6m
Draught: 3.43m/11ft 3in (maximum)
Armament: Mounting for 1 x CIWS
Machinery: 4 diesel engines driving 4 waterjets
Power: 28,348kW/38,000bhp for 47 knots (maximum), or 35 knots (loaded)
Fuel: 190 tons
Endurance: 7,360km/4,000nm at 20 knots
Protection: None
Complement: About 100
Capacity: 250 troops, or 500 tons cargo

Swimmer Delivery Vehicles (LSDV)

Landing special service personnel from submarines was commonly practised during World War II but, although techniques have since been greatly refined, they tend not to be kept secret. Of the two main types of wartime powered craft for swimmer delivery, the midget submarine was popular with the British, Japanese and Germans. What might better be described as "delivery vehicles" were developed successfully in the Italian *Maiale* (pig) and copied (less successfully) by the British and Germans.

During the 1990s, the US Navy operated a number of so-called Mark VIII LSDVs which, at 6.7m/22ft in length, were accommodated within dry superstructure extensions on SSNs and carried four equipped swimmers.

The current Advanced SEAL Delivery System (ASDS), however, is more sophisticated, a true midget submarine that can connect to a modified SSN via the common escape hatch also used by rescue vehicles. Larger than a wartime British X-craft, the vehicle can accommodate eight swimmers who enter and leave through a floodable trunk with hatches top and bottom.

Batteries powering all services are stowed individually in pressurized containers on the outside of the pressure hull. The craft is propelled by an electric motor and a single large-diameter, shrouded propeller. At bow and stern, retractable thrusters enable the craft to be positioned dynamically. There is no superstructure, but two fold-down masts support communications and monitoring antenna, together with an opto-electronic periscope. With a maximum of ten personnel aboard, the ASDS is also equipped with a life-support system.

Dimensions and weight are tailored to air transportation, and a force of six craft has been requested. It is reported, however, that the prototype craft are having problems both with inadequate battery capacity and in meeting limits for radiated noise.

Swimmer Delivery Vehicle (LSDV)

Displacement: 55 tons (surfaced); 60 tons (submerged)
Length: 19.82m/65ft (oa)
Beam: 2.44m/8ft (oa)
Draught: Not applicable
Armament: None
Machinery: 1 x electric propulsion motor, 8 x electric directional thrusters
Power: Not known
Endurance: 230km/125nm at 8 knots (designed)
Protection: Not applicable
Complement: 2 crew plus 8 special forces personnel

ABOVE: **USS *Greenville* (SSN-772), a nuclear-powered submarine at sea, with an LSDV on deck.** RIGHT: **An LSDV being loaded into the transportation container mounted on the deck of USS *Dallas* (SSN-700).**

LEFT: **A REMUS 600 being launched. The type can operate to a depth of 600m/1,969ft.**

Unmanned Vehicles (UV)

Without crew and associated safety systems, fighting vehicles can be made smaller, lighter and more cheaply. They can also be used with far greater risk and, potentially, more effectively. The US Navy's Drone Anti-Submarine Helicopter (DASH) of the 1960s was a first bold attempt but proved to be ahead of the technology of the time. The RQ-2A/B Predator, Unmanned Aerial Vehicle (UAV), capable of ship launch and recovery, is deployed operationally not only for reconnaissance missions but also as an effective missile delivery platform. The US Marine Corps has two squadrons devoted to defining uses in amphibious warfare.

In a maritime context, unmanned vehicles are divided between Remotely Operated Vehicles (ROV), linked to the controller by a trailing cable carrying command signals and data, and Autonomous Underwater Vehicles (AUV), which are pre-programmed and run independently until recovered. Free of any constraint, AUVs have a future bounded only by the systems and power source that can be packed aboard.

AUVs are already used widely in oceanographic work and, typically, have a three-day endurance and both an Inertial Navigation System (INS) and Global Positioning System (GPS). Larger AUVs are commonly used at a depth of 3,000m/9,843ft for scientific sampling, surveying, or search and salvage operations. Data are stored aboard for later downloading and analysis. Designed with a 2.75m x 324mm/9 x 1ft hull, such vehicles may also be launched from a torpedo tube.

In an amphibious warfare context, most current military interest resides in an AUV's ability to tow a high-definition sonar for the remote and unobtrusive detection and location of inshore mine fields. The state-of-the-art US-built REMUS 100 has been acquired in considerable numbers by both the US Navy and Royal Navy. Remote Environmental Measuring Units (REMUS) can operate autonomously for around 24 hours and are man-portable.

LEFT: **The REMUS AUV is pre-programmed to search underwater areas independently until recovered.**

Autonomous Underwater Vehicle (AUV), REMUS 100

Manufacturer: Hydroid LLC, Pocasset, Maine, USA
Weight: 37kg/81.4lb
Length: 1.6m/5ft 3in (oa)
Diameter: 190.5mm/7½in (maximum)
Propulsion: Brushless DC electric motor directly driving single propeller
Energy: 1 kW-h lithium-ion battery
Speed: Variable; 0–5 knots
Endurance: 22 hours at 3 knots
Maximum operation depth: 100m/328ft

LEFT: **Vehicles from a Ready Reserve Force (RRF) being unloaded on to LASH barges from a Combat Prepositioning Ship.**

Lighter Aboard Ship (LASH)

One logical offshoot from the "container revolution" that transformed much commercial shipping was the barge carrier, of which the best-known type was the Lighter Aboard Ship (LASH). Here, rather than 6–12m/ 20–40ft containers, the interchangeable modules were rectangular barges of 375 tons capacity. LASH ships were relevant to companies working between ports such as Rotterdam or New Orleans, which are located on major waterway systems. Barges would be taken aboard or discharged by the ship at a mooring, being moved singly or in groups by pusher tug.

Like that of an LSD, the after end on a LASH was a double-skinned, non-floodable docking well. Barges, stacked several deep, were stowed transversely and handled by a massive, 450-ton capacity gantry crane which travelled the length of the barge dock. The crane tracks were carried on beams which projected over the stern to allow a barge to be lowered into the water.

Beginning a massive acquisition of commercial tonnage during the 1980s, the Military Sealift Command took over four such ships. Following the disappearance at sea of a foreign-flagged LASH ship, the basic ship concept was abandoned.

The barge idea, however, was valid, the US Navy eventually progressing the type for second-echelon amphibious operation.

Under the label of the Improved Navy Lighterage System (INLS), an initial block of 23 dumb and six powered lighters had been acquired. All may be stacked, three deep, on a very large, flat-topped, seagoing dumb barge and towed to the operational area. Individual lighters can alternatively be transported in the docking well of an LSD or similar vessels.

On arrival, the barges are used for ship-to-shore movement of equipment (equivalent to the British "Mexeflote" system), being used as ferries, linked as causeways, or moored as pontoons for the repair of small craft.

ABOVE: **The Improved Navy Lighterage System (INLS) in operation. The US Navy ordered 23 barges and six powered lighters. Individual lighters can be carried in the docking well of an LSD-type vessel.**

Lighter Aboard Ship (LASH), *Green Island*

Tonnage: 32,280 tons (gross); 46,150 tons (deadweight); 62,310 tons (displacement, loaded)
Length: 243.03m/796ft 10in (oa); 272.29m/892ft 9in (oa)
Beam: 30.5m/100ft
Draught: 12.45m/40ft 9in (loaded)
Armament: None
Machinery: 2 sets steam turbines, single shaft
Power: 23,872kW/32,000shp for 22 knots
Fuel: 5,800 tons oil
Endurance: 27,600km/150nm at 22 knots
Protection: None
Complement: 27
Capacity: 90 barges

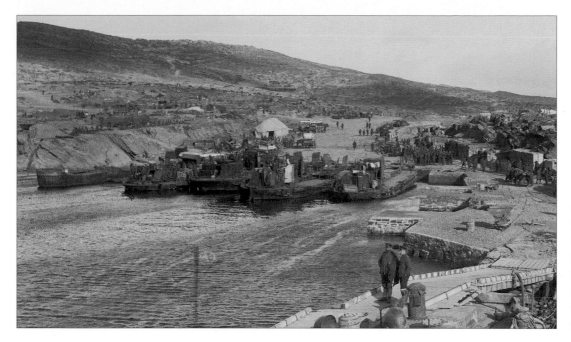

LEFT: **A row of X-Lighters ("Beetles") in the harbour at "A" West Beach, Suvla Point, on December 19, 1915, loaded and ready for the evacuation of Allied forces from Gallipoli.**

X-Lighters ("Beetles")

Early in World War I, the most cherished plan of the Royal Navy's First Sea Lord, Admiral Sir John ("Jacky") Fisher was his Baltic Project, whereby a Russian Army would be put ashore on the coast of Pomerania (divided between Germany and Poland) just 145km/90 miles from Berlin. Fisher's drive and fertile brain created many special craft, but there was overwhelming opposition from his more conservative colleagues, and he saw his "unparalleled Armada" being "diverted and perverted to the damned Dardanelles".

Among the 600-plus assorted craft of Fisher's "armada" were 200 craft built specifically to land personnel, horses, wheeled transport and artillery on the beach. Known as X-Lighters, numbered X1 to 200, all were powered, had a shallow draught and were fitted with a ramp. As the first series-built landing craft of modern times, the type deserves to be better recognized.

Not ordered until early in 1915, all were probably always destined for the Dardanelles, for which operational planning had already begun. A basic design brief was given to the small yard of Pollock at Faversham, Kent, which, within days, produced a proposal for a flat-bottomed, shallow barge with a pointed counter stern and a spoon bow. The latter was heavily flared to provide the necessary width for a 2m/7ft wide ramp. This was suspended around the centre of gravity by chains, attached to two manually operated pivoting beams. This characteristic feature, together with the curved cover fitted over the troop/cargo deck, brought about the craft's popular name of "Beetle". The cargo area was 18.28m/60ft in length, with a full-length centreline hatch 2.44m/8ft wide, with side decks each 1.98m/6ft 6in wide.

Unusually for the day, a diesel engine was specified, and sometimes two engines were fitted. A low coaming and short funnel covered the machinery space in the stern. Within six months, 220 had been completed.

ABOVE: **Another view of Royal Navy X-Lighters at Suvla Point, Gallipoli, awaiting evacuation.**

X-Lighters ("Beetles"), X1–200

Displacement: 160 tons (light); 310 tons (loaded)
Length: 32.14m/105ft 6in (oa)
Beam: 6.4m/21ft
Draught: 1.07/3ft 6in (light);
   1.98m/6ft 6in (loaded)
Armament: 1 x machine-gun
Machinery: 1/2 semi-diesel engines, 1/2 shafts
Power: 30–67kW/40–90bhp for 5–7 knots
Fuel: Not known
Endurance: Not known
Protection: Steering position only
Complement: 5

ABOVE AND LEFT: **HM Trawler** *Grimsby Town* **fitted for anti-submarine (note the depth charge racks at the stern) and anti-mine warfare. The vessel has a defensive armament of three Oerlikon cannon and a 4in naval gun.**

Auxiliary Minesweepers

As the greatest amphibious operation to date, the Dardanelles campaign of 1915, and its failure, were hugely influential on post-World War I thinking. The main objective (to place an Allied fleet at Constantinople) was not realized primarily because of a few lines of mines. These proved to be unsweepable and impassable, which demonstrated shortcomings in the Royal Navy's attitude to mine clearance.

Despite the success of Russian mining during the 1904–05 war with Japan, the British regular minesweeping force in 1914 was made up of only a handful of converted torpedo gunboats, with the first purpose-built craft (the original Flower-class sloops) on order. The reason for the delay was that commercial trawlers had been found to be ideal for the task, and also available in large numbers, together with skilled crews.

The work of deploying, towing and recovering sweeps, together with associated equipment, was little different to trawling, while the vessels had the necessary engine power. From 1911, therefore, the minesweeping organization for British waters was established, sufficient equipment being stockpiled to equip 250 trawlers immediately. This, however, was defensive minesweeping, with skippers and crews retaining civilian status but subject to naval discipline. In the fierce currents of the Dardanelles, and under heavy shore-based fire,

such trawler-minesweepers proved inadequate, and the naval high command appeared reluctant to use available converted destroyer-minesweepers.

Only a proportion of the British trawler fleet could be requisitioned, as the population still required to be fed. Large

numbers, however, together with their crews, were sunk by mines. Despite the availability of many more regular minesweepers in 1939, the fishing fleet was again raided for trawlers and personnel. Several large deep-sea trawlers served in the Falklands campaign of 1982.

ABOVE: **HM Trawler** *Ben Earn*, **one of the first of the type to be converted for anti-mine warfare. Note the minesweeping cable-winding drum mounted at the stern of the vessel.**

RIGHT: **Known popularly as the "Ellas", the distant-water trawlers of J. Marr & Company, a concern with a 100-year history in fishing based in Hull, East Yorkshire, served as minesweepers in the Falklands War, 1982.**

LEFT: **US Rangers embarked in British-manned LCAs in June 1944. Note the front protection for the helmsman and Bren-gunner. The ramps are fitted with rollers as an aid to beaching. The location is Weymouth Harbour, Dorset, and the craft are from HMS** *Prince Albert*.

Landing Craft, Assault (LCA, previously ALC)

What was then termed an ALC was defined in 1938 as a personnel assault craft hoistable by standard passenger liner davits. This limited the weight to 10 tons and defined the dimensions to accommodate crew, a 32-man platoon and five engineers/signallers. A 0.46m/18in beaching draught was specified. Cooperation between commercial interests and the Admiralty's Department of Naval Construction resulted in a strong and useful little craft.

Known after July 1942 as an LCA, the craft had virtually no rise of floor, the bottom curving upward at both ends. The double bottom gave reserve buoyancy in the event of a flooded deck

area, and was very shallow. Sheltered beneath narrow side decks, troops were seated along either side. Further seating along the centreline could be screened somewhat by adding raised coamings.

Behind the hand-operated forward ramp was a protective transverse armoured bulkhead with forward hinging doors. Much of the exposed hull was of patented bullet-proof steel. The helmsman occupied a cab on the starboard side. The cab had a lid so that the helmsman could stand on his seat to improve forward visibility. A similar port-side position was occupied by a gunner. Aft of the troop accommodation was an enclosed engine compartment containing two

Ford V8 petrol engines and fuel tanks. The twin rudders and propellers were protected by rather elaborate guards.

Designed as a ship-to-shore craft (and complementary to the vehicle-carrying MLC), the LCA was often used in circumstances for which it had been neither designed nor intended (notably cross-Channel to Normandy). The resulting shortcomings attracted unreasonable criticism. In many respects, the 1,900-plus that were built were stronger and superior to the 36ft LCVP that the US forces later used and preferred.

ABOVE: **US Rangers on board a Landing Craft, Assault (LCA) in Weymouth Harbour, Dorset, on June 4, 1944. The troops sat with their equipment in three rows in what were very cramped conditions.**

Landing Craft, Assault (LCA)

Displacement: 9 tons (light); 13 tons (loaded)
Length: 12.66m/41ft 6in (oa)
Beam: 3.05m/10ft
Draught (light): 0.33m/1ft 1in (forward); 0.53m/1ft 9in (aft)
Draught (loaded): 0.53m/1ft 9in (forward); 0.69m/2ft 3in (aft)
Armament: 1 x Bren gun, 2 x Lewis guns, 1 x 2in mortars
Machinery: 2 petrol engines, 2 shafts
Power: 97kW/130hp for 10 knots (light), or 6 knots (loaded)
Fuel: 64 or 98 gallons petrol
Endurance: Up to 147km/80mm at 7 knots (loaded)
Protection: 7mm/¼in plate to vertical surfaces
Complement: 4
Capacity: 37 troops plus 364kg/800lb equipment

Landing Craft, Tank, LCT (1) to (4)

After the Dunkirk evacuation, Churchill demanded the specification for a craft capable of landing tanks in numbers on the beaches of continental Europe. No such craft had ever existed, and designers worked from a blank sheet. A vessel of around 48.8m/160ft was specified to accommodate three 40-ton tanks and land them in 1m/3ft of water on a beach with a 1 in 35 (moderate) slope.

Production was rapid, with what became known as the LCT (1) appearing in November 1940. Major features included a tank deck, which could accommodate three 40-ton or six 25-ton vehicles. Running light, the bottom could be used for water ballast, while the side compartments could be sealed to give greater buoyancy in the event of the tank deck (which was below the load waterline) flooding. To lower the ramp, personnel had to go forward along the exposed side decks to operate the winches. A further winch, at the stern, operated a large kedge anchor, released on approach to

the beach and the cable kept taut both to maintain the craft's alignment to the beach and to facilitate reversing off.

To keep fully above the keel line, the two propellers were of small diameter. The relatively low thrust and a single rudder, combined with a shallow, beamy hull, resulted in difficult steering. The hull was built in four sections to permit transport as deck cargo.

The LCT (1) proved the principles adequately but it was apparent that a relatively small increase in dimensions would permit the loading of six 17.7-ton Valentine tanks. Mark 1 craft were, therefore, relegated to training duties in favour of the LCT (2). To achieve quantity production, this craft was assembled from modules prefabricated by non-shipbuilding companies.

Both LCT (1) and (2) were originally powered by aero-type petrol engines from World War I. Fortunately, the supply of these eventually ended, necessitating the adoption of the very

ABOVE: **A prototype LCT (2) during beaching trials. Intended to transport tanks from ship to shore, it was built to be capable of a Channel crossing.**

reliable 500bhp Paxman diesel engine. As the LCT (2) had three propellers, installed power was thus increased from 1,050 to 1,500hp, a 43 per cent increase, however this gave a speed increase of only half a knot. Fuel stowage became safer now that petrol was no longer used.

The Mark 3, or LCT (3), that followed was essentially an LCT (2) with an extra mid-hull module inserted to increase length by around 9.75m/32ft. Lines were also refined somewhat so that, even by reducing power to two engines, the type still made the same speed when loaded. This was partly by the design of the longer hull which also allowed simplified hull construction as well as saving a valuable engine. Steering remained erratic but was improved by the use of twin rudders.

LEFT: **Shorter and beamier than previous types, the LCT (4) was not designed to be covered. Note the open bridge and lack of armament.**

LEFT: **An early LCT (1), still carrying a "TLC" identifier. The vertical posts were supports for a portable metal roof. In these early craft, the whole of the open tank deck could be roofed over with a canvas cover.**

ABOVE: **An over-large funnel was a feature of the LCT (4). Camouflage shades were selected to blend with misty Channel conditions, the pattern designed to break up the vessel's outline.**

The LCT (3) could carry 11 Valentines, five Churchill tanks or 11 of the new US built Shermans. This was satisfactory, except that the capacity to carry tanks had increased more than vessel buoyancy. Inevitably, this resulted in deeper beaching draught. French beaches, the ultimate objective, were

known to have very shallow slopes, which would leave the craft grounded too far from the tideline. A shallower-draught version was obviously urgently required and allowed the chance to raise the tank deck above the load waterline for the first time, making it self-draining. The double-bottom was consequently a

generous 1.5m/5ft deep. Any improved stiffness that this gave was offset by the exceptional lightness of the construction. The hull did bend and twist quite alarmingly in a seaway.

Entering service in September 1942, the Mark 4, or LCT (4), was 1.5m/5ft shorter than the LCT (3), but 2.4m/8ft wider in beam. On these proportions, a reduction in speed had to be accepted and the craft could be beached satisfactorily on slopes of greater than 1 in 150. Vehicle-carrying capacity was again improved, while tolerable passage accommodation was provided for the crews of the vehicles carried.

ABOVE: **Note how the shallow-submerged propellers create an inefficient wash, and the large gallery that accommodates two single 2pdr "Pom-Pom" anti-aircraft guns on this LCT (3).**

Landing Craft, Tank, LCT (4)

Displacement: 200 tons (light); 585 tons (loaded)
Length: 57.11m/187ft 3in (oa)
Beam: 11.79m/38ft 8in
Draught (beaching): 0.56m/1ft 10in (forward); 1.22m/4ft (aft)
Draught (seagoing, full load): 0.94m/3ft 1in (forward); 1.29m/4ft 3in (aft)
Armament: 2 x 20mm guns (2x1)
Machinery: 2 diesel engines, 2 shafts
Power: 746kW/1,000bhp for 8 knots (sustained), or 9.5 knots (maximum)
Fuel: Not known
Endurance: 2,024km/1,100nm at 8 knots
Protection: 7mm/¹/₄in plate to wheelhouse
Complement: 12
Capacity: 6 x 40-ton, 9 x 30-ton or 12 x 3-ton tanks, or 350 tons cargo

Landing Craft, Tank, LCT (8)

Where British ideas much influenced early US thinking regarding amphibious vessels in general, the latter rapidly gained experience by virtue of massive construction programmes. By 1943, therefore, a reverse trickle of practical knowledge began to find its way into British design.

In the Landing Ship, Tank (LST), US forces found a most useful vessel that was particularly flexible in ballasting arrangements, which enabled safe ocean passages to be made as a cargo carrier. The vessel's draught could be differentially reduced to ground in shallow water to allow the discharge of heavy armoured vehicles.

LSTs were never available in sufficient numbers (many were "lost" in obscure military backwaters of the Pacific) and were relatively slow and vulnerable when deployed in an opposed landing. By the end of 1943,

therefore, the Landing Ship, Medium (LSM) was introduced – effectively a smaller LST but with the usefulness of a larger and faster type of LCT.

The extra speed was possible because the forward ramp was enclosed within LST-type bow doors. The raised forecastle, necessary to accommodate the length of the enclosed ramp and doors, was, to an extent, continued aft, with the resulting deep side compartments giving a higher degree of seaworthiness and, importantly, greatly improved longitudinal stiffness. There was no LST-type upper deck, so lack of torsional stiffness was still evident in rough seas.

Conceived as improved LCTs, all were in fact ordered as LCT (7), a designation that was never used in service since they were retitled LSMs. The replacement British LCT, then in the planning stage, thus became the LCT (8).

ABOVE: **The British-built LCT (4) was followed by the LCT (8), of which LCT 4001 (shown here) is an example. LCT (5), (6) and (7) were all US-built types.**

Like most British naval projects post-1943, the LCT (8) was designed with the intention of service in the Far East. Some 730 LCT (4) had been built. A number had failed structurally and required remedial strengthening. The LCT (8), therefore, had the same deep sides of the LSM, with bow doors enclosing the ramp and around an extra 12m/38ft of length. The two shafts were each powered by two Paxman diesel engines, giving a maximum speed of over 12 knots. Accommodation on this spacious landing craft was on a scale that allowed the ship's crew and the crews of the vehicles to be accommodated for seven days.

Only one LCT (8) was ever completed during hostilities, but around 24 served into the 1980s, refurbished

LEFT: **With the ramp enclosed and a longer hull, the LCM (8) was significantly faster. Increased depth gave the hull greater stiffness. HMS Bastion (L4040) was used during the Suez Crisis in 1956, and was sold to Zambia in 1966.**

to post-war standards and named. The names, such as HMS *Bastion* and HMS *Counterguard*, were mostly military fortification in origin, with one strangely named HMS *Arromanches*. Some remained un-named but, by the mid-1970s, all remaining craft carried battle names, commencing with the letter "A", from *Aachen* to *Audemer*.

All were now elderly, and the replacement, not on a one-to-one basis, was known as the LCT (9), although apparently not officially. It was of commercial design and, compared

with LCT (8) dimensions, it was a larger vessel. Despite engine power of 2,000bhp, the vessel could make only 10 knots. Two were built between 1977 and 1978, and were sometimes referred to as LSMs. Both could carry five 70-ton tanks, and the combined weight was equal to that transported in an LCT (8).

Operating under the Blue Ensign of the Royal Corps of Transport rather than by the Royal Navy, the craft were of novel design and ungainly appearance. The high forecastle, devoid of flare or sheer, supported the outer doors which

ABOVE: **Although built some 30 years later, the Ardennes class of the Royal Logistics Corps shows the influence of the LCT (8). Confusingly, HMS *Redoubt* (L4001) is numbered in the same series.**

protected the ramp. The tank deck ran almost to the after end of the high superstructure, which covered the deck. Deep longitudinal bulkheads flanked the tank deck, allowing headroom and improving stiffness to the hull. Externally, these formed high coamings with low, narrow side decks. The coamings could be roofed over, forming a flat centreline deck with an access hatch served by two 30-ton capacity derricks.

Most military stores were, by now, containerized. The low-density cargo containers could be conveniently carried on this forward deck. Tank crews were accommodated in the relatively spacious superstructure.

ABOVE: **The shallow draft of RASCV/HMAV *Arakan* (L4003) can here be appreciated. The high bow structure enables a maximum length of ramp to be stowed inboard. Note the sharp gradient of the ramp.**

Landing Craft, Tank, LCT (8)

Displacement: 660 tons (light); 1,010 tons (loaded)
Length: 68.63m/225ft (bp); 70.52m/231ft 2in (oa)
Beam: 11.9m/39ft
Draught (beaching): 0.96m/3ft 2in (forward); 1.52m/5ft (aft)
Armament: None
Machinery: 4 diesel engines, 2 shafts
Power: 1,373kW/1,840bhp for 12.5 knots (maximum)
Fuel: Not known
Endurance: 4,600km/2,500nm at 10 knots
Protection: Not known
Complement: 22
Capacity: 5 heavy tanks, or 350 tons cargo

LEFT: **L3507 and L3508, two Vosper-built craft, were prototypes for the LCM (9), the first class of British minor landing craft to be built since World War II. Commissioned in 1963, they had a more steeply housed ramp.**

Landing Craft, Medium, LCM (7) and (9)

Early Landing Craft, Medium, particularly the LCM (3) and (6), were designed to be set afloat empty using davits or cargo lifting gear, and then loaded alongside with heavy armoured vehicles. Clearances in the craft were critical across the beam while the fore-and-aft position of the load could be vital to stability. The situation was much alleviated by the introduction of the LSD, which permitted craft to be carried dry and pre-loaded before launching.

For US forces, the late introduction of the M26 Pershing tank in 1944 required a new landing craft to be designed. The British continued with medium tanks but required a craft more suitable than the LCM (3) and (6) for Far East use. Toward the end of 1944, a new LCM (7) was introduced, built of part-welded, part-riveted construction.

The LCM (7) dimensions of 18.35 x 4.87m/60ft 3in x 16ft and a weight of 28 tons did not allow it to be carried under standard davits. The beam appeared too large for the 13.42m/44ft width of the four Ashland-class LSDs being acquired through the Lend-Lease Program.

Able to carry a 35-ton tank, the LCM (7) closely followed the design principles successfully employed in the LCM (3). Externally, it lacked the distinct curve that characterized the shape of the upper edge on the coaming of the LCM (3). Only the mid-body was almost flat, with negligible rise of floor but with two shallow keels to prevent abrasion when grounding. Forward, the flat bottom was blended in a curve with the lower edge of the ramp. Aft, it swept upward to the lower edge of the square transom.

The tank deck rose in a near double curve to meet the sill of the ramp, avoiding the sharp step that characterized earlier craft, and which caused considerable problems to wheeled transport. The resulting deeper forward double bottom also counteracted tendency for the vessel to float bows-down when the vehicle deck

ABOVE: **A fully laden LCM (7) leaves the P&O liner SS *Canberra* during the Falklands campaign, with troops of the 5th Infantry Brigade destined for Blue beach on San Carlos Water.**

RIGHT: **An LCM (9) painted with "Arctic"-type camouflage during a pre-Falklands War landing exercise.**

was flooded. The crew of seven appears large but, even late in the war, manpower was cheaper than mechanization.

The LCM (7) programme was due to run to 250 craft but was cancelled in 1945. Several of these tough little craft were, nonetheless, still in service during the mid-1970s, overlapping the entry into service of the first post-war craft. Ten were built in the mid-1960s to be deployed with the two Fearless-class LPDs, and the docking wells on both could accommodate four. One was lost in the Falklands (where the type was generally referred to as Landing Craft, Utility [LCU]), but replaced by new craft built in 1986.

The LCM (9) was designed to carry a 54-ton Chieftain tank or 50 tons of cargo. During the Falklands campaign, however, LCM (9) proved to be very useful as a troop carrier. It was not meant for this usage and, following long passages in the Falklands winter, troops arrived wet, cold and very unhappy. The craft were subsequently equipped with a removable, inflatable shelter for the vehicle deck. The side coamings were also raised.

As built, all were fitted with twin propellers running in Kort nozzles to increase thrust. In the late 1990s, however, when most were approaching obsolescence, those in good condition were re-engined for waterjet propulsion. These propulsors not only removed vulnerable propeller shafts, A-brackets, propellers and rudders, but were unlikely to be clogged in shallow-water by weed. Before this, one LCM (9) was fitted with Schottel azimuth-thruster propulsion as a trials ship for a new LCM (10) craft, under design for use with the new Albion class. Ten were built between 1999 and 2005 and, larger again at 29.8 x 7.4m/97ft x 24ft 3in, they could transport a 70-ton armoured vehicle (a Challenger 2 tank weighs 62.5 tons). To facilitate docking, these craft are now fitted with bow thrusters. Of drive-through configuration, the craft is sufficiently different to be classed as an LCU.

ABOVE: **With the introduction of the LSD, the LCM, no longer constrained by davit limitations, became considerably larger in size. The LCM (9) weighed 115 tons.** LEFT: **The British LCM (9) dated from the mid-1960s, and was desiged to fit the docking well of the Fearless-class LPD. After 1999, the type was superseded by the larger LCU (10).**

Landing Craft, Medium, LCM (9)

Displacement: 115 tons (light); 165 tons (loaded)
Length: 25.7m/84ft 3in (oa)
Beam: 6.5m/21ft 4in
Draught: 1.7m/5ft 6in
Armament: Not armed
Machinery: 2 diesel engines, 2 shafts
Power: 462kW/620bhp for 10 knots (maximum)
Fuel: Not known
Endurance: 552km/300nm at 9 knots
Protection: Nominal
Complement: 7

Landing Craft, Gun (Large)/(Medium), LCG (L)/(M)

British LCGs were intended to cover the few minutes between the lifting of the preliminary barrage and the vulnerable assault craft actually hitting the beach. The type would be used to lead the first wave, with fire augmented by that of armoured fighting vehicles being carried in the craft. Before touchdown, the LCGs would be manoeuvred to the side of the attack to provide enfilading support fire more accurately than offshore warships.

During 1942, a total of 23 LCT (3) and 10 LCT (4) were converted, with the bows being sealed and an upper deck added. Two 4.7in naval guns fitted with gunshields were mounted along the centreline, firing over a deep, protective bulwark. The crew was increased to 39, many being gunners from the Royal Marines.

Unavoidably, large quantities of gun ammunition were carried above the waterline and, despite some armour protection, the craft proved vulnerable to mortar fire. Forced to remain beyond mortar range, the LCG (L)s proved to be ineffective.

This resulted in the LCG (M), purpose-built with a ship-type transom stern and a spoon-type bow to allow the vessel to be held against the shore. The two main types mounted two 25pdr or 17pdr Army guns in enclosed gun positions. The mountings were arranged at angles to allow both weapons to fire both ahead and to the beam. On the LCG (M), a major feature was the "central battery", an armoured structure, enclosing gun fire control, magazine and machinery space. The LCG (M) (1) had 52mm/2in sides, 25mm/1in deck plating and transverse bulkheads. On the LCG (M) (2), this was reduced to lessen weight and improve draught.

Considerable ballast capacity was incorporated, which allowed the craft to be flooded down to lay on the sand close inshore. This reduced the exposed hull cross-section to enemy gunners and provided a more stable gun platform.

ABOVE: **The Dieppe raid showed the need for close-in naval gunfire support to deal with strongpoints and armour. LCT (3) vessels were thus modified with a variety of medium-calibre guns.** BELOW: **The LCG (M) mounted two 25pdr or 17pdr guns in enclosed gun turrets.**

Landing Craft, Gun, LCG (M) (1)

Displacement: 308 tons (light); 339 tons (beaching); 381 tons (seagoing)

Length: 47.12m/154ft 6in (oa)

Beam: 6.81m/22ft 4in

Draught (beaching): 1.5m/4ft 11in (forward); 1.7m/5ft 7in (aft)

Draught (seagoing): 1.7m/5ft 7in (forward); 2.44m/8ft (aft)

Armament: 2 x 7pdr or 25pdr guns (2x1), 4 x 20mm guns (2x2)

Machinery: 2 diesel engines, 2 shafts

Power: 686kW/920bhp for 13.5 knots (maximum)

Fuel: 63 tons oil

Endurance: 3,183km/1,730nm at 12 knots

Protection: 50mm/2in vertical protection to magazines, engine room and conning tower; 25mm/1in to deck and control area deckheads; 6.5mm/¹⁄₄in to gun positions and compass platform

Complement: 31

LEFT: **The LCS (M) (2) was around 12m/40ft in length, and powered for a slow 9-knot speed. The sides of the hull and deckhouse were protected with 6mm/¼in steel plate.**

Landing Craft, Support (Large)/(Medium), LCS (L)/(M)

The need for close-in support fire to cover the first assault waves at the point of touchdown was evident pre-war, although it was envisaged that light automatic weapons and smoke would provide adequate cover.

Dating from 1938, the LCS (M) was simply a 41ft wooden LCA fitted with some vertical and horizontal 13mm/0.5in steel plate, and a steering position protected by the same thickness plate. In the cargo well were two pedestal-mounted 0.50in heavy machine-guns and a 4in smoke mortar. In the open hull, gunners were very exposed to enemy fire, and later a 20mm cannon with gunshield was fitted.

The Mark 2, or LCS (M) (2), was an improvement in providing an armoured deckhouse amidships on which was mounted a powered turret housing twin machine-guns. The mortar remained in the same exposed position. A final version, the LCS (M) (3), was similar except for a boat-shaped, hard-chine bow, which made little improvement to the maximum speed of the craft.

Although this Mark 3 remained in production throughout the war, the Dieppe raid proved the vessels' firepower inadequate against enemy armour. Although suitable to be transported under davits, a larger, more heavily armoured craft was obviously required.

A first attempt became the LCS (L) (1), only 1.8m/6ft longer than the LCS (M) but with the beam increased by 25 per cent. In appearance, the vessel resembled a small MTB, but was capable of only 10 knots. Mounted forward was the turret from a Daimler armoured car housing a 2pdr anti-tank gun. Aft was a square-shaped turret mounting two heavy machine-guns. Amidships protection was substantial for such a small craft.

The succeeding Mark 2 had less protection but was faster. Almost twice the size, it resembled a Fairmile "D" type, and mounted a 6pdr gun in a forward turret. Two 0.50in heavy machine-guns were mounted in a aft turret, and 20mm cannon fitted in side mountings. The wooden hull and petrol engines made the vessel vulnerable to enemy fire.

ABOVE: **This early version shows little refinement, with proper protection offered only for the helmsman. Rescue ropes with foot loops were often rigged along the sides.**

LEFT: **Sometimes dismissed as "Harry Tate's Navy", the inshore support craft matured into a formidable fighting force.**

Landing Craft, Support, LCS (L) (2)

Displacement: 84 tons (light); 116 tons (loaded)
Length: 32.04m/105ft 1in (oa)
Beam: 6.54m/21ft 5in
Draught (inshore): 0.69m/2ft 3in (forward); 0.91m/3ft (aft)
Draught (seagoing): 1.12m/3ft 8in (forward); 1.02m/3ft 4in (aft)
Armament: 1 x 6pdr gun, 2 x 20mm guns (2x1), 2 x 0.50in machine-guns (1x2), 1 x 4in mortar
Machinery: 2 petrol engines, 2 shafts
Power: 373kW/500hp for 15 knots (maximum)
Fuel: 18 tons petrol
Endurance: 1,288km/700nm at 12.5 knots
Protection: 13mm/0.5in special steel to deck, hull sides, bridge and gun positions
Complement: 25

Landing Craft, FlaK/Landing Craft, Tank (Rocket)/Landing Craft, Assault (Hedgerow), LCF/LCT (R)/LCA (HR)

Experience gained by the Royal Navy up until mid-1941 included the evacuation at Dunkirk of troops in the face of enemy air superiority. The RN had entered the war ill-prepared to meet the threat of air attack and temporary solutions were required.

The only potent long-range anti-aircraft (AA) mounting was the high-angle (HA) 4in gun which, to be effective, required director control. Air warning radar was still in its infancy and a destructive air attack often took the form of low-level passes with little or no warning. The close-range alternative, therefore, was barrage fire from numbers of automatic weapons. Excluding the ineffective 0.50in multiple-mounted heavy machine-gun, the choice was limited to the Oerlikon 20mm cannon (in very short supply) and the readily available Vickers 2pdr "Pom-Pom" gun.

June 1941 saw the commissioning of the first two Landing Craft, FlaK (LCF) converted from an LCT (2) for close support. The tank decks were covered, the space below allocated to magazines and accommodation for the gunners.

Armed with what was available, one had a twin 4in HA mounting and three single 20mm cannon. The other had eight single "Pom-Pom" guns and four single 20mm cannon. The first vessel became the forerunner to the LCS in having the firepower to attack strongpoints or enemy armour. The LCF thus continued as a type, later based on LCT (3) and (4) hulls, and were armed

ABOVE: **Modified as an LCT (R), an LCT (3) carried a load of 1,064 x 5in rockets. Fired in 24 rapid salvoes, these saturated an area of 685 x 146m/ 750 x 160yd at a fixed range of 3,200m/3,500yd.**

with a wide variation of weapon combinations. Also during 1943, the British experimented with covering an area with salvos of 5in artillery rockets, the idea being to detonate beach mines and to stun surviving enemy forces.

Six LCT (2) were fitted with a temporary upper deck to accommodate no less than 132 rocket launchers, firing projectiles each with a 13.2kg/29lb high-explosive head. With a fixed elevation of 45 degrees, theoretical range was 3,200m/3,500yd. The craft therefore had to be positioned and aligned accurately. All rockets were

LEFT: **A full salvo of 1,064 rockets being fired from an LCT (R) 125 during trials of the type in 1943.**

LEFT: **LCT (2) conversions carried only 792 rockets. Although the crew was increased to over 70, reloading took a considerable time.**

LEFT: **A profile view of an LCF (3) shows the wide distribution of the 2pdr main armament. Two 20mm cannon are mounted at the bow, and two are mounted behind the mast.**

"ripple" fired in seconds, saturating an area of 685 x 146m/750 x 160yd. One full reload was carried on board. Following the firing of the salvo, the craft was changed back to an LCT, the temporary upper deck and launchers being discarded.

The six prototypes proved valuable during the Operation "Husky" landings on Sicily, July 1943. A further number of LCT (3) were converted. These were, of course, larger and were able to carry up to 1,080 rockets, all of which had to be manually loaded.

The US military took up the idea in late 1944, using the LSM hull. Twelve interim-built craft retained the starboard

side superstructure but were fitted with an upper deck, a single 5in gun and two 40mm cannon. A full salvo of 480 rockets carried on 75 four-rail and 30 six-rail launchers could be fired in 30 seconds but it took 2½ hours to manually reload. Range was fixed at 3,685m/4,000yd.

Four further LSM (R) were each fitted with 85 improved 12-rail launchers. Range could be varied up to 4,801m/ 5,250yd by changing elevation. Firing 1,020 rockets took under a minute, but manual reloading was a lengthy operation. The "ultimate" LSM (R) arrived too late to see action (until the

Korean War), but featured launchers based on powered 40mm gun mountings, capable of being trained and elevated. The launchers were also mechanically reloaded, each twin launcher firing every 4 seconds.

The British-built "Hedgerow", or LCA (R), was a standard 13m/41.5ft craft modified to carry four rows of six "Spigot" mortars of the Hedgehog type used on anti-submarine escort ships. A 24-bomb pattern, when fired, greatly stressed even a frigate with the recoil force. An LCA suffered severely, several being sunk. The function of the LCA (R) was to blast a mine-free access across a beach, but the type was not a great success on D-Day.

ABOVE: **LCF (4) 24 moored to a buoy at a Royal Navy base on the River Clyde, Scotland, in August 1943.**

LCT (R), typical

Displacement: 640 tons (loaded)
Length: 58.56m/192ft (oa)
Beam: 9.46m/31ft
Draught: 1.04m/3ft 5in (forward); 2.03m/6ft 8in (aft)
Armament: 1,080 x 5in rocket projectiles, 2 x 2pdr or 2 x 20mm guns
Machinery: 2 diesel engines, 2 shafts
Power: 746kW/1,000bhp for 10.5 knots (maximum)
Fuel: 24 tons oil
Endurance: 4,968km/2,700nm at 9 knots
Protection: Blast reinforced wheelhouse, 6mm/¼in plate to bridge and gun positions
Complement: 51

LEFT: **Many LCI (L) built in the USA for the UK were completed as "Raiding Craft", fitted with a lower, elongated superstructure. Still retaining the portable gangways, this headquarters conversion is identified by the communications equipment.**

Landing Craft, Control/Navigational/ Headquarters (LCC/LCN/LCH)

Despite the title, these vessels were not landing craft as such, but were developed to carry the controllers of an operation. Hundreds of assault craft required marshalling into organized waves and needed to proceed, maybe in darkness and poor conditions, to the correct part of a multi-sector beach.

Exercises quickly showed the British the ease with which blocks of assault craft could become scattered, only to land at the wrong beach, with potentially disastrous consequences.

In January 1942, therefore, a number of LCP (L), now designated LCC, were fitted with extra navigational aids and, carrying specialist personnel, were used

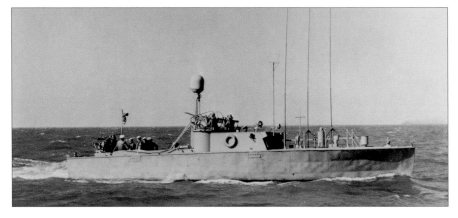

ABOVE: **Usually carried on the deck of an AKA or APA, the LCC (1) carried comprehensive communications equipment, including SO-type radar.**

to establish and mark exact start lines, as traffic control ships and to guide smaller craft. As standard Higgins boats, the LCCs quickly proved to be too small, and were replaced by the Fairmile B type, better known by the Royal Navy as Motor Launches (ML). The ML had a useful 20-knot speed and space for extra equipment, eventually including a radar "lantern" mounted on a sturdy lattice mast. The equivalent US Navy LCC, which entered service a year later, were smaller to allow transportation by AKA.

To approach close into the beach area to take a last sonar survey, act as static navigational marker or to provide smoke cover, the British Landing Craft, Navigational (LCN) was an LCP (L) conversion. The US Navy used the Landing Craft, Support (Small), or LCS (S), another modification of a Higgins boat.

The Landing Craft, Headquarters (LCH) had no direct counterpart in the US inventory. Converted from an LCI (an early version with a low-profile

superstructure), they were little changed externally except for the addition of a tall tripod mast amidships. Despite the imposing designation, the LCH was intended to act as a leader ship and communications centre for groups of larger landing craft.

ABOVE: **Converted from a Fairmile B-type Motor Launch (ML), the LCH was fitted to act as a communications vessel for large groups of landing craft. Note the winch and stern anchor.**

Landing Craft, Control (LCC), Motor Launch

Displacement: 75.5 tons (loaded)
Length: 34.16m/112ft (oa)
Beam: 65.64m/18ft 6in
Draught: 1.52m/5ft
Armament: 1 x 3pdr gun, 2 x 20mm guns (2x1), 2 x 0.50in machine-guns (1x2)
Machinery: 2 petrol engines, 2 shafts
Power: 836kW/1,120hp for 20 knots
Fuel: 10 tons petrol
Endurance: Not known
Protection: Nominal
Complement: Not known

LEFT: **All three of the Echo class moored alongside a jetty. The inshore minesweeper hull forms and the comprehensive electronics fits are obvious. Note the modern non-conformity in the shape of ships' crests mounted on the front of the bridge.**

Inshore Survey Ship, Echo class

Good hydrographic intelligence is essential to the successful planning of a major amphibious operation. To available knowledge of a prospective landing area must be added detailed data on rock ledges and offshore sandbars. Then there are the less familiar variables such as the load-bearing qualities of the beach, the exact slope, and the strength and direction of the local tidal stream and currents. To such detail the position of enemy underwater obstructions needs to be added.

The largely unknown hydrographic survey service of the Royal Navy deploys three major types of survey vessel – blue water, coastal and inshore. The last-named have hydrographic launches to extend

surveying up to the tideline, and may carry specialist teams to measure and reconnoitre the beach and beyond.

Following a landing, the service remains busy, using many techniques in common with anti-mine operations to chart obstructions in the approaches to, or in the basins of, essential ports.

World War II produced a number of improvised modifications which, by the 1950s, were being replaced by purpose-built ships. The inshore flotilla comprised three ships (HMS *Echo*, *Egeria* and *Enterprise*), which were built using the well-proven hull design of the Ham-class Inshore Minesweeper (IMS). To these were quickly added two more ships, HMS *Powderham* and HMS *Yaxham*, which later became HMS *Waterwitch* and HMS *Woodlark*

respectively, having been converted to the same high standard. All were commissioned between 1958 and 1959.

The large single block superstructure was devoted largely to the hydrographic office. At the rear of this, two short posts supported exhausts for the diesel engines, acting also as derrick supports for the survey launch. Sweep gear for checking the depth of obstructions occupied the space in the stern.

The Echo class had an open bridge and lattice mast. The Waterwitch type had an enclosed bridge with tripod mast. All were disposed of during the 1980s in favour of chartered commercial craft.

LEFT: **The modified sweep gear aft was not for minesweeping but for checking the depth of water over obstructions. The echo-sounding launch was a valuable auxiliary close inshore.**

Inshore Survey Ship, Echo class	

Displacement: 120 tons (standard); 160 tons (loaded)
Length: 32.57m/106ft 9in (oa)
Beam: 6.71m/22ft
Draught: 1.9m/6ft 3in
Armament: Usually unarmed; fitted with 1 x 40mm gun
Machinery: 2 diesel engines, 2 shafts
Power: 1,044kW/1,400bhp for 14 knots
Fuel: 15 tons oil
Endurance: 2,944km/1,600nm at 10 knots
Protection: None
Complement: 18–22

LEFT: **Some of the 1,000 Motor Minesweepers built were assembled in shipyards as far away as the Bahamas, Canada and Cochin (India).**

Inshore Motor Minesweepers (MMS/BYMS/IMS/CMS)

Badly run down after 1918, the minesweeping force of the Royal Navy was in poor shape by 1939. In larger "Fleet" minesweepers, numbers were reasonably adequate, the veteran "Smokey Joe" Hunt-class ships complemented by the new Bangor and Halcyon-class ships. Of the smaller specialist craft, however, there was an absence, it being assumed that, as in the previous war, a force could be created from requisitioned commercial trawlers and skilled crews. Britain, in the event, was faced with a starvation blockade, and many trawlers were required to carry on fishing in the interests of feeding the population. The shortage of auxiliary minesweepers was so desperate that even paddle steamers, typically associated with seaside resorts, were pressed into service.

More was required. The Germans used destroyers, E-boats and aircraft to lay mines in vital coastal shipping areas. These were technically advanced types, at first magnetic, later acoustic. Unexploded examples were collected for examination by eight drifters of the Mine Recovery Flotilla.

With the secrets of the magnetic mine revealed, several important programmes were initiated. The first was to "degauss" or "wipe" steel ships to reduce the magnetic signature. A second saw several east coast colliers converted to "mine bumpers", or Mine Destructor Ships, the forward cargo space carrying enormous electro-magnets. These certainly worked, but with the probabilty of serious damage to the ship and the crew.

The long-term solution, however, was the Double L (LL) sweep, whose two parallel cables were towed by drifters. Many more ships were, nonetheless, required and, for safety, these were to be constructed from wood.

ABOVE: **The hull of the "Mickey Mouse" was built from wood in yards specializing in fishing vessels. At the bow is the Kango-type anti-acoustic mine hammer. The A-frame pivoted downward.**
LEFT: **Two "Big Mickeys" moored alongside the quay in a Royal Navy yard. The class was numbered from 1001 to 1090.**

LEFT: **Hardly had the last wood-built types of World War II been disposed of than the outbreak of the Korean War triggered a huge new building programme for Coastal and Inshore Minesweepers. Many saw little or no service. HMS *Aveley* is an IMS in Royal Navy service.**

An order for 50 "cheap" 105ft motor minesweepers was mentioned as early as January 1940, together with a larger and faster (12-knot) variant capable of sweeping ahead of convoys. These materialized as 38.4m/126ft craft but with no extra speed. Both types were termed Motor Minesweepers (MMS), differentiated popularly as "Mickey Mice" and "Big Mickeys". The essential features of both were the large LL-type cable drum abaft the superstructure and an A-frame at the bows carrying a Kango-type hammer for the anti-acoustic mine equipment.

The first and follow-up orders for the 105ft type were shared among no less than 24 home and 25 overseas shipyards, the latter from the Bahamas to Beirut and from Canada to Cochin (India). The 126ft class had a small funnel and a raised forecastle in place of the steep bow on smaller ships.

As an example of the type's value and application to amphibious warfare, the prologue to the Normandy landings was the overnight creation of six safe cross-channel shipping lanes, each of some 80km/50 miles long, and 914–1,280m/ 1,000–1,400yd wide. Involved were 48 Fleet minesweepers, 42 MMSs and 45 trawlers, with specially fitted Motor Launches (ML) working close inshore.

The US Navy's equivalent programme was for the so-called Yard Minesweepers (YMS), which were of very similar dimensions to the "Big Mickey", and also built of wood. Many were transferred to the Royal Navy under the Lend-Lease Progam and, when lightly modified, known as BYMS. The type had twice the engine power of the 10-knot MMS, being capable of 10 knots. The BYMS were identifiable by a single large funnel. US Navy-operated examples had two, one or no funnels.

By 1950, with only 24 various MMSs and 10 BYMSs (due to be returned to the US) in Royal Navy service, the Korean War began. This alerted the UN forces to the threat of a Soviet-backed mining campaign.

The response included programmes for building 100 Coastal Minesweepers.

ABOVE: **HMS *Brinkley* was one of nine "M2001" vessels which differed from the other 80 vessels in the class in having wood-on-aluminium frame construction. The ships were painted black when being used as special diving tenders by the Royal Navy.**

Inshore Motor Minesweeper, 105ft MMS

Displacement: 163 tons (standard); 255 tons (loaded)
Length: 36.3m/119ft (oa)
Beam: 7.02m/23ft
Draught: 2.9m/9ft 6in
Armament: 2 x 20mm guns (2x1), 2 x smaller
Machinery: 1 diesel engine, single shaft
Power: Variable, between 205–373kW/ 275–500bhp for 10 knots (maximum)
Fuel: 22 tons oil
Endurance: Not known
Protection: None
Complement: 20

Griffon Hovercraft (LCAC)

ABOVE: **A Griffon 2000TD in service with the Royal Marines arriving on a beach in Basra, Iraq.**

For nearly 50 years, the hovercraft has been a mechanical principle looking for a useful application. A vehicle that can negotiate water, ice, swamp, foreshore or rapids, all with equal ease, must be useful. It was extensively trialled by US forces in Vietnam, where humidity and mud caused very demanding maintenance schedules. Exceedingly noisy, the general verdict was that, whatever the type was used for, a helicopter was better suited. The LCAC has, however, proved to be valuable, spearhead assault being left to helicopter-borne forces.

Smaller hovercraft have been considerably quietened by using a diesel engine and slower-turning, variable pitch airscrews. British special forces operate a number of Griffons alongside high-speed "fast transport craft". The latter are 45-plus-knot power boats, faster than the hovercraft in most conditions, but with smaller payload and less space.

The hovercraft's advantage is that it is, essentially, a floating raft. The cabin top, enclosing accommodation for 16 troops, may be removed to leave an open platform for loads of up to 2 tons. The strength of this type of vehicle really resides in that of the imagination of the people using them. It is of note that the Royal Marines have requested funding for larger versions, which would appear to be a small version of the LCAC, but able to carry troops as well as vehicles.

At the same time, larger Fast Transport Craft (FTC) are being sought, reportedly capable of maintaining 45 knots in Sea State 4 while carrying ten equipped troops or up to 2.5 tons of equipment.

LEFT: **An advantage of the hovercraft is that it is essentially a floating platform that can be left open for cargo-carrying or enclosed for personnel.**

Griffon Hovercraft (LCAC), Type 2000 TDX (M)

Weight/displacement: 6.75 tons (loaded)
Length: 11.04m/36ft 3in
Beam: 4.6m/15ft 1in; 5.79m/19ft (skirt inflated)
Draught (in rafting mode): 0.52m/1ft 9in
Armament: Not usually armed
Machinery: 1 diesel engine
Power: 265kW/355bhp for 40 knots, or 25 knots in Sea State 3
Fuel: 0.25 ton oil
Endurance: 522km/300nm at 40 knots
Protection: None
Complement: 2
Capacity: 16 troops, or 2 tons equipment

Landing Craft, Tank (EDIC/CDIC)

Until the commissioning of a French-designed class during the early 1960s, the French Navy operated LCT (4) built by the British in World War II. The new craft were of identical size to an LCT (4). The Ouragan-class LSDs, which were being constructed at the same time, were designed to carry two of the type.

Typically, the French have their own categorization, the craft being EDICs (*Engins de Débarquement d'Infanterie et de Chars*), i.e. craft for landing troops or tanks. Identified initially as EDIC 1-10, confusingly L9000 numbers were used in the series still carried by surviving British-built LCT (4).

Most EDIC vessels were flush-decked. Masts, tetrapod or lattice were located adjacent to the funnel casing. The loading ramp folded in two sections for extra length and appeared to be assisted in operation by a set of light sheerlegs.

From the mid-1970s, the class was reduced by scrappings and sales abroad, the retirements heralding the construction of a new type, again of similar dimensions. Only four, however, were completed for the French Navy. Two in 1988, later taking the names FS *Rapière* and FS *Hallebarde*, were designed specifically to fit in the docking well of the Foudre-class LSD, then under construction. Of orthodox

layout, the new craft had a low superstructure and folding mast. Although of similar size and function to the earlier type, all were termed CDIC, "C" representing *Chaland* (barge).

The two sister ships, completed first, were of modified layout, differing externally in a higher superstructure and a hydraulic crane forward. Later named FS *Sabre* and FS *Dague*, both were fitted for tropical service, and deployed to Tahiti and Djibouti respectively. Known perversely as EDIC II, or EDIC 700s, the type also attracted export orders for Senegal and Lebanon.

Landing Craft, Tank (CDIC)

Displacement: 750 tons (loaded)
Length: 59.4m/195ft (oa)
Beam: 11.9m/39ft
Draught (beaching): 1.1m/3ft 7in (forward); 1.76m/5ft 9in (aft)
Armament: 2 x 20mm guns (2x1)
Machinery: 2 diesel engines, 2 shafts
Power: 806kW/1,080bhp for 11 knots (maximum)
Fuel: 20 tons oil
Endurance: Provisions for 15 days, or 5,960km/3,250nm at 9 knots
Protection: Nominal
Complement: 18

ABOVE: **An *Engin de Débarquement d'Infanterie et de Chars* (EDIC) could carry 350 tons of cargo. Here, in ideal conditions, the vessel is beached in a light swell.**

LEFT: **CTM 1**, the first of the type, was built from steel and entered service in 1965. On March 31, 1982, the vessel was scrapped after 17 years usage with the French Navy. **CTM 29**, *Nué Dho*, built from aluminium alloy, was delivered on June 23, 1988, and remains in service.

Landing Craft, Medium, CTM/LCM (8)

The general-purpose LCM (8) began to enter US service around 1949. Because the steel-built Mod. 1 weighed 56 tons unloaded, it was complemented by the 34-ton aluminium-alloy hulled Mod. 2, light enough to be carried aboard some AKAs.

For such an apparently simple craft, the LCM (8) caused considerable design problems. The 22.4m/73ft 6in length was quite critical to safe trim, the designed working load being that of a main battle tank of the time. To reduce resistance, the ramp was stowed at the unusually shallow angle of 35 degrees to the horizontal. Further variants showed the difficulty of deciding between the economy and robustness of steel (Mods. 1, 3 and 5) and the lightness, greater expense and relative fragility of aluminium alloy (Mods. 2 and 4).

The French built 16 steel-hulled LCM (8) under licence during 1966 and 1967. Known as CTM (*Chalands de Transport de Matériel*), they were reportedly capable of carrying 90 tons. This corresponded to a full load of around 150 tons, whereas the US Navy rated their craft, both steel and alloy, at around 60 tons, with full-load figures of 116 and 121 tons respectively. A further identical 15 CTMs were built between 1982 and 1992, during which time the earlier craft were disposed of mainly by transfer to friendly states, where five of the type still serve. Numbered CTM 17 to 31, many of the later craft have since been given Vietnamese themed names.

The CTMs, although with limited remaining service life, are the preferred craft for the new Mistral-class LH which, alternatively, can carry a single CDIC. No less than ten CTMs could be loaded on a Foudre-class LSD. The docking well on the Mistral class is designed to carry two US-built LCACs and can only carry four CTMs.

ABOVE: **Designated *Chalands de Transport de Matériel* (CTM), the type first entered service in 1965. CTM 21 *Guéréo* is one of the second series built between 1982 and 1992.**

Landing Craft, Medium, CTM/LCM (8)

Displacement: 150 tons (loaded)
Length: 23.4m/73ft 6in (oa)
Beam: 6.35m/20ft 10in
Draught: 1.25m/4ft 1in (beaching)
Armament: 2 x single 0.50in machine-guns can be fitted
Machinery: 2 diesel engines, 2 shafts
Power: 336kW/450bhp for 9.5 knots (maximum)
Fuel: 3.4 tons oil
Endurance: 736km/400nm at 8 knots
Protection: Nominal
Complement: 4
Capacity: 90 tons

ABOVE AND LEFT: **Ever more sophisticated, mines are increasingly required to be identified and destroyed manually. The Vulcain-class tenders were designed to support 12 clearance divers and two medical personnel.**

Mine Countermeasures Divers' Tenders, Vulcain class

To create and maintain a mine-free route, it is necessary first to conduct a thorough survey, followed by the removal of all obstructions. A final survey then provides a datum condition, recorded by a combination of high-definition sonar backed by considerable computer capacity. All remaining features being thus accurately defined, it is a relatively simple task to keep the route open, with electronics immediately indicating any new obstructions on the seabed.

Before any major operation, such procedures would be followed only as far as practicality allowed. The operations

BELOW: **FS *Vulcain* has a clear afterdeck with a 5-ton capacity crane. The gap between the funnels suggests the location of the decompression chamber.**

are now conducted on a regular basis to guarantee safe routes for ballistic missile submarines needing to transit the relatively shallow continental shelf waters separating their base from the open sea. In addition to mines, active or passive, uninvestigated objects en route might also comprise devices to monitor ship movements and to record the radiated noise characteristics of a specific craft.

Clearance work is demanding, involving teams of divers or specialist Unmanned Underwater Vehicles (UUV) to investigate and, probably, remove each unknown object. Diving teams and their equipment are too space-consuming to be accommodated aboard a standard MCSO. The first vessels modified for the task were ex-US Navy MSCs.

In 1980, a thorough trial conversion was made of the French auxiliary vessel FS *Isard*. This defined the necessary accommodation required, including a decompression chamber, lifting gear, ROV, small craft and helicopter spot.

The requirements established the design for the four Vulcain-class ships ordered in 1984 and based on the hull of *Isard*. This features a short, raised forecastle and a long amidships block incorporating accommodation. A two-man decompression chamber, rated to a 150m/492ft depth, is carried. The clear afterdeck has a 5-ton SWL hydraulic crane, used for recovery work or handling small craft and ROV/AUVs.

Mine Countermeasures Divers' Tenders, Vulcain class

Displacement: 409 tons (standard); 490 tons (loaded)
Length: 36.96m/121ft 4in (bp); 41.6m/136ft 6in (oa)
Beam: 7.5m/24ft 7in
Draught: 3.2m/10ft 6in
Armament: 1/2 x 0.50in machine-guns can be fitted
Machinery: 2 diesel engines, 2 shafts
Power: 1,641kW/2,200bhp for 13.5 knots (maximum)
Fuel: 90 tons oil
Endurance: 5,244km/2,850nm at 13.5 knots
Protection: Nominal
Complement: 15 plus 12 divers and 2 medical personnel

LEFT: **Working with a Eurocopter Panther, the dayshapes for a vessel with restricted manoeuvrability are carried on the mast of FS *Antarès*. Note the two sonar towfish stowed on the starboard side of the afterdeck, with two Oropesa floats to port.**

Mine route survey craft, Antarès class

The three ships in this class complement the Vulcain-class diving tender in being the vessels used to survey proposed mine-free routes. For this role they are equipped with a comprehensive range of aids and, for the size of the vessel, a large crew.

Adequate working space was a design requisite, solved by the adoption of a trawler-style hull already used successfully for the Glycine-class navigational training vessel. The high-freeboard hull has a long forecastle and a low working deck aft, largely enclosed by high bulwarks. The large deckhouse incorporates a wheelhouse and navigation facilities.

The main electronics system is currently a DUBM-41B sidescan sonar, a high-frequency, high-definition, short-range set operating at 500 kHz. The towfish can be utlized at up to 10 knots and will scan up to 200m/656ft either side of the ship's track, in depths of up to 80m/262ft. Unusually, the towfish is stabilized using Oropesa-type floats more often associated with "traditional" minesweeping. The vessels are also fitted for the very similar task of streaming a sweep wire to define water depth over large obstructions. The stern carries two light cranes, floats and sweep gear, standard fitments on a minehunter.

Search results are input to a specialized Syledis route-recording system, which produces the baseline route condition against which all subsequent scans are compared. The ships have inherited the deep draught and relatively large-diameter propeller of the trawler. A bow thruster is fitted, but such a device is primarily an aid to low-speed manoeuvring, having little effect when a ship has significant forward speed. The ships are also used for offshore patrol.

RIGHT: **The hull of the FS *Altair* shows a distinctive trawler origin. The same trawler-style hull was successfully used on the Glycine-class navigational training ships.**

Mine route survey craft, Antarès class

Displacement: 295 tons (standard); 340 tons (loaded)
Length: 28.3m/92ft 9in (oa)
Beam: 7.7m/25ft 3in
Draught: 3.8m/12ft 6in (maximum)
Armament: 1 x 0.50in machine-gun
Machinery: 1 diesel engine, single shaft
Power: 597kW/800bhp for 10 knots
Fuel: 50 tons oil
Endurance: 6,624km/3,600nm at 10 knots
Protection: None
Complement: 24

Inshore Minesweepers (IMS), Yevgenya/Lida class

ABOVE: A Lida-class inshore minesweeper, known to the Russian Navy as the Sapfir class. The glass-reinforced plastic (GRP) hull has a slightly arched appearance aft. The usual degaussing girdle is not fitted.

Although expert in mine warfare, the Russian Navy is vulnerable, and has produced many types of countermeasures vessel for both defensive and offensive operations.

With Inshore Minesweepers (IMS), the then Soviet Union followed the West in adopting glass-reinforced plastic (GRP) as a non-magnetic and easily repairable building material. The first product of a new facility at Kolpino, near Leningrad, was a series of some 90 Korund-class minehunters, built between 1969 and 1985, and known in the West as Yevgenya.

The hull had a pleasing sheerline, with a low-forward bulwark to improve dryness. A single-block superstructure had accommodation for the entire crew. The relatively spacious afterdeck allowed deployment of sweep gear for all usual types of mine. Several crew members were clearance divers, and used follow-up markers dropped by a television-guided ROV.

Designated as Roadstead Minesweepers, the Yevgenya class was equipped with a small high-frequency dipping sonar for the detection of hostile Unmanned Underwater Vehicles (UUV). Explosive charges were carried to attack such types.

All the Yevgenya class were retired by 2005, having been superseded by the Sapfir type (codenamed Lida).

Similar in layout and appearance to the earlier craft, the Lida class are, nonetheless, almost 9m/29ft longer and proportionately wider. The earlier pole mast was replaced by a tripod type, but the major external difference is the helmet-type mounting for a 30mm Gatling-type gun in place of the original twin 25mm weapon mount.

On-board equipment is largely updated versions of those on the Yevgenya class, with the addition of removable rails for inshore minelaying. Intended mainly for export, the class appears to have been terminated in 1996.

ABOVE: This Sapfir class (codenamed Lida) is fitted with the normal degaussing girdle around the deck edge. The common practice of painting the after hull to disguise exhaust stains has been used.

Inshore Minesweepers (IMS), Lida class

Displacement: 135 tons (loaded)
Length: 31.45m/103ft 1in (oa)
Beam: 6.5m/18ft 7in
Draught: 1.58m/5ft 2in
Armament: 1 x 30mm Gatling-type gun, shoulder-launched SAMs, mines
Machinery: 3 diesel engines, 3 shafts
Power: 671kW/900bhp for 12.5 knots
Fuel: Not known
Endurance: 736km/400nm at 10 knots
Protection: Nominal
Complement: 14

Landing Craft, Air Cushion (LCAC)

The Russian equivalent to Marines are the Naval Infantry. During World War II, the force were shown to be adept at using the sea for outflanking movements or conducting numerous raids. Post-war, the amphibious element of the Soviet Navy was, for long, somewhat neglected, as the emphasis was placed on defensive measures. This was mainly to counter the threat of major landings by the West's powerful amphibious fleets covered by battle-tested carrier and surface support groups. Hundreds of missile-armed minor warships of numerous classes were built over the years, the aim being to swamp the defences of an amphibious attack with sheer numbers. Most of these types had conventional planing or semi-planing hulls, but hydrofoils were also used. The more recent is the Dergach, a rigid sidewall surface effect vessel.

Air cushion craft go back rather further in the amphibious force, which saw much improved funding from the late 1960s. Innovation produced three major similar designs during the 1970s: the Gus, Aist and Lebed. Since then, however, the only significant new design has been the Zubr class (NATO codename Pomornik) of the early 1990s.

Similar to an enlarged British-built SRN6, the 27-ton (loaded) Gus is capable of transporting 24 equipped troops at around 50 knots, and equates to a personnel-only assault landing craft. A canopy may or may not be fitted over the personnel section. In having to uses ladders to disembark, troops are vulnerable. Around 32 Gus types were reportedly built between 1969 and 1976. Any craft remaining in service are most likely to be used in the training role.

The Aist class, of which 18 are believed to have entered service between 1970 and 1985, is similar to the

ABOVE: **The Zubr class (NATO reporting name Pomornik) is a joint Russian and Ukranian design, and is the largest LCAC in operational use.**

British-built BH7, but again larger. The class was tested extensively for use in mine countermeasures, and proved not only to have an almost undectable signature but also to be relatively immune to mine explosion. Large, the type is fitted with a ramp at each

ABOVE: **The Zubr class is powered by five Kuznetsov MT-70 gas-turbine engines, two for lift and three for propulsion. The type has been in service with the navies of Russia, Ukraine and Greece.**

LEFT: In the same class as a US Navy LCAC, the Lebed type entered service in 1975. The 20 built were powered by MT-70 gas-turbine engines for lift and to drive the two four-bladed variable-pitch propellors. By 2005, only three remained in service with the Russian Navy.

end and has a 74-ton cargo capacity. Alternatively, around 220 troops can be transported for over 322km/200 miles at 40 knots. A small number of the Aist class are belived to remain operational.

A Lebed class, dating from 1982 to 1985, is half the size of an Aist class and has a bow ramp only. More compact in appearance, four pylon-mounted, open airscrews have been changed to two quieter ducted units. Although capable of transporting 35 tons of cargo or 120 troops at 45 knots, all of the class have been retired.

At 550 tons loaded, the Zubr class is by far the largest air cushion assault craft in the Russian inventory, and only three, already over 15 years old, appear to be operational. Four further vessels have reportedly been sold for commercial use. The Zubr class has a flat-topped, rectangular-section central hull with a ramp at each end. This "cargo compartment" is bordered by two low side decks which form the tops of the wing compartments. The very spacious upper surfaces appear under-used due to limited weight restrictions. The solid, two-level

bridge structure supports the fire directors for two 30mm Gatling-type guns. Near the bow, two multi-rail rocket barrage launchers are mounted. The major feature on the Zubr, however, is the row of three ducted airscrews which produce directional thrust for steering, rather than conventional rudders.

None of the current Russian designs appear to have progressed beyond the experimental stage, being unsuitable for series production. From the design aspect, the capacious box-shaped hulls offer little inherent stiffness and are very liable to vibration problems. Weight was critical, requiring the use of aluminium-alloy hull components.

ABOVE. **Russian Naval Infantry coming ashore from a Zubr-class LCAC during an exercise on the Baltic coast.**
BELOW: **With ramps forward and aft, the Aist class superficially resembles the earlier British-built BH7.**

Landing Craft, Air Cushion (LCAC), Zubr class

Displacement: 340 tons (light); 550 tons (loaded)
Length: 57.3m/187ft 10in (oa)
Width: 25.6m/83ft 11in
Draught: N/A
Armament: 2 x quadruple SA-N-8 ("Gremlin") SAM launchers, 2 x 30mm Gatling-type guns, 2 x 22-round barrage rocket launchers
Machinery: 5 gas turbines; 2 for lift fans, 3 for propulsion
Power: 45,133kW/60,500hp for 63 knots (maximum); 37,300kW/50,000hp for 55 knots (sustained)
Fuel: 56 tons kerosene
Endurance: 552km/300nm at 55 knots (loaded)
Protection: Nominal
Complement: 31
Capacity: Up to 36 troops, or 10 LVTs, or 3 main battle tanks

Landing Craft, Medium (LCM), Ondatra/Serna class

ABOVE: **Twenty-nine Ondatra-class LCMs are known to have been built from 1979 to serve with Ivan Rogov-class LSDs. Only one of the latter remains in service, and most of the LCMs have been scrapped.**

Around 80 T-4-type LCMs were built between 1968 and 1974. Pre-dating LSDs in the then Soviet fleet, their dimensions of 20.4 x 5.4m/66ft 10in x 17ft 8in were based on lifting 50 tons. The size was somewhat less than that of the LCM (8) in US Navy service, which can carry 60 tons on 22.43 x 6.43m/73ft 6in x 21ft 1in. Reportedly, the T-4 can make 10 knots in light condition with an installed power of only 300bhp. This speed is unattainable by an LCM (8) with 1,080bhp.

The T-4s were starkly rectangular, lacking sheer or flare, but the Ondatra class that superseded the T-4 between 1979 and 1991 has a slight forward sheer, emphasized by the deeper coamings, which also acts as an upper support for the longer ramp. Dimensions of the T-4 allow six to be carried in the docking well of an Ivan Rogov-class vessel.

Apparently undergoing long evaluation is the Serna-type fast LCM, a private venture craft available on the open market. With a 50-ton load capacity, this 25.65m/84ft craft has a semi-planing, wave-piercing hull the underside of which is an air cavity, a principle similar to that which the US military proposed for the fast LCU 1682 class, which was cancelled in 2006. The contained air cushion may provide some upthrust, but is primarily to reduce suction between hull and water, permitting the craft to plane with relatively low engine power. Once on the plane, wavemaking resistance drops considerably, while the significant decrease in draught (some 14 per cent) reduces wetted area and lowers skin resistance. Also of light alloy construction, the craft is claimed to be able to make 30 knots with only 2,462kW/3,300bhp of engine power. Speed is emphasized by the raked-back styling, the hull sides being full depth and lacking the usual narrow side decks outside a deep coaming.

Landing Craft, Medium (LCM), Ondatra class

Displacement: 107 tons (loaded)
Length: 24.5m/80ft 4in (oa)
Beam: 6m/19ft 8in
Draught: 1.55m/5ft 1in
Armament: None
Machinery: 2 diesel engines, 2 shafts
Power: 448kW/600bhp at 11 knots
Fuel: Not known
Endurance: 505km/275mm at 10 knots
Protection: Nominal
Complement: 5
Capacity: 1 x 40-ton vehicle, or 50 tons distributed cargo

ABOVE: **The Serna-class fast LCM is being evaluated by the Russian Navy. The vessel, which was developed as a private venture, is capable of 30 knots when loaded.**

ABOVE: **The 10m Shohatsu type could accommodate 35 troops.** LEFT: **Attrition rates in small assault craft were always high. A stranded steel-built 14m Daihatsu shows the main features. Note the characteristic continuous sheerline.**

Landing Craft, Tank (LCT), Daihatsu types

Extended operations in China during the 1930s saw the Imperial Japanese Army identify the need for a craft capable of landing personnel, artillery and vehicles "over the beach". Certainly uninfluenced by early British trials in this direction, the Daihatsu was produced to serve as the landing craft aboard the *Shinshu Maru*. Such craft appeared subsequently aboard a range of Japanese merchant vessels which had been converted to transport and attack cargo ships.

"Daihatsu" refers incorrectly but conveniently to a series of craft. Built in vast numbers, most were 14m and 17m craft. With the shortage of steel from 1944, the wooden 15m craft was built. More rarely 10m and 13m craft were encountered.

The design owed much to traditional Japanese working craft, and was completely open except for a protective shield in front of the helmsman. The hull had a continuous sheerline, with a flat cargo/vehicle deck, a short forward ramp and rounded stern. Usually loaded alongside larger vessels, the sides were protected by heavy rubbing strakes. The Daihatsu type was powered by a variety of engines and proved to be the lifeline of Japanese island garrisons, particularly in the bitterly disputed Solomons.

Only the 14m and 17m vessels can really be considered LCTs. The Pacific theatre was ill-suited to tank warfare, the Japanese using mainly the manoeuvrable Type 95 KE-GO light tank, which was easily transported on the 14m craft. With the arrival of the US-built Sherman, the Type 97 CHI-HA became more common. A medium tank, it was transportable only on a 17m Daihatsu.

Also worth mentioning was the so-named Umpoto-powered pontoon, a three-sectioned raft supported on two longitudinal submerged metal buoyancy tanks fitted with de-rated torpedo motors. The 21 x 4m/70 x 14ft craft carried 15 tons of cargo, was virtually silent and had a low silhouette.

ABOVE: **So uncoordinated were Allied forces opposing them that the Japanese were able to rapidly overrun much of the Far East. Recapturing the taken land and islands would take a long time.**

Landing Craft, Tank (LCT), Daihatsu types ●

	Displacement (light) tons	Length (oa)	Beam	Draught (mean)	Speed (knots)
10m type	6.5	10.6m/34ft 9in	2.44m/8ft	0.58m/1ft 11in	7.5
13m type	16	13m/42ft 8in	2.9m/9ft 6in	0.79m/2ft 7in	8
14m type	21/22	14.57m/47ft 10in	3.36m/11ft	0.76m/2ft 6in	7.5–8.5
15m type	17.5	15m/49ft 2in	3.63m/11ft 10in	0.53m/1ft 9in	8
17m type	33/38	17.61m/57ft 9in	3.71m/21ft 2in	1m/3ft 3in	8–10

Mine Countermeasures Drones and Control Ship

TOP AND ABOVE: **Designed and built in Sweden, these Self-propelled Acoustic, Magnetic (SAM) drones are in service with the Japanese Navy.**

Because of the increasing intelligence and lethality of modern mines, techniques for surveying by Autonomous Underwater Vehicles (AUV) and investigation/demolition by Remotely Controlled Vehicles (ROV) are evolving continuously. Swept channels, or areas designated for search, can be marked inconspicuously with transponders laid by swimmers. Such devices transmit only when signalled, and will be used only when simpler means do not suit the nature of the operation. By "simpler means" it would usually imply visual markers, i.e. moored buoys. Most visual among these is the simple Dan buoy, as used on fishing craft over the centuries.

In the suspected presence of mines, Dan buoy-laying is as hazardous as any activity and, during the early 1980s, the Swedish Navy developed the Self-propelled Acoustic, Magnetic (SAM) craft to both sweep and mark clear channels under remote control. Japan acquired six SAMs, which are used in pairs from the converted Hatsushima-class minehunters *Kamishima* (MCL 724) and *Himeshima* (MCL 725). In calm conditions at least, paired drones are transported to the area of operation by being secured alongside the parent ship, rather than being towed.

The drones comprise a rectangular, non-magnetic platform which is supported clear of the surface by two longitudinal, cylindrical buoyancy tanks. The tanks are inflated and, being flexible, are virtually immune to mine explosions. The shock wave of an explosion will expend much of its energy by momentarily deforming the cylinders, little being transmitted to the platform.

A rectangular cabin on the raft houses acoustic equipment, power generators and the diesel engine which drives the single Schottel azimuth unit. The shrouded propeller may be swiveled through almost 360 degrees. Eight Dan buoys, each with a radar reflector, are racked across the stern and are released by remote command.

ABOVE: **A Hatsushima-class minehunter operating as control ship for SAM drones, which are used in pairs to sweep and clear channels.**

Mine Countermeasures Drones and Control Ship

Displacement: 20 tons (loaded)
Length: 18m/59ft 1in (oa)
Beam: 6.1m/20ft
Draught: 0.7m/2ft 3in; propeller extends to 1.6m/5ft 3in
Armament: None
Machinery: 1 diesel engine driving Schottel azimuth thruster
Power: 157kW/210bhp for 8 knots
Fuel: Not known
Endurance: 607km/330nm at 7 knots
Protection: None
Complement: None

Landing Craft, Utility (LCU), Yura and 1-go class

Landing Craft, Utility (LCU) have replaced the older Landing Craft, Tank (LCT), the different designation reflecting greater flexibility. War-designed craft are intended for cheap and rapid series production, where parameters hold higher priority than hydrodynamic efficiency. Peacetime standards, however, allow for hulls of improved shape, but at the expense of more components requiring complex curvature. This, coupled with higher power, enables current Japanese LCUs to make 12 knots. This may not appear a very impressive increase over the 10–10.5 knots of the original LCTs but, for this type of hull, it represents considerable improvement.

The JMSDF currently operates just four LCUs. The first two, ambitiously labelled Landing Ship, Utility (LSU),

also take landing ships' 4,000-series numbers. Of a late 1970s design, they are the *Yura* (4171) and *Noto* (4172). Despite being classed as "ships" (as opposed to "craft"), both feature an open vehicle deck and are single-ended. The usual high forecastle supports the ramp and two clamshell-type outer doors. Although there is no upper deck, accommodation is provided for 70 troops. This does necessitate a relatively large superstructure. The Osumi-class LSDs, designed to carry two LCACs, thus cannot accept a Yura-type LCU, which is some 4m/13ft longer in total, and has too much height.

The new 1-go class, designated LCU 2001 and LCU 2002, were built between 1988 and 1992, and are

ABOVE: LCU 2002, a 1-go class of the JMSDF about to land during an earthquake relief exercise at Yokosuka on September 1, 2008. In the background is USS *Essex* (LHD-2), which was also involved in the exercise.

more compact than the Yura-class vessel. Some 6m/20ft shorter overall, the type has no forecastle, the ramp being stowed at a much shallower angle and without outer doors. A permanent light full-width gantry is used when operating the ramp. Without accommodation for troops, the superstructure on the vessel is one level lower. Air draught is reduced further by folding masts.

Landing Craft, Utility (LCU), 1-go class

Displacement: 420 tons
Length: 52m/170ft 8in (oa)
Beam: 8.7m/28ft 6in
Draught: 1.6m/5ft 3in (aft, beaching)
Armament: 1 x 20mm Gatling-type gun
Machinery: 2 diesel engines, 2 shafts
Power: 2,238kW/3,000bhp for 12 knots
Fuel: Not known
Endurance: Not known
Protection: Nominal
Complement: 28

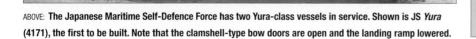

ABOVE: The Japanese Maritime Self-Defence Force has two Yura-class vessels in service. Shown is JS *Yura* (4171), the first to be built. Note that the clamshell-type bow doors are open and the landing ramp lowered.

Siebel Ferries and F-lighters (MFP)

Until the surprise demand to mount the eventually aborted Operation "Sealion", the *Wehrmacht* had been concerned only with water crossings no larger than those of the major European rivers. Assault crossings were spearheaded in *Sturmboote* (assault boats), propelled by an outboard motor and transported by road. On the assumption that bridges would be either destroyed or outflanked, powered pontoons were developed to follow up with vehicles and heavy equipment. These broke down into road-transportable modules, and were assembled on site.

The "Sealion" exercise had graphically demonstrated the need for specialist craft if larger-scale operations were ever to be considered. If the Germans had any knowledge of British experiments with assault landing craft, it is not obvious by their response, which was highly individual. As a matter of some urgency, two types of craft were produced, both of which were subject to much variation.

The first, the Siebel Ferry, was credited to Wilhelm Siebel, a future aircraft designer who, at that time, served as a major in the *Luftwaffe* reserve. Like most good ideas, his

ABOVE: **Note the very shallow vehicle deck on the MFP, the upswept sheerline and the lack of means by which troops could leave the upper deck.**
BELOW: **A damaged and disarmed F-lighter. The long arch of the coamings stiffened the shallow hull with minimum addition to weight. The bow ramp is in the closed position.**

was simple, using two sets of existing pontoons in parallel, and bridging both with a flat vehicle deck to form a large and very stable catamaran. Simplicity was everything, and the ramps were removable, to be attached by man-power for loading and discharge, a weak point in the face of an opposed landing. A wide ramp gave forward access for larger vehicles. Smaller vehicles could pass either side of the aft-located superstructure to use quarter ramps. The superstructure was no more than a protected wheelhouse flanked by platforms, usually for quadruple 20mm FlaK mountings.

Called a *Heeres-Transport-Fähre*, the Siebel Ferry could lift around 230 tons. When assembled, the vessel measured 32.3m x 14.7m/106ft x 48ft. The ungainly shaped vessel could travel at a creditable 10 knots, powered by four 620hp diesel engines. Readily transportable, the Siebel Ferry was deployed on coastal and inland waters anywhere from Lake Ladoga, near St. Petersburg, to the Caspian Sea. Defensive firepower, augmented by that of vehicles and artillery carried on deck, could be formidable.

The name *Marinefahrprähme* (MFP) indicated the role of a seagoing lighter, but the Allied forces that regularly encountered the type referred to them

simply as "F", or "FlaK" Lighters. The type resembled an LCT, but with an enclosed vehicle deck and unobstructed side decks fitted with minelaying rails. The hull was, of course, shallow and, to achieve the required headroom on the vehicle deck, high coamings to the hull were necessary. The line of these sloped down at the forward end, meeting at the bows with the upswept forward sheer of the hull. The overall effect was to give the vessel a strange humped profile. The square bows supported protective doors and a short ramp that, when in use, usually required an extension. During load and discharge of vehicles, the forward sections of deck roof needed to be removed.

The control position was a small three-level, open-bridge tower. As the type was used more in combat situations, the bridge structure became flanked with various arrangements of platform to support whatever armament was available. Typically a single 8.8cm (the much-respected "88") would be mounted, and also one 3.7cm high-angle gun and twin or quadruple 2cm FlaK mountings.

Where the early craft (hull numbers to 626) had a mean draught of only 1.8m/5ft 10in, which made them virtually immune to torpedo attack, additions in

ABOVE: **Simply a deck overlaying two sets of rectangular pontoon hulls, the Siebel Ferry was treated with respect by Allied light forces owing to the firepower frequently transported. This example has an 8.8cm FlaK at each corner.**

armament and 25mm/1in protective plate gradually increased the draught to 2.7m/8ft 11in. Standard MFPs were 49.8 x 6.6m/163ft 6in x 21ft 8in, and displaced some 200 tons. There were shorter and beamier variants, the *Marinenachschubleichter* (MNL) "supply lighter" of 280 tons and, smaller but wider again, the purpose-built *Marineartillerieleichter* (MAL). The latter was intended as an escort for the MFP which were, unlike Siebel Ferries, unable to rely on the armament of vehicles carried on the deck.

MAL

Displacement: 180 tons (loaded)
Length: 35.5m/116ft 6in (oa)
Beam: 8.6m/28ft 3in
Draught: 1.80m/5ft 10in
Armament: 2 x 7.5cm Army guns (2x1), 6 x 2cm guns (1x2/4x1), 1 x 8.6cm mortar
Machinery: 2 diesel engines, 2 shafts
Power: 403kW/540bhp for 8 knots
Fuel: 4.2 tons oil
Endurance: About 920km/500nm at 6.5 knots
Protection: 25mm/1in
Complement: 28

ABOVE: **During the run-up to Operation "Sealion",
nearly 1,300 barges were collected in Channel
ports, over 80 being visible in this group alone.**
LEFT: **At the top of the picture it can be seen
that the bows of these barges have been
removed and replaced by ramps.**

Inland Waterway Barges

Operation *Seelöwe* (Sealion), the projected German invasion of Britain in 1940, was ordered at short notice and without specialist assault craft. In order to land 16 divisions over three days, it was thought that 1,277 inland waterway barges would be needed. Towage was common on European waterways, so many of these were unpowered, requiring a total of 471 tugs to be requisitioned.

A typical Rhein *Schleppkahn* (literally "towbarge") was little different to the powered craft so familiar today. When loaded, the sidedecks were just above the water, with the hatch cover supported on high coamings. Forward freeboard was low, there being no forecastle. Ground tackle was primitive and usually hand-powered. Most carried stern anchors,

which would have been used to prevent broaching in surf. The protruding barn-door-type rudder was highly vulnerable.

Never intended to operate far from a river bank, few safety features were incorporated. To maximize carrying capacity, the double bottomed hull was very shallow. Depth of hull at the sides was some 3m/10ft, while headroom under hatches at centreline was around 4.5m/15ft. High-sided transport would have required open hatches.

The hull being long and shallow, designed for the distributed load of a bulk cargo, would have had to be loaded carefully. In the absence of ballast capacity, this would have been exacerbated by the need to achieve a low forward-beaching draught.

Modification to the vessels was extremely basic, the bows being cut away to the width of the coamings and to a level just above the load waterline. The resulting gap was filled by a flap which was lowered to permit a ramp to be manually run out (under fire).

ABOVE RIGHT: **Unsuitably
clad German troops
manhandling a 75mm
field gun into a converted
barge that lacks even
basics such as a winch.**
LEFT: **Fast assault craft
for river crossings
made good propaganda
material. The helmsmen
and the early outboard
motor appear vulnerable.**

Inland Waterway Barges	

Displacement: 3,630 tons (loaded);
  3,000 tons (cargo deadweight, maximum)
Length: 105m/344ft 8in (oa)
Beam: 13m/42ft 8in
Draught: 3m/9ft 10in
Armament: None
Machinery: None
Power: N/A
Fuel: N/A
Endurance: N/A
Protection: None
Complement: 3–4

ABOVE: **Type 393** *Nixe* at anchor with others of the class. The Ariadne class were named after cruisers that had served with the German Imperial Navy (1871–1919).

LEFT: *Perseus* of the Type 340/341 group has a different style of bridge structure.

Inshore Minesweepers (IMS), Types 340 and 394

With origins going back to the 1920s, the R-boat (*Raumboot*) was developed rapidly during World War II. The vessel had excellent seakeeping qualities and served variously as minesweeper, minelayer, convoy escort or light gunboat. Variants ranged from 26–41m/85–136ft in length, with a displacement of 60–175 tons. The design of the largest, the so-called "GR" type, took the multi-purpose ethic just too far, being criticized as being "too costly for minesweeping, too slow for an MTB, too

lightly armed for an MGB of her size, and too fast for a pure convoy vessel". Restricted by what could be built in the early post-war era, however, the German Navy contracted the original shipyard, Abeking & Rasmussen, to produce a coastal and inshore minesweeper design that could be used in other roles with minimum alteration.

Differing only in the type of propulsion, the design of the larger 340 and 341 types was clearly based on the R-boat. Abeking & Rasmussen built 21 of the total of 28

"patrol minesweepers" between 1959 and 1963. Built of wood, the type had similar operational capabilities to the R-boat but was slower and, at 47.5m/156ft overall, somewhat larger. Unusually, the vessel was fitted with two cycloidal propellers.

More truly inshore minesweepers were the 18, again very similar, Type 393 and 394, between 1961 and 1968. These, also constructed of wood, were built by Krögerworft of Rendsburg. The hulls, with a pronounced chine and near full-length rubbing strake, again echoed their origin. The relatively large superstructures were similar to those on the defensively orientated craft which, as IMSs, were also deployed as patrol boats. All the crew could thus be more safely accommodated above the upper deck when engaged in mine clearance.

Abeking & Rasmussen completed a smaller version in 1966. It was intended as the first ship for a series of 20 which was, however, cancelled.

ABOVE: *Gemma* was fitted for minesweeping rather than as a patrol craft. The T-shaped davit for handling Oropesa-type floats was very distinctive.

LEFT: The Type 340's R-boat origins are clearly visible here. This is *Jupiter*, fitted out as a fast minesweeper.

Inshore Minesweeper (IMS), Type 394

Displacement: 238 tons (standard); 246 tons (loaded)
Length: 38.01m/124ft 9in (oa)
Beam: 8.03m/26ft 4in
Draught: 2.1m/6ft 11in
Armament: 1 x 40mm gun
Machinery: 2 diesel engines, 2 shafts
Power: 1,492kW/2,000bhp for 14.5 knots
Fuel: 30 tons oil
Endurance: 1,196km/650nm at 14 knots
Protection: Nominal
Complement: 24

Landing Craft, Medium/Mechanized (LCM), Yuqing/Yuchai and Yunan class

These useful craft have been produced in very large numbers, however in the absence of LPD-type ships for transportartion in a pre-loaded condition, all appear not to have been used for conventional amphibious warfare but rather for the day-to-day policing and control of a nation with a long coastline and vast internal river system. The nation's coastal waters are uniformly shallow, while those inland waterways not yet canalized are subject to great seasonal fluctuations in depth.

For all practical purposes, the Yuqing class (1960s) and the improved Yuchai type (1980s) are identical. A total of at least 70 of these types are believed to remain in service. The design is reportedly based on that of the Soviet-built T4, with the same beam but with length increased by 44m/14ft 6in. As the cargo deck is an identical 9.5 x 3.9m/31ft 2in x 12ft 10in, the extra length is in the larger two-level

ABOVE: **A total of some 250 of the Type 067 Yunan-class LCMs were built by the early 1990s. Since then, many have been withdrawn from service and placed in reserve by the People's Liberation Army.**

accommodation superstructure, which accommodates more than 20 crew and vehicle personnel.

Either type is designed to carry a medium tank, the vehicle deck being accessed via a bow ramp. Unusually, the vehicle deck is covered, with flat roller-type hatch covers that stack at the rear during loading, or to accommodate high vehicles. The coamings are proportionately lower

LEFT: **A Type 068 Yuqing-class LCM at a naval base in China.** BELOW: **Marines of the People's Liberation Army embarking on a Type 068 Yuqing LCM during an amphibious landing exercise.**

than on a T4, but headroom has been maintained internally through the higher freeboard of the hull.

Built in parallel with these classes over a 20-year period was the somewhat larger Yunan type, of which production ceased only in the early 1990s. Of an estimated 280 built, the great majority are surplus to requirements and maintained in reserve. With an extra 2.7m/9ft of length overall, the vehicle deck is considerably increased to 15 x 4m/49ft 3in x 13ft 1in. This results in a smaller accommodation superstructure carried a little further aft.

Landing Craft, Medium/Mechanized (LCM), Yunan class

Displacement: 133 tons (loaded)
Length: 27.50m /90ft 3in (oa)
Beam: 5.4m/17ft 9in
Draught: 1.4m/4ft 7in (seagoing)
Armament: 2/4 x 14.5mm machine-guns (1/2x2)
Machinery: 2 diesel engines, 3 shafts
Power: 448kW/600bhp for 10.5 knots
Fuel: Not known
Endurance: 920km/500nm at 10 knots
Protection: Nominal
Complement: 6
Capacity: 1 heavy tank, or 46 tons distributed cargo

TOP: **The Wosao class was a Chinese-built replacement for the Sasha class.** ABOVE: **Based on Western practice, the Wonzang class is the latest Coastal Minesweeper (MSC) of the People's Liberation Army (Navy).**

Coastal Minesweepers and Drones (MSC and MSD), Wosao and Futi class

The Chinese Navy does not operate Inshore Minesweepers (IMS) for shallow-water countermeaures, preferring to deploy larger Coastal Minesweepers (MSC), standing off and controlling drone craft. Despite a great tradition of small-craft construction, Chinese-built MSCs are not wooden-built, surprisingly. Western practice, adopted by the then Soviet Union, favoured wooden MSCs with high forecastles and low working decks aft (typified by the British-built Ton class and Soviet-built Sonya class). As a model, however, the Chinese Navy preferred the 45.1m/148ft steel-built Sasha, a design dating from the mid-1950s and already being phased

out in the 1980s when the Wosao class entered service.

The Wosao class is flush-decked, with sheer at either end but what appears to be inadequate freeboard. Unusually, from the survivability aspect, there is a row of large open scuttles, around 1m/3.3ft above the normal waterline. The type lacks the 57mm gun as mounted on the Sasha class. There is no funnel, this being replaced by a large compact superstructure.

The clear afterdeck is fitted for sweeping the common range of mines. Surveying to establish clear routes involves the ship deploying boom-mounted towfish, which carry sidescan sonar, and this increasingly hazardous

practice led to the development of purpose-designed drone craft. Details of these, known as the Futi class, are uncertain but, at 21m/61ft overall, the type is smaller than a German-built Troika and larger than a Swedish-built SAM. The 47-ton displacement, however, suggests a hull of orthodox shape. Fabricated in GRP, the type can, like the Troika, be manually controlled, but they are intended to be remotely operated from a distance of around 4.8km/3 miles. On passage, the Futi class is powered by two diesel engines but, when minesweeping, electric power is used.

ABOVE: **The Soviet-built Sasha class minesweeper was constructed on a steel hull.** LEFT: **Seen on the left are Futi Type 312 drones in service with the Pakistani Navy. The type can be manually or remotely controlled from a command vessel.**

Coastal Minesweeper (MSC), Wosao class

Displacement: 310 tons (loaded)
Length: 44.8m/147ft (oa)
Beam: 6.2m/20ft 4in
Draught: 2.27m/7ft 6in
Armament: 4 x 25mm guns (2x2)
Machinery: 2 diesel engines, 2 shafts
Power: 1,492kW/2,000bhp for 15.5 knots
Fuel: Not known
Endurance: 920km/500nm at 13 knots
Protection: Nominal
Complement: Not known

Landing Platform, Dock (LPD), Type 071

China has recently completed an LPD-type vessel with an estimated 17,500-ton displacement, making it significantly larger than the Dutch MV *Rotterdam* and its derivatives. The practice is to size docking wells to suit multiple stowage of large air cushion craft or LCUs. Existing craft in these categories appear to be unsuitable. Chinese-built LCAC-type craft have been tried but, presumably unsatisfactory, were quickly scrapped.

BELOW: **This helicopter deck appears to have temporary markings. The small crane does not appear to have a hatch connection to the docking well.**

The largest current deployable air cushion craft, the so-called Payi type, is tailored to LSTs and has a capacity of just 10 troops. Eight Russian-built LCACs, classified LCUA, have been acquired but have four times the footprint of US forces equivalent, in addition to having too great an air draught to be LPD-transportable. Existing LCUs are also unsuitable.

The category can vary widely, for instance the standard US Navy LCU 1610 class is around 41m/135ft in length, and the British LCU (10) is only 30m/98ft. A basic Yuling of a design dating to the 1970s, however, is over

56.5m/185ft. Its exact form remains vague but, if its credited 15 knots is achievable, this indicates a hull form rather more refined than that of the average tank landing craft. Some 24 Yulings were constructed, and probably provided the design baseline of the Yuhai class, their successor.

Landing Platform, Dock (LPD), Type 071

Displacement: 20,800 tons (estimated)
Length: 210m/680ft (oa)
Beam: 26.5m/86ft
Draught: 7m/23ft
Armament: 1 x 76mm DP gun, 4 x 30mm CIWS, 4 x 120mm rocket launchers
Speed: 20 knots
Capacity: 500 troops, 15 EFV, 2 LCAC (estimated)
Aircraft: 2–4 helicopters
Complement: Not known

Inshore Minesweepers (IMS), Bay class

Coastal, as opposed to ocean, minesweeping was not specifically addressed by the Royal Australian Navy (RAN) until the mid-1950s, when a projected domestically built class of ships was rejected in favour of acquiring six British-built Ton-class vessels. Purchased in 1961, these served through to the 1980s and were replaced only at the turn of the century by six Italian licence-built Gaeta class, significantly larger vessels.

ABOVE AND BELOW: **The high superstructure of the Bay class results from all power generation and accommodation being located topside. Catamarans require careful hydrodynamic design to avoid interaction between the hulls. A retractable sonar is mounted in the port hull. A hydraulic crane is mounted aft to handle towfish.**

Inshore mine countermeasures, essential to any intervention warfare, were addressed in 1980. Two prototype craft, to be followed by a class of six, were ordered. The type selected was a catamaran which, for the size of the craft, gave the largest useful upper deck working area.

Known as the Bay class, the first two (HMAS *Rushcutter* and HMAS *Shoalwater*) were constructed of glass-reinforced plastic (GRP), an expensive choice. The further six vessels were cancelled.

The superstructure included a diesel generator compartment, supplying power to the propulsion motors located in each hull, which drove Schottel-type azimuth thrusters. Between the hulls, the upper deck extended down in a boat shape, designed to reduce pitch by entering the water and momentarily increasing forward buoyant upthrust. For rigidity, the hulls were linked at keel level by a faired transverse strap, probably far enough aft to limit emergence and slamming in head sea conditions. Of note was the demountable operations/control room, located at the rear of the superstructure.

Apparently unsatisfactory, the two vessels had a relatively short service life, both being decommissioned in 2001. Since then, the RAN has favoured reliance on Craft Of Opportunity (COOP), and acquired a number of commercial fishing vessels to evaluate their suitablity for inshore mine countermeasures.

Inshore Minesweepers (IMS), Bay class

Displacement: 100 tons (standard); 170 tons (loaded)
Length: 31m/101ft 9in (oa)
Beam: 9m/29ft 6in
Draught: 1.8m/5ft 10in (mean)
Armament: 2 x machine-guns
Machinery: 2 diesel engines, 2 electrically driven azimuth thrusters
Power: 134kW/180hp for 10 knots
Fuel: Not known
Endurance: 2,208km/1,200nm at 10 knots
Protection: Nominal
Complement: 13

Glossary

AGC Amphibious Command Ship (US); LCC from 1969.

AKA Attack Cargo Ship (US); LKA from 1969.

ALC Earlier designation of LCA.

"Amtrac" Popular term for LVT.

APA Attack Transport (US); LPA from 1969.

APD Auxiliary Personnel Destroyer (US); later High-Speed Transport Destroyer.

ARG Amphibious Ready Group (US).

ATG Amphibious Task Group.

AUV Autonomous Underwater Vehicle.

ballast Additional weight taken aboard to improve stability, to correct trim or to modify ship movement.

bandstand Raised island platform for gun mounting.

beam Width of hull at waterline at Standard Displacement.

bhp Brake horsepower. Power available at output of a diesel engine.

bunkers In the modern sense, fuel, rather than the compartments in which it is stored.

BYMS British Yard Minesweeper Variant on YMS (US).

C3 (C-3) US Marine Commission designation for a cargo ship of between 137–152m/450–500ft waterline length and carrying less than 100 passengers. Note also

the "C" referred to standard cargo vessels of under 122m/400ft, C2 of 122–137m/400–450ft, and C4 of 152–168m/500–550ft.

camber Transverse curvature of a ship's deck.

cantilever Overhung structure supported at only one side or end.

casing (funnel) Outer plating surrounding exhaust end of uptakes.

CATF Commander, Amphibious Task Force (Naval).

chine Line of intersection between sides and bottom of a flat-bottomed or planing craft.

C-in-C Commander-in-Chief.

CIWS Close-In Weapon System. Close-range, anti-missile defence of automatic guns and/or missiles on single mounting.

CLF Commander, Landing Force (Marine).

CTOL Conventional Take-Off and Land.

Daihatsu Common name for a range of Japanese landing craft.

DASH Drone Anti-Submarine Helicopter.

DD tank Duplex-Drive amphibious tank.

deadweight (tonnage) Actual carrying capacity of a cargo ship, expressed usually in tons of 2,240lb. Abbreviated to "dwt".

derrick Pivoted spar, fitted with winches, for lifting loads. In US, a "cargo boom".

displacement, full load or "deep" Weight of ship (in tons of 2,240lb) when fully equipped, stored and fuelled.

displacement, standard Weight of ship less fuel and other deductions allowed by treaty.

draught (or draft) Mean depth of water in which a ship may float freely.

DUKW Amphibious truck, commonly known as a "Duck".

ECM Electronic Countermeasures.

ELINT Electronic Intelligence.

endurance Usually equal to twice the operational radius.

EOD Explosive Ordnance Disposal.

ESM Electronic Support Measures.

flare Outward curvature of hull plating.

freeboard Correctly, the vertical height between the waterline and the lowest watertight deck. Commonly, the vertical height of the shell plating from the waterline at any particular point.

gross registered tons Measure of volumetric capacity of a merchant ship. One gross ton equals 100cu ft (2.83m³) of reckonable space. Abbreviated to "grt".

"Hedgerow" "Hedgehog"-type anti-submarine spigot mortar adapted for beach mine clearance.

horsepower (hp) Unit of power equal to 746 watts.

ihp Indicated horsepower. Specifically, the power delivered by the pistons of a reciprocating steam engine.

IMS Inshore Minesweeper.

knuckle Line of change in direction of shell plating. Usually a signature-reduction measure, but also reduces excessive width of upper deck in hulls of pronounced flare.

LAMPS Light Airborne Multi-Purpose System.

LASH Lighter Aboard Ship.

LCA Landing Craft, Assault.

LCA (HR) Landing Craft, Assault (Hedgerow).

LCAC Landing Craft, Air Cushion.

LCC Landing Craft, Control (UK); AGC after 1969 (US).

LCF Landing Craft, FlaK.

ABOVE: **The Royal Navy aircraft carrier HMS *Ark Royal* conducting a Replenishment at Sea (RAS) with the Royal Fleet Auxiliary supply vessel RFA *Wave Knight* in the North Sea. HMS *Ark Royal* was withdrawn from Royal Navy service in October 2010.**

LCG (L)/(M) Landing Craft, Gun (Large)/(Medium).

LCH Landing Craft, Headquarters (UK); British equivalent of AGC/LCC (US).

LCI (L)/(S) Landing Craft, Infantry (Large)/(Small).

LCI (R) Landing Craft, Infantry (Rocket).

LCM Landing Craft, Mechanized.

LCN Landing Craft, Navigation (UK).

LCP (L)/(M)/(S) Landing Craft, Personnel (Large)/(Medium)/(Small).

LCP (R) Landing Craft, Personnel (Ramped).

LCS (L)/(M)/(S) Landing Craft, Support (Large)/(Medium)/(Small).

LCS (R) Landing Craft, Support (Rocket) (UK).

LCT Landing Craft, Tank.

LCU Landing Craft, Utility.

LCV Landing Craft, Vehicle.

LCVP Landing Craft, Vehicle, Personnel.

length (bp) Length between perpendiculars. Customarily the distance between forward extremity of waterline at standard displacement and forward side of rudder post. For US warships, lengths on designed waterline and between perpendiculars are synonymous.

length (oa) Length, overall.

length (wl) Length, waterline. Measured at standard displacement

LSC Landing Ship, Carrier (Derrick Hoistings) (UK).

LSD Landing Ship, Dock.

LSDV Swimmer Delivery Vehicle.

LSF Landing Ship, Fighter Direction.

LSG Landing Ship, Gantry (UK).

LSH Landing Ship, Headquarters (UK).

LSI (L)/(M)/(S) Landing Ship, Infantry (Large)/(Medium)/(Small) (UK).

LSM Landing Ship, Medium.

LSM (R) Landing Ship, Medium (Rocket).

LSS Landing Ship, Sternchute (UK).

LST Landing Ship, Tank.

LVT Landing Vehicle, Tracked.

MAB Marine Amphibious Brigade (US).

MAF Marine Amphibious Force (US).

MAU Marine Amphibious Unit (US).

MCMV Mine Countermeasures Vessel (UK).

"Mexeflote" Powered pontoon used also as causeway unit (UK).

MGB Motor Gun Boat (UK).

ML Motor Launch (UK).

ABOVE: **A Landing Craft, Air Cushion (LCAC) from USS _Bonhomme Richard_ (LHD-6) of Expeditionary Strike Group Five (ESG-5) supporting Operation Unified Assistance, the humanitarian operation effort in the wake of the tsunami on Sumatra, Indonesia, January 10, 2005.**

MLC Early designation of LCM.

MMS Motor Minesweeper (UK).

Monitor Shallow-draught vessel with heavy armament.

MSC Military Sealift Command (US).

MSB Minesweeping Boat (US).

MTB Motor Torpedo Boat (UK); US equivalent PT.

NATO North Atlantic Treaty Organization.

NGS Naval Gunfire Support.

OTH Over The Horizon.

PCF _see_ Swift Boat.

PDMS Point Defence Missile System. Rapid-response, close-range anti-air missile system.

Plan Orange US plan for war against Japan.

protection In this context, usually only splinter-proof, but variable.

RAF Royal Air Force.

RCT Royal Corps of Transport.

RFA Royal Fleet Auxiliary.

ROV Remotely Operated Vehicle. Usually with umbilical.

SAM Surface-to-Air Missile.

sheer Curvature of deckline in fore-and-aft direction, usually upward toward either end.

shp Shaft horsepower. Power at point in shaft ahead of stern gland. Does not include frictional losses in stern gland and A-bracket.

sided Situated at sides of ship, usually as opposed to centerline location.

SIGINT Signal Intelligence.

ski jump Pronounced upward curvature at forward end of flightdeck, to enhance effect of short take-off run.

SSM Surface-to-Surface Missile.

stability range Total range through which, from a position of equilibrium, a vessel is stable in the static condition.

STUFT Ships Taken Up From Trade.

SWATH Small Waterplane Area, Twin Hull.

Swift Boat Otherwise PCF; 50ft coastal surveillance boat (Vietnam).

TF Task Force.

TG Task Group.

trim Amount by which a vessel deviates, in the fore-and-aft axis, from the designed draught.

TU Task Unit.

turbo-electric Propulsion system in which a steam turbine drives an electrical generator. This supplies energy via a cable to a propulsion motor coupled to the propeller shaft.

UAV Unmanned Aerial Vehicle.

uptake Conduit exhausting products of combustion to the funnel.

volume critical Vessel whose design is driven by space rather than weight considerations.

V/STOL Vertical or Short Take-Off and Land.

Warsaw Pact Eastern military bloc, essentially a counter to NATO.

weight critical Vessel whose design is driven by weight rather than space considerations.

Index

BELOW: **A Sugashima-class minesweeper of the Japanese Maritime Self-Defence Force (JMSDF).**

Key to flags

For the specification boxes,
the national flag that was
current at the time of the
vessel's use is shown.

 Australia

 China

 France

 Germany – World War II

 West Germany – post-World War II

 East Germany

 Italy

 Japan

 The Netherlands

 Soviet Union

 United Kingdom

 United States of America